Social
Role
Valori~

The R...g.... p

Social
Role
Valorization

and
The English Experience

David G Race

Whiting & Birch Ltd
MCMXCIX

Published by Whiting & Birch Ltd,
PO Box 872, London SE23 3HL, England.
USA: Paul & Co, Publishers' Consortium Inc,
PO Box 442, Concord, MA 01742.

British Library Cataloguing in Publication Data.
A CIP catalogue record is available from
the British Library

ISBN 1 86177 027 8

Printed in England by Watkiss Studiios

Contents

Prologue

The need for this book

Fifteen years ago, at Castle Priory College, Susan Thomas, co-author with Wolf Wolfensberger of the then new evaluation tool, Program Analysis of Service System's Implementation of Normalization Goals (1983), hereafter PASSING, gave two days of presentations that were to precede a five day PASSING workshop. Many of the audience, including myself, had experience of various forms of training under the general heading of 'normalisation' and many were under the impression that they were to hear Wolfensberger's latest thinking on the subject at this event. Well they did, but what they also heard, most of them for the first time, was that the ideas were now to come under a different heading, something called 'Social Role Valorization'. Many of the overheads at Susan Thomas's presentation had the word 'normalization' etched out and the words 'Social Role Valorization' inserted, and we were to hear later that the whole PASSING instrument, with its 510 page manual, would have referred to 'Social Role Valorization' rather than 'normalization' had it not been in too far advanced a state of publication to recall. (what the acronym would have been is open to speculation; perhaps PASSIS, though French speakers may have had some associational problems with that).

The practical point of Susan Thomas's workshop was, as we shall elaborate in chapter 1, that the new name came at the same time as a social movement was beginning to take root in the world of learning disability services. This movement was largely generated through training events in the eighties, following a relatively influential academic movement in the previous decade, both based on something called 'normalisation'. Its influence was to be considerable, and would produce an equally powerful backlash, from the service world and also from certain academic quarters. At the same time, the author of this key version of normalization, and the one which was at the heart of the social movement, was attempting to go well beyond a renaming of his set of ideas and into a whole reconceptualisation. Over the fifteen years that have followed that original presentation of SRV, as it became known, the reconceptualisations have resulted in what its author claims to be a fully fledged social scientific theory, that is applicable to a whole range of groups at risk of devaluation. Wolfensberger's theory has been taught and written about in several different countries in that time, most notably Australia, New Zealand and Norway in addition to the USA and Canada, where a strong culture already existed, and a literature, both critical and supportive, has paralleled the development of a training culture. The 'English experience' as will be elaborated at various points in this book, especially chapter 1, has been somewhat different, with the academic response being mainly to 'normalisation' and the training culture being dispersed, sometimes affected by mutual antagonisms, and ultimately marginalised. At the same time many things have been achieved that are very much in accord with the basic impetus to SRV, the address of devaluation.

Hence the need for this book. Though Wolfensberger and his network of supporters have made efforts, particularly since the International Conference, 'Twenty-Five Years of Normalization and Social Role Valorization - a Retrospective and Prospective View' held in Ottawa in 1994, to publish even more and to engage in international discussion, the events of the years since 1983 have resulted, in my view, in a lack of availability of a detailed explication of SRV theory in England. The third edition of Wolfensberger's introductory monograph (Wolfensberger 1998) goes a long way to filling this gap, and should ideally be read in conjunction with this book, which follows the same structure. What is, hopefully, important about this book to an English audience is its two main objectives. First, both for readers unfamiliar with either normalization and SRV, and for those who have had some contact with those ideas, the book attempts, in an English context using mainly English writings as evidence, to lay out my interpretation of SRV theory. This is, of course, far from definitive, and I believe only the originator of the theory himself could produce such a work, but it is meant to be sufficiently detailed to enable those new to the theory to see whether it has something to offer them, and for criticism and debate to be focused on the theory itself, rather than on some of the misunderstandings and misinterpretations that have occurred in this country.

The second objective follows from the last point above, and is my attempt, in the course of the explication of SRV, to address as many of the academic critiques of the theory (or more usually of the English experience of 'normalisation') as possible, so that the current 'accepted wisdom' might be challenged. I believe that SRV theory offers both important and deep insights into the situation of many people whom society places into a state of devaluation, as well as offering some key strategies for addressing that devaluation. It is therefore an academic theory that can be tested at both the level of ideas and in terms of practical application, as well as being set alongside other theories that inform the world of human services; not as a rival, or with any sense of superiority, but as part of a range of perspectives. It is hoped that what follows goes some way towards these two objectives, and that it will be read with them in mind.

A note on spelling

Lest readers are already confused, I will be using the arbitrary device of talking about *normalization*, and the *normalization* principle to refer to that version of the ideas propounded by Wolf Wolfensberger in his writing and his and his Training Institutes teaching, and *'normalisation'* to refer to the collection of ideas, from both the Scandinavian origins and also from interpretations of Wolfensberger's work, that were discussed and taught in the 'English experience' It is hoped that the distinction will be useful, rather than confusing, as this has particular significance in the transition from normalization to SRV and the English experience of that transition.

Acknowledgments

In some ways acknowledgment for the ideas in this book go back many years, particularly to Alan Tyne and Paul Williams, whom I have known for over twenty years and who have been a source of constant discussion and inspiration to many people, not just myself. Thanks are also due to my former employers at the Children's Society, especially Ian Sparks and David Lovell, for giving me the chance, in the eighties, to be both part of a growing social movement, to let it influence their organization and to allow me to expand the horizons of my contacts beyond these shores, especially to attend events and discuss issues with Professor Wolfensberger and his colleagues. I am also indebted to John O'Brien, not only for his comments on chapter 1, but also for many years of discussion, debate and humour, to which I fear I have given scant justice in this book.

More immediately, thanks go to the Research Committee of Stockport College, for funding me to continue my involvement with the international SRV network, but particularly for assistance with the more detailed work for this book, most notably my visits to Plymouth and Syracuse. In the former, the help and invaluable information from Paul Jenkins, as well as access to his important archive, has been an key aspect of my understanding of the 'English experience' of SRV. During the latter, discussions with Wolf Wolfensberger and Susan Thomas were an important means of firming up the ideas for this book.

Beyond that visit, of course, my debt to Wolf Wolfensberger, as author of the ideas of SRV and so much else that has influenced my life over the past fifteen years, goes far beyond the specific acknowledgment of his comments on the final draft and his permission to use material. Without his work, so many things, both for individuals and whole devalued groups, especially people with learning disabilities, would have been very different, and, I believe, much worse.

Discussion, teaching and writing over the years about SRV has also involved many other people in influencing what was in my head as I wrote what follows, so specific acknowledgments of particular parts is difficult, though the overall framework follows closely the one used by Wolf Wolfensberger in his monograph, referenced in the Prologue and elsewhere.

Beyond SRV, but highly relevant to this book, has been my contact with Oxana Metiuk and Ruth Abrahams. As friends and as colleagues trying to raise awareness of Wolfensberger's work, they have played a prominent role in deeper insights into devaluation and measures to counter it, and I thank them sincerely.

Finally, to my wife Deborah, for keeping my flights of writing fancy to understandable levels, and for twenty-five years on the beginnings of an exploration of what life has to offer, I dedicate this book, with much love and thanks for constantly reminding me, through herself and my four sons, what is really valuable.

1

'Normalisation' and SRV: An English experience

Introduction

In 1978 I shared my first, and, to date, last platform with a Government Minister. At a conference organised by the 'Midlands Society for the Study of Mental Subnormality' I was representing a DHSS sponsored research unit evaluating a large scale 'experiment' in services for people with learning disabilities, known as the 'Sheffield Development Project'. Roland Moyle, the Minister of Health in the Labour government, listened to two presentations, one by a consultant psychiatrist on 'fashions in care', and one by myself on 'the research viewpoint.' He then proceeded to present government policy for 'the mentally handicapped' which consisted of a summary of the targets in the White Paper *Better Services for the Mentally Handicapped* (DHSS 1971), and the three 'initiatives' set up in 1975 by his previous senior minister, Barbara Castle.

That a minister should appear on a public platform (in a public house in fact, which happened to be the location of the conference) and answer unprepared questions from the floor, as well as respond to our two papers, which he had not seen, says much about the relaxed media management of governments at that time. What is more relevant to this book, however, was that such an event was, in theory, covering issues at the leading edge of services for people with learning disabilities, that the government of the day actually had a policy specifically for this group of people, and that virtually no mention was made of the word normalization. As a member of a research unit I had, unlike many people in England outside of academia, read the 1972 text of that name, written by Wolfensberger with other contributions, as well as examining the 1975 evaluation tool, written by Wolfensberger and Glenn, *Program Analysis of Service Systems*. I had also, again unlike many at the conference, visited the much vaunted services for people with learning disabilities in Sweden, on which many of the physical buildings in the

Sheffield Project were based, and experienced first hand their service system based on 'the normalization principle'. All of this had led me, along with a number of others (e.g. Shearer 1972), to the conclusion that the 'leading edge' of services in the UK, consisting as it did of a continuing dominance by hospitals and abnormal sized buildings, was not the real answer for people with learning disabilities, but that a service free of the ties of competing generic departments, and based on ordinary housing, would represent a real 'experiment.' I said as much in my presentation, and had already written more extensively on the same theme (Race 1977), but the fact that my views were taken in entirely different ways by the conference organiser and the minister again speaks volumes for the relative weight of different influences on services (as opposed to academic ideas about them) of more pragmatic and interested considerations. With hindsight I can see that I was talking about a new service based on Wolfensberger's elaboration of the normalization principle, though I hardly articulated it in that way at the time.

What the organiser of the conference, a consultant psychiatrist who was later to become a prominent figure in Rescare, a pressure group opposed to hospital closure (Cox & Pearson 1995), thought I was talking about was the empirical inadequacy of the proposals in the White Paper for reducing the hospital population by half. What the minister thought I was talking about was a critique of the ability of the newly created generic Social Services Departments to provide adequate services for people with learning disabilities, or to work in harmony with the local Health Department. Both were more concerned with issues to do with power and responsibility of different professional groups than with the reality of life as it was lived in the service world of 1977, still dominated by institutions, large and not so large. That reality, described and experienced vividly by workshops teaching about 'normalisation' only five years later, was what was at the heart of the normalization principle, and yet its realisation at that point was only in a small number of academics and pressure groups such as Campaign for the Mentally Handicapped (CMH).

This chapter describes from a personal perspective, the development of the English experience of 'normalisation': firstly as it was taken up by a few academics, and influenced thinking about services; then as it was taught through training events, and influenced the values that informed services, and more directly the pattern of services; and finally, academic and service confusion about the notion of a 'social science theory' called Social Role Valorization, which applies, not just to services for people with learning disabilities, but to the much larger group of people at risk of societal devaluation. That the confusion persists is, as noted in the prologue, one of the reasons for this book, and one of the reasons why I feel it is necessary to precede the fuller exposition of SRV theory in subsequent chapters with a look at the history of the interface between academia, 'normalisation', SRV and services for people with learning disabilities. Like the ways to explain devaluation and SRV that will follow, the interactions of the various elements of this history overlap and feed back on one another, and there is no attempt to say which had more or less effect on the misunderstandings that I believe exist about SRV, merely to describe what happened as I saw it, and as the literature reveals. This is also why the chapter tends to move from discussing 'UK' academia and services to 'English' academia and services, since the experience of the rest of the UK seem to be rather different. Appearances and contacts suggest perhaps more influence of 'normalisation', and certainly SRV, in Wales and less in Scotland and Northern Ireland than the 'English experience', at least in terms of services. Those countries are also less a part of this English writer's experience, with the same applying to those English academics that form a large part of the critical mass that continue to denounce or dismiss 'normalisation' and the address of whose criticisms is the secondary object of the book.

It is salutary to think that, despite having now had twenty-one more years of exploration of the ideas, and innumerable conversations, teaching and writing on this and related subjects, far less opportunity to share a platform with a minister would be forthcoming today, either for me or anyone else who wanted to talk about SRV. Even some one who wanted to hear about government policy for people with learning disabilities would have waited a long time, though there are signs from the new Labour government of some developments along those lines. In the brave new world of the service marketplace, only slowly changing as a result of a change of government in 1997, the unconscious self interest and pragmatism displayed 21 years ago is still there, the only differences being that politicians and services now seem much more open about it. When all this is combined with a sense that nobody currently has an overall strategy, however misguided, for anything to do with human services, there is an even greater need for the understanding and address of devaluation, such as is found, though not exclusively, in SRV theory. This understanding, and the English experience of it, is what the rest of this chapter, and this book, is all about.

Table1.1 below attempts to provide an overview timeline of the various developments in the three main themes of this chapter. As with the history as a whole, others would put different events in this framework, but it is hoped that it will aid the reader in getting some sense of the interactions, at least in terms of their relative timing.

Beginnings of the English experience: 'Normalisation' , UK academics, and services for people with learning disabilities

In a review of his time in the service world, Wolfensberger (1991) remarked that forty years ago you only needed to have read roughly twenty

Table 1
Timelines of the interweaving themes of chapter 1

	Normalization and SRV	Academia	Services
1960	Scandinavian Services based on 'normalization'	Leaders in learning disability, Tizard, Clarkes, O'Connor publish research on 'trainability'	Most people at home or in hospital
	Visits by English Academics and NHS staff to Scandinavia	more research on 'small units'	Some growth in adult training centres
1968		Small international Group looking at normalization based services, Morris's *Put Away* published	'Experimental units' set up. Richard Crossman takes personal interest.. 'Ely scandal' report
1969	*Changing Patterns in Residential Services*		*Seebohm Report* on social services
1971	CMH formed	Wessex Research Unit publish paper on the feasibility of locally based hospital units	First Wessex Units opened
	Anne Shearer critical of normalisation		*Better Services* White Paper
	Wolfensberger published normalisation	Various other research units set up	Social Services Departments set up
1974	CMH publish an account of ENCOR	Behaviourism becomes significant	
1975	Third edition of PASS	Little reference to normalisation in textbooks	NDG, NDT and the Jay Committee set up by Barbara Castle
1977	Links made between CMH and the normalisation movement in the US	NIMROD project set up by Mental Handicap in Wales Applied Research Unit	
			Jay Committe Reports
			Thatcher Government elected
1980	CMHERA set up	Still largely dominated by behaviourists	Some health plans include normalisation eg NWRHA
	First PASS workshop held in England		
	An Ordinary Life published	Academic disdain for PASS	
1983	PASSING published		Ordinary housing projects begin

	Normalization and SRV	Academia	Services
	First PASSING workshop in England	Some research on ordinary housing eg Wells Road Project	General cuts in welfare services
			some residential units close
	SRV now used by Wolfensberger		Movement out of hospital gathers pace
1985	First Wolfensberger visit to England for 20 years	Textbooks begin to recognise the power of normalisation	Real work project begins
			Audit Commission report on Community Care
	Further visits by Wolfensberger		
	Workshops on advocacies, deathmaking and moral coherency		
1989	Frequent PASS(ING) workshops by various presenters		
		Textbooks become more critical of normalisation	NHS and Community Care Act
1992		*Normalisation: A reader for the nineties* published	
	Ottawa Conference '25 years of Normalisation'	Social theory of disability propounded as an alternative	Full implementation of Care Management and Purchaser/ Provider split. The 'Care Market' in full swing
	SRV as social science theory		
1995	First presentation of ten themes of SRV in Newcastle, England		Made to Care - Argument for village communities
	UK SRV study group newsletter launched	Review of research of people coming out of hospital – no mention of SRV	Labour Government elected
	Growth of interest in SRV from other fields		
		Event celebrating 20 years of NDT is highlighted	
1998			Various policy initiatives on welfare in general and on social inclusion including inclusion in schools

publications to be a world authority on 'mental retardation'. Looking at the UK scene in the fifties and early sixties, the same statement would largely hold true. At that time, UK academic literature on learning disabilities was very limited in quantity and what did exist consisted almost entirely of medical text books(e.g. Tredgold 1956, Hilliard & Kirman 1965). Only a small group of academics from beyond the medical world, predominantly psychologists, had been publishing material on 'mental subnormality' and only a few of these remotely suggested alternatives to the medical model of care. Even these 'radicals' (e.g. Clarke & Clarke 1958), were writing largely for an academic audience, rather than for direct service managers, planners or providers, though O'Connor and Tizard (1956), with their work on learning of industrial tasks, did begin, to some extent, to apply academic work to services. Tizard, in fact, bemoaned the lack of academic interest, in a review of research in 1972 '...few scientists in universities have as yet interested themselves in health service and social services problems' (p 12).

'Normalisation', as has been noted elsewhere (Race 1995, Wolfensberger 1991) had impinged on a few in this group through reading about, and visiting Scandinavian services, and by the connections between academics in the UK, Scandinavia and the US. Ironically, the late sixties may also have seen the strongest influence of academics on the development of services in the UK. The psychologists group, represented by Tizard in particular, but also by the Clarkes and others, (Tizard 1967, King et al 1971, Clarke 1966) made their influence most keenly felt when Richard Crossman was Minister of Health, and when he was looking to respond to the first of a series of scandals in 'Mental Subnormality Hospitals', as they were then called (Howe Report 1969).

It needs to be remembered that almost 90 per cent of learning disability services at this time were controlled by the Minister of Health, through Regional Health Boards and Local Hospital Boards of Control. A similar percentage of people with learning disabilities in residential care were in hospitals, and these were predominantly the large institutions that had been set up or expanded in the early part of the century when the full force of the eugenics moment was recognised in legal terms through the Mental Deficiency Act, 1913.

Two decades after its inception therefore, in the late sixties, Crossman was taking on an entrenched part of the NHS, as well as having to deal with the career civil servants who headed the service from London. He therefore looked to 'outside' academics for help. It is clear from his diaries (Crossman 1977), that the work of Tizard and others, including Morris's *Put Away* (1969), an unusual entry by a sociologist into the field, was used in a powerful way to make changes within NHS services. Research on 'small' residential facilities, particularly for children (King et al. 1971) led not only to 'Crossman Units' in hospitals, but also to notions of 'care in the community', a phrase that has obscure origins but which has since remained, with immense variations in interpretation, a byword for policy. In Crossman's day it led to the White Paper mentioned earlier, *Better Services For The Mentally Handicapped* (DHSS 1971). This document, for the first time, set out specific targets for the transfer of people from hospitals to 'the community'. Though the academics had undoubtedly influenced this policy, the impact of 'normalisation' was somewhat indirect, largely consisting of Scandinavian 'models of service', in the form of hostels and day centres, being proposed as the alternative to hospitals, though mentions of 'locally based' also had roots in the anti-institution movement.

Some growth in academic work

Perhaps because of the influence on policy of 'leaders' in the learning disability field such as Tizard, or perhaps more simply because of the general growth of psychology as an academic discipline in the UK, the early seventies saw a modest rise in academic activity in the field of learning disabilities. A number of research units, staffed mainly by psychologists, were set up or expanded, and again these had considerable effect on services. Kushlick's work in Wessex, from the sixties, and the 'models of service' provided by his 'locally based hospital units' were widely referred to in the still limited literature (Kushlick et al 1976). Since Kushlick, as a protégé of Tizard, was one of the group of academics who had been involved with 'normalisation' in the sixties, elements of 'normalisation', again largely with Scandinavian rather than North American origins, were present in these 'leading edge' models, at least in the sense of physical integration and attempts at 'normal patterns of life'. Such models were also a strong influence on the 'experiment' of the 'Sheffield Development Project' mentioned in the introduction, which consisted of a range of architectural designs, from 96 bedded 'hospitals' through twenty four bedded 'hospital hostels' and 'Social Services hostels' to a few unsupervised 'group homes', to accommodate the entire population of people with learning disabilities in Sheffield identified as being in need of residential care (Heron and Myers 1983)

At the same time other psychologists were making their presence felt, most notably the behaviourists. Though Kushlick's unit had also looked at the behaviour modification scene in the US, in particular early intervention with children, Smith et al (1977), writings in the general psychology literature at this time include reports of a number of demonstration projects of behaviourist approaches, (e.g. Klein 1973, Pizzat 1974). The research units would therefore tend to include behavioural psychologists in their teams and behavioural techniques, more or less thoroughly taught, became a key element of services, both in hospitals and the new community care hostels and day care centres (Kiernan & Woodford 1974, Comley 1975). The setting up of the British Institute of Mental Handicap added to the impact of behaviourist thinking on the academic world (e.g. Capie et al 1980). There was therefore a rather more varied, though still small, literature on learning disability in the academic world as the seventies progressed.

There were still only two specialist UK journals. *The Journal of Mental Deficiency Research* (funded by the National Society for Mentally Handicapped Children), largely discussed medical research findings or reports on various behaviour modification techniques.The only real mention of 'normalisation' comes in the *British Journal of Mental Subnormality* (BJMS). In 1970, the BJMS included a 'symposium on normalisation'. This perhaps shows how little the ideas had taken hold in UK academia by then, as apart from an editorial and article by Gunzburg, all other contributions are from overseas. That Gunzburg's editorial also reveals the degree of difference in interpretation even amongst those who had heard of 'normalisation.'

Schools, institutions, hostels, lodgings, whatever facilities are provided, should therefore become stepping stones within a programme of normalisation, which will set everyone on the road to normal life conditions, even though the majority of our people will never reach to normal life conditions, even though the majority of our people will never reach 'passing out' standard (Gunzburg 1970a, p56).

Gunzburg's (1970b) contribution to the symposium, entitled 'The Hospital as a Normalising Training environment' confirms the Scandinavian influences as does Nirje's (1970) contribution which talks of adopting the principle in institutions. Shearer's critique, (1972, p2), mentioned in the introduction, attacks 'normalisation' for being 'used to shore up and justify the basically abnormal situation that mentally handicapped people are living in'. She, too, cited the above quotation from Gunzburg as supporting evidence, and was critical of Scandinavian services which he, like the others, had visited and admired. She does not refer to Wolfensberger's formulation, though in highlighting 'integration' as the key to a better life for people she is echoing the prominent place of this idea in the 1972 text that he and others had just produced. As well as its scarcity in the journals, UK textbooks too, despite the publication in Canada and then international availability of the 'Normalization' book mentioned above, and despite it later being identified by an international survey of 'most cited works' as a 'seminal text', Heller et. al. (1991), refer hardly at all to 'normalisation' and when they do, it is usually again to Scandinavian experiences (Gunzburg 1973, Clarke & Clarke 1974, Gunzburg & Gunzburg 1973).

Changes in services in the seventies

Within services, a more significant event affecting their delivery was the setting up in 1973 of Local Authority Social Services Department following the Seebohm Committee Report (Home Office 1968). The significance of these new departments for learning disability services was two fold. First they were controlled by Local Authorities, with locally elected councillors having, at least theoretical, control over policy, and locally based officers running the organisations. This differed from the centrally organised and funded NHS which, though it had regional and institution based officers, was at least in policy terms fairly monolithic. Second, Local Authorities had little experience of learning disability services, either at councillor or officer level. Professional managerial and front-line staff in the new departments would usually have been trained specifically in child care or services for elderly people, with the occasional person involved with mental health issues Social workers qualifying after the Seebohm Report would have a generic training, with very little input on learning disability, especially the radical ideas of 'normalisation'. Many Social Services Departments, therefore, turned to the national Department of Health & Social Security, and their consultation papers and circulars (Llewelyn Davies et al 1971, DHSS 1973), particularly on building design, did much to determine the physical shape of the new hostels and day centres.

It was not surprising that movement to meet the policy targets of the 1971 White Paper was slow, nor that, when Labour were returned to power in 1974, the Secretary of State, Barbara Castle, sought to re-introduce the impetus that Crossman had created in the field of learning disability with the three 'initiatives' mentioned in the Introduction. With the first, by putting psychologist Peter Mittler at the head of her newly created policy advisory body, the National Development Group, she was clearly influenced by the growth of his profession's academic credibility in the learning disability field. By also having a psychiatrist and nurse on the group, however, she was acknowledging the political power still retained by the medical establishment, which went with the vastly greater numbers of people with learning disability for whom the NHS was still responsible.

The second initiative, the setting up of an inspectorial group, known as the National Development Team, which could call on experts from round the country to supplement the main team, was a re-creation of Crossman's Hospital Advisory Service. Again, however, by appointing the psychiatrist Gerry Simon, who was also on the NDG, the medical dominance and assumptions were still powerful.

The growth of pressure groups

This relative lack of challenge from the NDG contrasts with the other key group to influence thinking about services in the seventies, Campaign for the Mentally Handicapped (CMH) was first set up in 1971 as a pressure group on the hospital closure issue, but expanded its scope to all services for people with learning disabilities. It consisted initially of a few people from a variety of backgrounds, including a journalist, Anne Shearer, who did much in the media and at conferences to highlight learning disability issues. They had close connections with the growing normalization movement in the US, and were the first to publicise in the UK the ENCOR project, a full scale service in Nebraska based on normalization that had been developed in the late sixties (Thomas et al. 1978). In terms of the academic learning disability world, however, they were seen as something of a bunch of well meaning amateurs. Their own newsletters were written non-academically, and they published little in the academic journals. Despite academic disdain, the circulation of the newsletter grew rapidly within the service system and as most services were still controlled centrally by the DHSS, CMH had a narrow target for pressure. In one of their specific campaigns CMH had wider support from other pressure groups, who then formed a specific group of their own, called 'Exodus' aimed at getting all children out of hospital, recalled much later by Jay (1996) A widely read book by Maureen Oswin (1971) gave this group some academic backing, though even her publication was cited more often by service personnel than academics.

Ironically, the rising influence of pressure groups in the seventies, and CMH in particular, also meant that the fledgling Local Authority Social Services Departments, instead of being seen as the instigators of the way forward, came under pressure from two sides, especially in their use of the residential model of the hostel. From CMH Tyne (1978), came stories about life in hostels, including, most radically, stories from residents themselves, CMH (1973), that had many echoes of the institutional models whose origins were described by Wolfensberger (1969), and then criticised in the full normalization text (Wolfensberger 1972). On the other hand, from the medical learning disability establishment came many papers about the 'unqualified' nature of Local Authority hostel staff, and the undesirability of people being placed in the community (e.g. Shapiro 1974). It took an academic from the discipline of sociology, Michael Bayley, to raise the more fundamental questions of the difference between care in the community and care by the community, something that was to bedevil 'normalisation' based services, and even the ideas of SRV itself, well into the future (contrast Bayley 1973 with Bayley 1991).

The Jay Committee: public endorsement of 'normalisation?'

Returning to the practical level, however, Barbara Castle's third policy initiative in 1975, the setting up of the Jay Committee of Enquiry into Nursing and Care, provided perhaps the greatest chance for 'normalisation' ideas to be incorporated into policy. It should be noted that the period (1975-1979) during which the committee was working was unusual for the number of attempts at cross disciplinary discussion and debate, both within the academic world, narrow as that still was, and among the widening range of professionals involved in learning disability. Gunzburg attempted a new international journal, *Research Exchange and Practice*, which had contributions from many disciplines. An organisation, The Association of Professions for the Mentally Handicapped, was set up with members from nursing, social work and the academic world. Research units began to include individuals from a wider range of disciplines. There was therefore, in a short space of time, much airing of new ideas on development in services.

Among these, 'normalisation', and especially its implications for the undesirability of institutions, be they large hospitals or 'small' hostels of 24 beds, was very much to the fore. In fact many articles in the *British Journal of Mental Subnormality*, still the most widely read journal within the academic learning disability world almost took it for granted that 'normalisation' was now an accepted influence on policy (e.g. Gunzburg 1978).

Little, if any, of the discussions centred on the ideas themselves however, and the distinctions between Wolfensberger's development of normalization and the Scandinavian formulations were rarely made. Instead the main debate centred around submissions to the Jay Committee. At one end of the scale were those which represented a growing consensus on the desirability of a move away from the medical model towards a social model, which usually included references to 'normalisation' for support (e.g. Kushlick et al 1976). At the other end of the scale were submissions, with suggestions for minor reforms in the centre, from the various professional bodies in charge of the existing system (e.g. Royal College of Psychiatrists 1976).

The Jay Committee Report (1979), and what happened to it in terms of implementation, represents in my view a watershed in the connection between the academic world of learning disability, normalisation, and the development of services. The broad 'principles' laid out in section 89 of the report seem to represent an acceptance by at least some of the committee of 'normalisation' ideas.

Section 89 states,

> (a) *Mentally handicapped people have a right to enjoy normal patterns of life within the community.*

(b) *Mentally handicapped people have a right to be treated as individuals.*

(c) *Mentally handicapped people will require additional help from the communities in which they live and from professional services if they are to develop to their maximum potential as individuals.*

This is reinforced by the Service Principles of Section 93.

(a) *Mentally handicapped people should use normal services wherever possible. Special provisions tend to set apart those who receive them and may therefore increase the distance between mentally handicapped people and the rest of society.*

(b) *Existing networks of community support should be strengthened by professional services rather than supplanted by them.*

(c) *'Specialised' services or organisations for mentally handicapped people should be provided only to the extent that they demonstrably meet or are likely to meet additional needs that cannot be met by the general services. Often these specialised services will be required only intermittently or as one component in a more general service. Often the aim will be to provide 'back-up' to a more general service. Wherever possible the special services should be delivered in integrated settings. In the past such services have often been specialised only in name, they have not met defined special needs.*

(d) *If we are to meet the many and diverse needs of mentally handicapped people we need maximum co-ordination of services both within and between agencies and at all levels. The concept of a life plan seems essential if co-ordination and continuity of care is to be achieved.*

(e) *Finally, if we are to establish and maintain high quality services for a group of people who cannot easily articulate and press their just claims, we need someone to intercede on behalf of mentally handicapped people in obtaining services.* (Jay Committe 1979, pp 35-37)

Many now working in learning disability services would love to have as clear a statement of principles guiding their services. They might also claim, if they do have anything like them, that such statements stem from the growth of 'normalisation' teaching in the eighties. That the statements were made before the teaching therefore suggests an influence of the ideas published and discussed in the seventies by academics and others.

Unfortunately the recommendations of the Jay Committee were not put into effect and, to quote an author writing six years later were 'quietly buried' (Ryan & Thomas 1987). The victory of the medical and nursing establishment that this represented also marked, in my view, the beginning of the decline in academic influence on policy and, most significantly, the start of the most radical changes in public services and their ethos brought about by the incoming Thatcher government. Given that 'normalisation' was to have its full impact in challenging peoples' values (not hitherto a factor in the academic discussions) at the same time as these other changes, this set the scene for a completely different service world for people with learning disabilities. Though its recommendations, especially about a common training for those working with people with learning disabilities, were never put into effect the principles of the Jay Committee still had some impact, especially when they were allied with further publications advocating ideas based on 'normalisation'

An Ordinary Life: 'Normalisation' into practice?

While the Jay Committee had been sitting, and subsequently, another group was meeting at the Kings Fund Centre in London. The group, consisting mainly of people from the services world, but also including some academics, eventually published a report, An Ordinary Life (Kings Fund 1980). Though with the imprimatur of a reputable research and information body, the report was not, as with CMH publications discussed earlier, fully accepted as a 'academic' report. Many of the journals and textbooks ignored it but radicals in the wider service world, still loudly debating the Jay Committee Report, looked on it as providing a model that they could work to. In certain places An Ordinary Life formed the basis of official policy documents (e.g. North Western Regional Health Authority 1983, South Western Regional Health Authority 1986) and since it included express references to the influence of 'normalisation', so too did the policy documents. What these policy documents did not contain however, was a more detailed exposition of 'normalisation' ideas, particularly as they explored issues beyond the mere undesirability of institutions and the desirability of ordinary housing.

In fact the phrase 'an ordinary life' was to become an 'English shorthand' for 'normalisation' and 'ordinary life principles' referred to as an alternative to 'the normalisation principle'. This was to have important consequences later as academics sought to come to terms with the power that 'normalisation training', especially through PASS and its successor PASSING workshops (Wolfensberger & Glenn 1975, Wolfensberger & Thomas 1983) was to unleash. On the academic side in the eighties, however, minds were more concentrated by threats to the very existence of the welfare state coming from the Thatcher government, and from thinkers of the 'new right'. This occupied many of the learning disability research units in trying to prevent (or often failing to prevent) their own demise, rather than leading services into new developments. One exception to this was the Mental Handicap Applied Research Unit, which had begun to develop the NIMROD service in Cardiff in the late seventies, very much in parallel with the Jay principles and An Ordinary Life, and hence with 'normalisation'

(Blunden & Smith 1988). That Wales also saw a great increase in funding and activity in the eighties, in what became known as the Welsh Initiative, makes the development of services in that country something of an exception to the general description in this chapter. That several key people in the 'normalisation movement' also moved into positions of influence in Welsh services is also significant, and is one more reason for our focusing here on the 'English experience', leaving the 'Welsh experience' for others to describe. In England the 'exceptions' were fewer, initially being only individual researchers, such as Linda Ward in Bristol and Jim Mansell in Kent, though their connections with 'normalisation' contributed to the development of some original service practices and the reputations of their places of work. In fact the growth of a jointly funded post in Kent into what was to finally be called the Tizard Centre, and from an individual piece of research in Bristol to the major development of the Norah Fry Research Institute in Bristol, says much for those individuals, and a few others, sticking out against the grain of academic trends.

The development of 'normalisation' training

The ideas represented by the Jay Committee Report and *An Ordinary Life* now began to be put into effect in some places. The detailed history of Tyne and Williams' visits to the USA and the visits to the UK of O'Brien, Osburn and others is documented elsewhere (Williams 1995a), but from the point of view of service development, I would argue that the foundation of the Community and Mental Handicap Education and Research Association (CMHERA) in 1980 described initially as the 'training arm' of CMH, and the introduction and development in the UK of workshops based on PASS (Wolfensberger & Glenn 1975) was the most significant event of the decade. That the development took place through training and consultancy, rather than through the more traditional academic route, is also significant. As the Jay Committee's recommendation for a unified training for workers in learning disability was rejected, no standardised courses, academic or otherwise, were readily available to impart 'normalisation' ideas. There was thus neither control over who got to hear about 'normalisation' nor the teaching of any 'standard' version of normalisation. The academic learning disability world, even in the early eighties, was still medically oriented, though psychologists, especially behaviourists, had made inroads. Reports of the studies into the few real projects based on the 'normalisation principle' began to appear (e.g. Ward 1987) but the learning disability academic establishment were on the whole somewhat scathing about the 'unscientific' nature of PASS, and the 'evangelism' of the workshops given by CMHERA (e.g. Heron & Myers 1983.). Within services however, in some parts of the country, hearts rather than, or sometimes as well as, minds were being reached. Leaving later arguments over the presentation of workshops aside for the present, the undoubted result of CMHERA's programme of work and its follow-up by key local individuals meant that the full effect of services on people's lives (not just people with learning disabilities, and not just institutions) was revealed to a many in the service system by the intensity and thoroughness of the PASS workshop process (Tyne 1987). Given that services were still largely controlled by a few people in any one locality, i.e. a few key individuals in a Local Authority and a similar number in managerial positions in the Health Service, it was possible for major changes in thinking to be introduced in certain areas. It is my view that the key element in these changes was the realisation, noted above, of what the lives of people who received services were like. This then challenged individuals at all levels in the service hierarchy to make reference to values, which in many cases were not explicit in the services themselves; to realise that changes were needed; and to use the tool of PASS and other consultancy work by CMHERA and their network to develop those changes The fact that the response was made initially on a values basis does not, of course, mean that 'normalisation' *was* a set of values, or was taught as such, but the use of phrases like 'values based training' and organisations including 'values' in their titles gave an impression that there was a set of values being taught or, in some people's view, imposed. The fact of values challenge and the myth of 'brainwashing' on workshops led to a growing belief that what was being taught was not a set of ideas, still less a social science theory, but an ideology (e.g. Lindley & Wainwright 1992). Still further, the absence of any new version of 'normalisation' ideas in the same form as Wolfensberger's 1972 text led to understandable assumptions that PASS was the embodiment of those ideas as a set of rules, and that the objective of services should be solely to maximise their PASS ratings. This also fuelled the notion that, since PASS and PASSING had been primarily developed to evaluate professional services, 'normalisation' had no applicability to informal services, or to devaluation in the world at large. Academics, particularly those from the behavioural psychology side who still had some influence on services, struggled to come to terms with the development of what clearly was in Tyne's (1992) words a 'social movement'. They could not however, deny its power.

The development of SRV: A peculiar English experience

What the 'social movement' itself was to be less clear about, as the eighties progressed, was the development by Wolfensberger of his version of normalization into the 'theory' of Social Role Valorization. Whilst UK teachers on PASS and other workshops had, like those in the US, suffered all the frustrations of counter arguments to normalisation based on myths about 'conformity to the norm' and 'what is normal anyway?', those had been dealt with, more or less successfully, by the power of the workshop process getting to the heart of people's lives. That workshops were now talking about 'SRV' and yet still using, even with the new instrument of PASSING (Wolfensberger & Thomas 1993), a document that referred to 'normalisation', was a confusing issue for both the trainers and the trained. Later publications by Wolfensberger (1992a for example) and Lemay (1995) make clear the key changes in emphasis and conceptualisation that meant that SRV was not just a 're-naming' of normalisation, and this is covered in detail in chapter 5, but at the time no real discussion of this took place in the wider English learning disability scene, many parts of which were still coming to terms with, and in some cases resisting, 'normalisation'.

SRV made little impression on the academics who had not been involved in the training process of 'normalisation' and PASS(ING) workshops, but who saw the influence that they were having on services. Some dismissed it as a further attempt by Wolfensberger to distance himself from the real lives of people by jargon and 'professional' language (Booth 1988). Others sought to come to terms with the academic theory yet were frustrated by a lack of written material to get their teeth into (Burton 1994)

Other interweaving factors now led to more confusion and dispute, both within the 'social movement' and outside. It should not, of course surprise those who have been involved with devaluation and responses to it that a good deal of this confusion, and even acrimony, should have come about as a result of perceptions of the situation, rather than matters being clarified through face to face discussion. One strand of this upheaval concerned the differences in presentation of SRV between the US and the UK. With the exception of the visit by Susan Thomas, mentioned in the Prologue, to present an SRV workshop followed by the first PASSING workshop at Castle Priory in 1984, teaching of 'normalisation' had, as we have seen, been either through short lectures based on an individual teacher's reading and understanding of the available published material or, much more powerfully, via a self-contained PASS workshop. In the UK this workshop would include presented material on 'normalisation,' simulation exercises, one site visit to a human service, evaluation using the PASS instrument and a verbal feedback to the practice site. As Williams (1995a, op.cit) notes, this style of workshop had developed from work with John O'Brien, when he was a close associate of Wolfensberger's Training Institute. In the US, presentation of SRV ideas in two or three day lecture formats, sometimes but not always linked to a PASS workshop, became the Training Institute's preferred form, (Wolfensberger 1983). PASS, and then PASSING workshops were distinct events from these SRV presentations, though the presentations were a prerequisite for attending the workshops. In Training Institute supported PASSING workshops, which became the key workshops for exploring SRV ideas further in the US, two sites, as opposed to the one in the UK, were used for practice evaluations, and written feedback after the workshop, rather than verbal feedback during the workshop was provided to the practice sites.

Having participated in events on either side of the Atlantic, it is my view that each have advantages and disadvantages, and the difference between the PASS(ING) events themselves is not particularly significant particularly to those relatively new to SRV. What does appear to have been important in these differences, however, was the lack of detailed presentations of SRV ideas, as they developed and were modified from normalisation, and the adoption in the US and elsewhere of a predominance of PASSING, rather than PASS, as the preferred evaluation and training tool. In the US, in Canada, and then later in Australia, a 'training culture' developed around SRV presentations, using Training Institute materials, giving a perception within the attending population of at least some connection to the 'authors' of SRV. It also gave a perception to the network in England that their way of doing things was not 'approved' by the Training Institute, and that they were setting up a selective hierarchy of trainers and others, to which English trainers were not invited. At the same time, however, others in the English scene who wanted to pursue the Training Institute process had the perception that it was CMHERA who were resisting changes to their process, and maintaining their own selective hierarchy, with the added twist, in those times of great debates about political correctness in the late eighties, that it was perceived to be a heavily male dominated hierarchy. Whatever the truth of these various perceptions it is ironic that Wolfensberger should be totally blamed, as he is in a number of academic articles that began to appear in the late eighties, for keeping 'control' over the SRV material when, in fact, some of the material that was 'controlled' was that presented by CHMERA. As in England, of course, some people involved with SRV in the USA and elsewhere presented versions of it that were totally unlike those written by Wolfensberger but only in England was it hard to find individuals who did present the full Training Institute version of SRV, and as the SRV training culture in other parts of the world took account of the various developments in the Training Institute materials, the gap between English presentations of the theory and others elsewhere increased.

What did happen in the UK was that both PASS and PASSING workshops continued into the late eighties, though now referring to SRV rather than normalisation. A distinct format for PASS workshops was also introduced by Kristjana Kristiansen, which differed from those produced by CHMERA and attempted to insist on SRV training as a pre-requisite. Unfortunately, as we have seen, Training Institute style three day SRV training did not really take place at this time. This also did not prevent, as noted above, many people who had attended PASS(ING) workshops (and some who had attended the few full SRV events in the late eighties) seeking to teach their own version of SRV and these versions began to appear in professional training courses, especially in nurse training in the state sector.

Some have argued, of course, that the distinctions between SRV and normalisation are less than the Training Institute would suggest, but that debate was not really held in any sort of public or published forum. Instead, those services which had been active in developing services from a normalisation standpoint began to face a backlash, particularly as over zealous use of PASS(ING) ratings as if they represented mandates for action became commonplace. Added to this, the promotion by CMHERA of O'Brien's workshop 'Framework for Accomplishment' (O'Brien & O'Brien 1989), and then many others taking from this the list of 'Five Accomplishments' gave the movement and the services, as well as a very useful developmental tool, a much less painful analysis than PASS(ING) and the sort of language that can be much more readily put into service planning documents and statements of vision. The fact that O'Brien made clear the distinction between normalisation and his formulation of accomplishments (O'Brien & O'Brien 1989 op.cit) did not prevent a widespread acceptance of his ideas as being an 'alternative version' of normalisation. (e.g. Emerson 1992).

As well as the debates over training, which might not have been that apparent to those outside the small number of people closely involved, another dimension arose in the late eighties and into the nineties which was to cause yet more dissension and confusion, both within the narrow circle of the 'movement' and in the wider service and academic world. This dimension was the series of visits from the mid eighties onwards, to initially large audiences, of Wolf Wolfensberger to England. Because of the power of the 'social movement' even by 1985 when he first came, and certainly by the later visits towards the end of the eighties, very many people were interested in listening to Wolfensberger's presentations. The problem, as I see it, of those visits, as far as the development of SRV was concerned, was that his presentations did not deal with SRV, but instead focused on Wolfensberger's wider, some would say higher level concerns, with the changing values of western society, with the growth of what he termed the Post Primary Production Economy, and with the massive increase, as he saw it, in the threat to the lives of vulnerable people. Though these views were published variously, the real impact on the 'social movement' came from the actual presentations.

First, the style was similar to the Training Institute style for SRV theory events, with extensive lecture style presentations and use of multiple overhead projectors. This, as we have seen was unfamiliar to the English scene. More importantly, the views presented, especially on 'deathmaking' as far as many feminists were concerned, and on higher order issues of beliefs, as far as agnostic, atheist or other religious sceptics were concerned, presented a major challenge to the values of his audiences. Of course many other listeners agreed with a great deal of what he was saying, and still others took them as an interesting set of views to put alongside other worldviews, but what, again in my view, was most significant about these events as far as the 'movement' was concerned was the combination of an apparent 'orthodoxy' on SRV or 'normalisation', either from Wolfensberger or from CMHERA depending on the perceiver, with a powerful challenge to the highest order beliefs of people in the network coming from Wolfensberger's public presentations. To those on the edges of the 'social movement' it often appeared that they were being asked to take Wolfensberger 'all or nothing' though he made strenuous efforts to separate out the developing theory of SRV from his other views.

The English academic backlash: Critiques of 'normalisation' or SRV?

As noted above, therefore, later developments by Wolfensberger, in the early nineties, of SRV into a full-blown social science theory, which emerged formally at the 1994 Ottawa conference 'Twenty Five Years of Normalization, Social Role Valorization and Social Integration: A Retrospective and Prospective View.' went largely un-noticed in the training world, and even less in the academic world. The confusion about 'normalisation' and the effect of Wolfensberger's other views was then strongly reflected in the academic literature of the late eighties and early nineties. Like many other areas of life in the England at this time, a much more competitive market place had been created in academia, in particular for publication. In learning disability, as elsewhere, academics responded to this market place by an increase in quantity, if not necessarily quality. Academics in the learning disabilities field could not deny the impact of 'normalisation', via CMHERA's influence in particular, on services. Yet they could not, with a few exceptions (e.g. Alexewski and Ong 1990) discuss the ideas themselves and particularly the notion of SRV as a significant development from 'normalisation', since they had little UK or any other material to work with. Research reports of 'new' services developed under 'normalisation principles' could be carried out, and were (Alexewski & Ong 1990; Ward 1987). So too could writings based on the growing attempt to hear the stories of people with learning difficulties, (Brechin & Walmsley 1989) and those in turn would occasionally acknowledge the influence of 'normalisation' in seeking to obtain such stories. At the more academic level, however, critiques of the ideas began to appear which, whilst perhaps valid as critiques of 'normalisation', used as their sources material which Wolfensberger himself had already acknowledged as being earlier foundations and ideas (Wolfensberger 1985). In particular, academic writers were basing their critiques on one or more of the following: a) experiences of PASS(ING) workshops, which as we have seen did not give lengthy expositions of SRV ideas and which were not generally experiences that academics could relate to, particularly the degree of effort involved; b) the PASS(ING) manuals themselves, which are tools for evaluation based on normalization and SRV and not statements of rules about what should happen; c) a return to earlier publications, especially Wolfensberger's 1972 text, instead of;. d) attendance at, or hearing accounts of, Wolfensberger's other events in England.

Many articles in the journal *Disability, Handicap and Society* (now *Disability and Society*) are particularly vehement in this area, though other journals have their own pieces. Late eighties and early nineties text books also take a swipe at 'normalisation' (e.g. Baldwin & Hattersley 1991). Issues of importance, such as a feminist critique of normalisation, (Brown & Smith 1989) are thereby intermingled with almost personal attacks on Wolfensberger (Jackson 1994). Nearly all discuss the interpretation of the ideas in training events or in services rather than the ideas of SRV itself. In particular the use of 'An Ordinary Life' as a phrase to represent SRV and to criticise it, though usually still under the name 'normalisation', has become frequent, despite Wolfensberger having apparently never used the term. Even in one of the few attempts at an academic evaluation that goes beyond the confines of UK publications (Pilling 1995) the focus is on the PASS and PASSING instruments, rather than the ideas, and the author still uses the umbrella term of 'normalisation'. So although her chapter finds empirical evidence to support certain aspects of SRV contained in PASSING, in particular the themes of expectancies, imagery and integration, and deals cogently with the academic critics mentioned above, the idea of SRV as a distinct theory is still not brought out. Nor, curiously, is this particular evaluation often cited in later critiques of normalisation by English academics.

The broader English experience: Some effects of Thatcherism

At the same time, and interwoven with the academic confusion about what SRV ideas are really about and how these are distinct from, yet relate to, normalisation (or O'Brien's accomplishments) came the much broader force of the Thatcher government's policy on welfare services, and the declining extent to which academic thinking was referred to in determining that policy. The debates of the seventies in the learning disability field had been fairly fierce, even vituperative, but they were debates about ideas as well as profesional and organisational power. The fact that they were also

debates that could reach the relatively few people who controlled services made them potentially more influential. The impact of CMHERA in the eighties, also exerting pressure for services to examine the values on which they were based, had in its turn had a powerful impact, especially on practice. Moving into the nineties, however, with government policy becoming clearer, two key factors, in my view, diminished still further the declining impact of 'normalisation' on services (or any ideas based on the development of planned, values based, and safeguarded public services) .

The first was what Butcher (1995) described as the move from a notion of 'public administration service' to a welfare market. Successive changes in welfare services culminating in the impact of the NHS and Community Care Act, 1990 have meant that there is no longer an identifiable or even a manageable number of people in control of what happens in service development (Lewis & Glennerster 1996). These changes have also separated the purchasers of service from the providers, typically with the purchasers of learning disability services being non-specialists. This is especially so in Health Authorities, where learning disability will only be part of a much broader brief. Local Authorities, though they too have purchasing responsibility, and often 'lead' responsibility, are increasingly being forced to purchase services from organisations from the independent sector over whom they have no real control, other than very broad specifications, often confined to basic physical standards. All the work in the eighties to spread 'normalisation' ideas, had therefore resulted in some improvements in terms of physical settings, particularly in residential care. Staff performance improvements, however, in terms of the quality of service, and even those physical setting themselves, are now under threat. This threat is from purchasers of services who have little experience of learning disability, let alone 'normalisation', and certainly not SRV. This has tended to lead to a response based on financial, rather than values led forces.

The second key element to add to the confusion was the continuing decline of academic influence on policy. The refusal of Oxford University to award an Honorary Degree to Margaret Thatcher in the mid eighties was symbolic of a belief, from the traditional heart of academia in England, that respect for ideas was not a priority for her government. The irony that university departments would be formally judged (and financed) on their research and publication output as opposed to their teaching, and yet that published output would be ignored if inconvenient to ministers, has resulted in a mushrooming of publications, including those already noted critiques of normalisation and SRV, but precious little influence on services. This of course is not unique to services for people with learning disabilities, but the potential for SRV ideas to influence policy was weakened by the combined effect of academic disdain within the still small group of learning disability academics, the notion within the wider academic world that SRV is a learning disability theory, and the lack of listening by policy makers. Such an effect was exemplified clearly by the publication in 1996 by Hatton and Emerson, two leading academics in the learning disability field, of what was described as a 'comprehensive review of research' into residential care for people with learning disabilities. This review, commissioned by the national Department of Health was intended to bring together all the research on residential care. It had, as an advisory body, an eminent panel of other academics in learning disability and therefore would have been expected to have covered the full range of academic thinking in this field. What emerges in the publication, however, would give the impression to an outside reader that 'normalisation', and especially SRV, had not existed as a force for change in residential services. This is despite a number of research reports included in their review being on services that specifically came about as a result of the influence of CHMERA and the 'social movement' of the eighties. Nor is any reference made to accounts of services by people themselves, despite many having been published as a result of the 'normalisation' movement. Nor are published evaluations using PASS (e.g. Williams 1995b) or accounts of 'normalisation's effect on service agencies (e.g. Williams and Race 1988) included in this review. Not only does this reveal the extent to which a received wisdom has emerged as to what are or are not 'respectable' publications, but it also adds to the impression that 'normalisation' and SRV have 'been done' and therefore have little to contribute to the debate over service provision.

It is ironic that there is currently a move within the NHS and Social Services Departments to ascertain and favour 'evidence based practice' and yet those projects within learning disability services that emerged from the power of the teaching of PASS(ING) workshops by CHMERA have not been evaluated by PASS(ING) or where they have the evaluations have not been considered reputable enough to publish in a 'comprehensive' review of research and evaluation.

Conclusion: The need for this book

It is now difficult to fill places on PASS and PASSING workshops in England. Even the promise of the first public airing in the world of a revised and fully developed SRV theory in 1995 failed to attract more than around 30 people from all over the UK. Virtually none of these were academics, still less those publishing continuing critiques of normalisation based on out of date sources (e.g. Chappell 1997).

Even were there more interest in SRV ideas by academics, it is doubtful that they would have the influence on services that either the early ideas of normalisation, as discussed and promoted by academics, did on the Jay

Committee and the Kings Fund Group or that the experience of peoples' lives did on considerable numbers of service staff, of all levels, carers and service users who attended CMHERA workshops in the eighties. Considerable changes occurred as a result of both of those two forces, and the individuals who then moved from that starting point to related responses to devaluation in such areas as advocacy and the inclusion movement. While SRV as an academic theory may still find a place worldwide, not least through the third (1998) edition of Wolfensberger's monograph, and the development of the international journal *SRV/VRS*, what is unlikely to occur, in this author's view, is a change either in hearts or minds of those currently shaping services for people with learning disabilities in England.

Unless the new government alters the attitude to academia, and unless the organisational changes within the service system brought about by its predecessors can be harnessed to bring values back to the forefront, the continuation of what has been described elsewhere as 'chaos' in community care services, (Race 1999) will continue. For services for people with learning disabilities, the situation may be even worse, since a belief within the service system that they have had their 'period in the sun' in the heady days of 'normalisation', is still strong.

It is therefore only a small hope that SRV may be given a fair hearing as a result of the small but growing SRV network in the UK (perhaps drawing strength from work in Wales) and from other applications of SRV, in the fields of mental health and services for older people. The rest of this book is an attempt to play a part, at least at an academic level, in that hearing.

2

Social Devaluation:
The foundation of SRV

Introduction

Perhaps the most significant impact of 'normalisation' and then SRV, on people working in English services was, as we discussed in the last chapter, a much fuller realisation of what the lives of people who used services were like. Much of this realisation came through spending time with people on the site visit of a PASS or PASSING workshop and then setting that experience against the sharp focus of a group assessment. Much of the subsequent action, however, stemmed from an individual's choice of path, having reached what O'Brien (in press) describes as the 'turning point' between 'detachment', i.e. removing oneself from paid human services and either making an individual commitment to someone or simply getting involved in something else entirely, and 'creation', i.e. trying to work in new ways within the service system to better the lives of users, whilst acknowledging its shortcomings. Many people took one or the other path, while others did not acknowledge the reality of the experiences they had observed and continued as they had before the workshop.

Few people turned their minds to the theoretical foundation of both normalization and SRV in social devaluation, and this may, as noted above, have led to a number of academic critiques based on second hand information about the detail and scope of normalization and SRV. This in turn tended to result in particularistic actions being taken, and particularistic examples being used in academic analysis. Some of the actions merely consisted of 'stopping things', for example, taking down pictures deemed to give a bad image, or preventing service users going out with other service users because this constituted 'congregation'. The 'stopping' was, unfortunately, not always replaced with any alternative. Similarly a number of the academic critiques focused on such specific actions, or on elements of the PASS or PASSING manuals instead of examining the broad scope of the ideas. Thus attention was diverted from the part individuals and groups, as members of a professional service culture but more importantly as human beings and members of a particular society, played in social devaluation.

This may, to some extent, have been the result of the teaching process purposely focusing on ideas for action for people working in services through the PASS(ING) analysis, with only a limited time on a more detailed academic analysis or exposition of the ideas, unlike the three or four day SRV presentations in other parts of the world. More broadly, however such lack of introspection on the scale of the devaluing process and one's own part in it seems to come from a very human reaction to the mass of information, both within the service system and in the wider world leading to the adoption of one of two views: either, that devaluation is something that other people do, on an individual basis, which can be trained out, legislated out, or 'procedured out'; or that it is the result of the massive forces of capitalism, racism and male dominance of society and that one should do nothing unless it actively challenges these malevolent forces, otherwise one is 'colluding in oppression.'

What this chapter will attempt to do is to convince the reader that social devaluation, which is the foundation of both normalization and of SRV, is universal, present in all societies at all times. It is also contended that devaluation is part of the human condition, and thus whilst its expression is heavily influenced by social and economic conditions and the various power groups in society, it will, as the Bible says of the poor, always be with us. A corollary of this is, of course, that whether one likes the fact of devaluation is irrelevant to its being present, and that no amount of denial of unpleasant things will make them go away. Critics of SRV who therefore see it as irrelevant to, or at worst conniving with, injustice and oppression will therefore be addressed.

Devaluation: Some initial clarifications

What, then, do we mean by devaluation, and societal devaluation in particular? As with many issues surrounding SRV we have first to deal with the matter of language. Because of the acknowledged connection with the sociological theory of 'deviancy,' the language used in a number of writings on normalization, (e.g. Wolfensberger 1972), includes the words 'deviant' as in 'deviant behaviour' or 'deviancy' as in 'deviancy image' i.e. an image that gives out a message of deviancy. This has been the cause of some criticism from a number of directions. Some, especially feminist, sociologists have argued that the theory of deviance, according to which societies needed to create and punish 'deviants' as a means of social control to maintain the status quo, was 'outdated' and part of 'male functionalist' explanations of society (Chappell 1992). Though this view has been taken up in some discussions of 'normalisation' it is far from agreed amongst sociologists (see, for example Hirschi and Gottfredson 1994, for continuing analysis of 'the generality of deviance'). Nonetheless, the implication drawn in England was that, by its association with deviancy, normalisation was a redundant theory. Similarly, sociologists from the growing disabled people's movement looked at the notion of their being seen as 'deviant' as yet another example of an attribute, supposedly intrinsic to their identity, which amplified society's disabling tendency towards them (Barnes 1990). Whatever the validity of these criticisms, and there will be much more said about them later, it is important to be clear that, as long ago as 1979, and certainly in his articles analysing his reformulation of normalization into SRV, Wolfensberger (1985), in Lemay's words 'changed the focus of the principle of normalization, leaving behind its reliance on the sociological concept of deviancy, and turning to the concept of social devaluation' (Lemay 1995, p517)

Though clearer and more easily examined, the language of devaluation has also had its problems. One, continuing from the 'deviancy' critiques, claimed that SRV was implying that devalued people were intrinsically so, i.e. it was part of them, rather than being something which society imposed on them. I hope that it will be clear as this chapter proceeds that it is the position of SRV theory, as it was with normalization, that devaluation 'is in the eye of the beholder' (a phrase much used at SRV theory presentations). Whether that 'beholder' is an individual or a group of people, or even the majority of a society is, as we shall see, important as to the effects of devaluation, but whether one person or a million devalues a person does not say anything about their inherent worth, at least as far as SRV theory is concerned. In this respect the analysis of the social theory of disability (Oliver 1990), whereby the actions of a capitalist society imposing a view of the reality of disability as played out in the so-called 'medical model', is in accord with SRV theory, though SRV would look for a broader source of devaluation than simply the need for capitalism to create a pool of individuals surplus to the economic system. Again, much more will be said later on the connections and differences, both real and perceived, between SRV and the social theory.

A further clarification of language is to state unequivocally that devaluation is not the same thing as dislike. Many valued people in any society may be disliked, even by quite a few others. Current examples would include 'fat cat' utility operators, politicians of various parties, sports stars (especially if one supports another team) and so on. Equally there are few individuals who are not liked, or even loved, by somebody, though they may be the subject of intense and systematic devaluation, such as we will describe later. Given the above clarifications we are now in a better position to look in more depth at social devaluation.

The devaluation process

Devaluation as universal to humans

At the heart of the devaluation process is the perception of difference .If a person or group of people are, or become, different from others in ability, behaviour, or appearance and that difference is valued negatively by the majority or by powerful groups in society, that person or group becomes not only different but devalued. This can then lead to many additional handicaps and negative experiences for that person or group. We will say more about the last point in the next chapter, but first let us examine the elements of the seemingly obvious statement at the beginning. Why should some differences be valued negatively? Are there some basic elements of human experience that cause us to devalue others? Here we are into some very fundamental issues of human behaviour which have been the subject of much study at the personal level by psychologists, at the societal level by sociologists, and at the level of values by political and philosophical analysts. Unfortunately they all seem to want to stick to their own field and rarely is there a crossover of findings and views looking at the empirical fact of devaluation and using evidence from all these fields to support the notion of its universality. SRV leads us to do this, and it is in this sense a 'superordinate' theory, i.e. one which covers a wide range of empirical evidence from a number of disciplines (not, and here we get into language traps again, a 'superior' theory - merely one which seems to address a wider range of perspectives).

So from psychology we can draw the notion that human perception is essentially evaluative; 'we perceive to learn, as well as learn to perceive' as Gibson (1991, p616) has it. Some psychologists have even argued that this evaluative nature of perception is instinctively negative, since fear of strangeness and strange people is an adaptive response for survival (Lycan 1990). If this is a correct analysis then we must also note here the importance of what is perceived, as opposed to what might actually be there, and pay attention to all the processes of perception, and the different media through which our perceptions may be formed, when we come to look at how and why persons or groups are devalued.

We can add to the basic point that perception is evaluative the view, from sociology and social psychology (Woodward 1997; Abrams and Hogg 1990) that humans have a basic need for definition of who we are – our identity, both as individuals and as groups. From this need come attempts, which have occupied thinkers for centuries, to define what humanness is, what constitutes human worth, and what are the essential boundaries of societies and their sub-groupings. Many of these attempts have been not only for identity, i.e. asking the questions 'who am I', 'what makes me a worthy person' and what makes my group (tribe, nation, religious sect, etc.) unique; but for security, i.e. 'I am safer in being me if I can identify why I am not you', 'I am safer if I am more worthy than you' and 'I am safer being part of a group which is more worthy than another group'. It is therefore in my interest to have at least one other person who is not only different, but inferior, since that reinforces my sense of who I am, i.e. not them. Abrams and Hogg (1990, p3) in discussing how 'one' might wish to belong to an 'in-group', propose that 'to the extent that the in-group is perceived as both better and different than the out-group, thereby achieving positive distinctiveness, one's social identity is enhanced'. Again, we should note that we are trying to look at the reality of human experience, not what we might like it to be, so the fact that we may find it undesirable that humans seem to have behaved in this way for many generations should not blind us to the existence and power of this way of thinking..

An extension of this identity and security argument also comes from social psychology and covers the human tendency to release the tension we feel when things are not going as we would like by blaming somebody else (Brown 1996). This can be the human equivalent of 'kicking the cat' i.e. just hitting out literally or metaphorically at a conveniently available weaker person or group, but can, and does, become much more serious and far-reaching when this tendency is used, at the level of a community or even a whole society, to legitimise the scapegoating of sub-groups as being responsible for the ills of the whole. Many examples abound of this tendency, with the treatment of ethnic or religious minority groups in all societies and over all times standing out in its frequency.

When the above processes that enhance the tendency for devaluation are combined with the observations that scholars, and probably more powerfully artists (especially novelists), have made of the seemingly endless quest for power and privilege that make for social stratification, then our evidence for the universality of devaluation is reinforced still further. Some critics of SRV (or, in reality, 'normalisation') have accused it of not providing a 'materialist' analysis of devaluation (Chappell 1992) and thus not addressing the true reality of power, which they see as resting in the possession of material wealth and its associated privilege. Some come at this from a Marxist perspective, seeing the basis for human relationships as predicated on the unequal distribution of wealth, others from a feminist perspective, seeing the basis for human relationships being the unequal power position of men and women, and others combining the two, to explain stratification in society by men's dominance of both material and physical power (Brown and Smith 1989).

I would argue that, far from ignoring the role of that social stratification in devaluation, SRV's analysis includes its influence as a key process that leads to, and reinforces devaluation, but does not hold the view that it is the sole causal process. SRV goes further, by breaking the elements of stratification into at least those of economic stratification and that of class and status. The first is clearly a worldwide phenomenon, as many analysts of current and past world economic structures have pointed out, e.g. Dawson (1996). The latter two, whilst also present in all societies have, I believe, an enduring and unique influence over English society, sometimes to the point of being more important a cause of stratification, and certainly of devaluation, than simple economic differentials. The maintenance of England as a society obsessed with class, though increasingly unconsciously, still contributes most powerfully to the setting up of criteria for judging people. This is despite English participation in the more global phenomenon of a greater plurality of class divisions (Laclau 1990), and therefore the stratification being more complex than that which informed Marxism. The very use of the word 'class', in everyday English discourse, to describe things and people of high value is just one example of how certain behaviours and attributes can maintain certain people in status positions, sometimes regardless of their economic wealth, and keep others in low status positions, equally regardless of wealth. One only has to read the tone of certain newspapers with regard to winners of the National Lottery, if they are from a 'working class' background, to realise how many and how deeply ingrained are the indicators of class, and therefore of status, in English society. The Thatcher years may have made some people a lot richer, though the overall gap between rich and poor actually increased, but most people were still very aware of the hollowness of John Major's notion of a 'classless society'.

Now it could, and has been, argued that stratification and hierarchy are essentially male concepts (Maclean and Groves 1991) and that differentials of wealth and status are the result of centuries of domination of men, imposing across the world through physical and economic power the notion of competition as the intrinsic part of human nature that guides, and should guide human relationships. This argument goes further to state that, since men make the rules of the competition, they have legitimised, and taken into people's unconscious assumptions, whole varieties of criteria by which women in particular, but also other groups who do not fit the criteria for competition, are placed in positions of devaluation. A look worldwide at the status of women would tend to support this view, and a view of history in terms of conquest, warfare and the placing of people from different cultures as 'inferiors' or, worse, 'inhuman' would also seem to be a corollary. As a critic of this situation puts it, 'the integrity of the nation becomes the integrity of its masculinity. In fact it can only be a nation if the correct version of gender hierarchy has been established and reproduced', (Gilroy 1997, p333). Those who hold those views who have also had some contact with SRV then accuse its analysis of devaluation as 'not addressing' the issues of gender and race. It is true that the analysis of devaluation at the root of SRV does not specifically ascribe those devaluing attributes of human behaviour described above to 'mankind' as opposed to 'humankind.'

It is a moot point, however, and one which is beyond the scope of SRV theory, as to whether those devaluing human processes, which empirically can be seen to be carried out by both women and men, have, in effect, been 'imposed' on women by men as being what is somehow 'natural' or whether they are in fact features of 'humankind' as a whole. Whatever is the case, such arguments do little to deny the universality of devaluation, only to raise as speculation whether it would still exist were the power to be equalised, or handed over to women. Similarly, the devaluation of imperial subjects by the colonisers, and the devaluation of immigrant groups by the host country seems to have been unaffected by whether the colonisers or the immigrants were of one ethnic group or another, if one takes a long view of history, rather than just looking at the past two hundred years or so, or just focusing on Western imperialism.

SRV therefore posits that devaluation is universal, and has been and is carried out in all societies and at all times in history. The corollary of this, which again has caused controversy, is that devaluation is carried out by everybody.

Devaluation is carried out by everybody

In our earlier discussion we noted two views on devaluation prevalent in the human service system and in wider society. One, that devaluation is something done by other people, and that it can be socially or legally 'engineered out' of people, and two, that it is so endemic to western male capitalism that only an overthrow of that, or at least mass resistance, will address the problem. The perceptive reader may also have picked up, at the beginning of the section on the process of devaluation, that it is the positive or negative perceptions of the majority or powerful groups in society which turn difference into devaluation. So is devaluation therefore only the responsibility of, or is it only enacted by, certain sections of society? If this were true, then theoretically the more enlightened could, through education or legislation, change the perceptions of the majority or the powerful groups. The evidence seems more to point towards everybody being involved in some form of devaluation, but the effects of that devaluation varying with a number of factors. The first is the four way split between who is doing the devaluing, and who gets devalued. If an individual devalues another individual, then the form and power of the effects of that devaluation will be very idiosyncratic, perhaps not amounting to no more than an avoidance of one person by another. On the other hand such devaluation can be very significant if the devaluing individual has power over the individual being devalued. Obvious examples are wife-beating husbands or abusive parents, where devaluation can become life-defining or even life taking. Similarly, the devaluation by an individual of a group or class of people will vary in its effects dependent on the power of that individual over the group, and the opportunities for the individual to become involved in group to group devaluation. So an individual racist may be considerably less influential than one who inspires other racists to action, or one who joins a racist group, though individuals can still very powerful in certain situations, e.g. as a lone village schoolteacher or prison governor.

Because of the obvious extreme examples it is often difficult for many people, who would see themselves as aware citizens totally unlike such extremists, to come to terms with their own participation in devaluation. However, in many exercises at SRV workshops and elsewhere it is very revealing for participants to look into themselves honestly, and think of individuals or groups that they do, in their heart of hearts, devalue. Even where this is very idiosyncratic, there is within people a great reluctance to acknowledge such feelings, particularly if they are part of the service culture, since many parts of that culture now have policy statements to 'procedure out' such feelings. It is rare, however, when people are asked to look at their feelings in private, for devaluation of groups or individuals not to emerge.

If this is true for individuals, who have limited, though not insignificant, power to put their devaluation into effect, then when it comes to collective devaluation, by a group or class, the potential for a much greater effect is realised. Collective devaluation of an individual tends to be rarer than collective devaluation of another group, but can be devastating in its effects, amounting almost to demonisation. This has been demonstrated in recent years in England in the cases of certain sex offenders being obliged to notify the police of where they are going to live on their release from prison. Regardless of the values issues here, those people have been so devalued by the media that 'action groups' appear at whichever town they propose to stay, making them virtual prisoners after their release from gaol.

That example is also one where an individual becomes an embodiment of a class or group which is devalued by a significant group in the wider society, and so we get on to the main focus of SRV, which is the systematic social devaluation of a group or class of people. This can also be another way of looking at devaluation overall, i.e. as being essentially rooted in group to group devaluation, but carried out in practice depending on the power relationships in the individual/group two by two matrix. Therefore the effects of group to group devaluation, being at the core, is likely to be both more powerful and more widespread. This focus of SRV also addresses, in the English experience, the tendency, noted in the introduction to this chapter, to reduce analysis and criticism of SRV to its effects at the individual level only. To do so is to miss a number of points, not least the fact that SRV as a social science theory only claims to be empirically testable at the probabilistic level. In other words it will apply in the long run and over a large number of examples, and thus individual exceptions are inevitable. It also misses the point, made in Wolfensberger's 1995 paper on the teaching of SRV that SRV does not 'tell people what to do' in any particular set of circumstances, but merely points out the likely effects of certain actions, leaving people to weigh the effects against the 'costs' by reference to their values, which will be the ultimate guide to action. This contrasts with the analysis of certain critics (Robinson 1989) who, by using individual situations where the 'desirable' action, i.e. action taken on the basis of a person's values, differed from what the authors interpreted as what SRV 'said' should happen, have thought to thereby 'disprove' SRV. More than ever in individual situations, but no less in considering the effects on groups, SRV is clear about the necessity of a detailed and accurate assessment of the social situation to judge the likely outcomes of any action, which action should then be weighed up by reference to values. Therefore blanket prescriptions are not what SRV is all about, even though what has been said and occasionally done in its name may lead to the opposite view.

The filters of social judgment

If we therefore grant for now that devaluation is universal, that it is carried out by everybody, at an individual and collective level, and that while individual devaluation can have powerful effects the devaluation of groups of people by other groups (including majorities, powerful groups or even whole societies) has a more devastating effect on large numbers in any society, we can begin to look in more detail at the significant elements of the devaluation process.

Table 2.1 below, which has featured in SRV theory events for many years, and is adapted with permission from Wolfensberger (1998), provides us with a way of doing so. It proposes that the judgment of an observer, who again may be an individual or a group, will be influenced powerfully by four factors, which we will examine in turn below. Before that, however, it is important to try and clear up some confusions and objections to this analysis which, in the English experience, may have resulted in a lessening of its impact.

First, and this is really a repetition of the 'individual case defeats overall theory' argument discussed above, because some people may not consider that they are influenced by some or all of the factors listed this does not invalidate the analysis. It may well be that certain people have refined their own views and values to such a level that they are capable of forming judgments totally without external influence. If such people exist, they are rare, if the evidence from the advertising industry, let alone more academic studies from perceptual psychology are taken into account (Alvarado and Thompson 1990). Even were they to exist, the fact that the effects of collective devaluation only require a majority, or a powerful minority, to

Table 2.1
How a Person or group (the observer) will form a social judgement about
another person or group

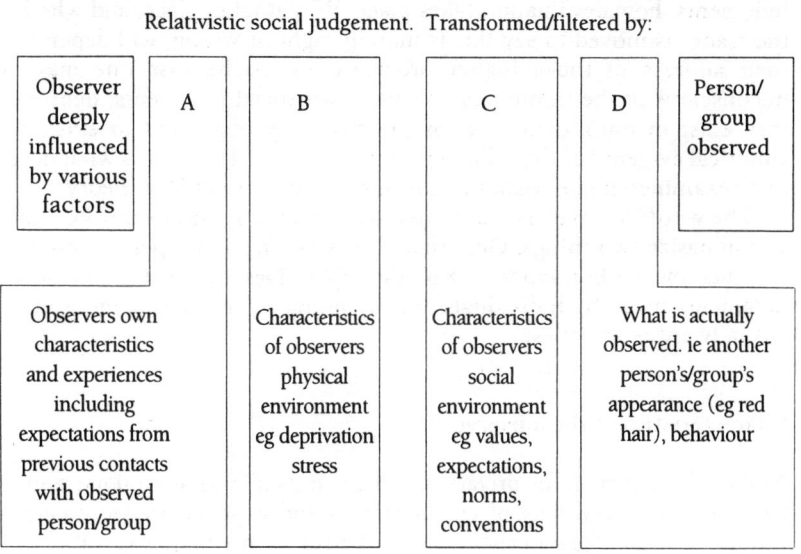

Relativistic social judgement. Transformed/filtered by:

Observer deeply influenced by various factors	A	B	C	D	Person/ group observed
Observers own characteristics and experiences including expectations from previous contacts with observed person/group		Characteristics of observers physical environment eg deprivation stress	Characteristics of observers social environment eg values, expectations, norms, conventions		What is actually observed. ie another person's/group's appearance (eg red hair), behaviour

make negative judgments about a group would still make such an analysis worthwhile. What is probably more at issue with such critics is that they do not like the way people and groups make social judgments because it offends against a value position that people ought to judge people for 'who they are' rather than be influenced by external factors. This point, or a close variant of it, will occur time and again in the English experience of SRV. It has occurred elsewhere, of course, but the particular combination of the timing of the introduction of normalization/ SRV, especially during the years of Thatcherism, and the political and philosophical orientation of academia at the time, especially the increasingly influential feminist perspectives, makes it crucial to an understanding of English reactions to SRV.

Ironically, this very dislike of social judgments being based on external influences can be traced to a reaction to thousands of years of that very process dominating English society. The very words 'position in society' will bring out some very deep reactions in anyone over twenty-five or so, and the effect of those words in defining people's lives is embedded in the collective unconscious. These questions, however, relate to higher order values about how we see our fellow human beings, and the history of English society is one of tension between different answers to them. SRV does not operate at a high enough level to deal fully with these complex issues, or even with how those value positions affect devaluation. All it seeks to do is help us to understand, by looking at the influences on social judgments, how devaluation takes place. Why it takes place, and whether the reader is moved to say this is morally right or wrong, will depend on their address of those higher order values. So because one may be unconscious of the influences on one's own social judgments, deny that they exist in one's own case, or say that they ought not to exist, the empirical evidence of the influence of the factors of Table 2.1 is what needs to be examined if one wishes to consider the validity of SRV theory.

The word 'observer' is put in inverted commas in the ensuing headings to emphasize two things. One, that SRV is talking about perception, and not just mere observation. Two, that SRV does not just cover social judgments made by individuals, but by groups of people, ranging up to virtually entire societies.

Characteristics of the 'observer'

As the advertisement for private healthcare puts it, 'you are unique' and in terms of a whole variety of characteristics and experiences every person making a social judgment about another will do so in a unique way. Previous contact by the observer with the person or group observed will therefore also have been experienced in a unique fashion, and will have set up particular expectations with regard to that person or group. As noted earlier those experiences, as well as being about perception, are about evaluation, and will therefore have formed a positive or negative expectation of the next encounter. In addition to direct experiences of a person or group, however, an observer will be very likely to have had other experiences, especially in what they may have been indirectly, or even systematically, taught. Impressions picked up in the formative years are very powerful and so what is said about another person or group by one's parents and other childhood influences can be highly significant in the characteristics that one brings to a social judgment. Many studies of racism, for example, point to the influence of parental opinions (Kushnick 1998). The observer's more general physical and mental characteristics, though again influenced by both personal experiences and teaching, will affect how they regard their fellow human beings, not just the group in question. This is also relevant here, in giving a range of predispositions from positive to negative.

Characteristics of 'observer's' physical environment

Psychologists are well aware of the effect that any particular physical environment has on an individual's behaviour (Evans and Garling 1991), including the result of altering the physical constitution of the person, as by deprivation of food or inducement of stress. In collective contexts, too, such as warfare or rioting, behaviour, and of course the perceptions of the situation that lead to behaviour, are significantly affected by the physical environment in which they take place. Social judgments, central as we have said to devaluation, are no exception to this observed pattern. In warfare, any stranger is more likely to be interpreted as an enemy; on depressed housing estates, young people in a group are likely to be interpreted very differently than a similar sized group would be at a school open day. Individuals or groups operating under stress will form rather different views of other people in the same stressful situation than the same people in a more relaxed environment. Again, whether they ought to feel this way is not material to this argument

Characteristics of 'observer's' social environment

Here again certain critics of 'normalisation' (Brown and Smith 1992a) have laid the charge that only the dominant social environment is considered to be important, or that 'normalisation' assumes that there is one homogeneous social environment, thereby not allowing for the diversity of many societies (Gilbert 1993). This is not the case. By asking the reader to consider the effect of the social environment on people's social judgment of others, SRV is explicitly acknowledging the diversity of cultures, and the diversity of groups and sub-groups within those cultures. It is also acknowledging, along with a great wealth of sociological and social psychological literature, the influence that values, norms and expectations have on the members of any one group or sub-group of a given society. It also then goes on to suggest that such values, norms and expectations produce a range of social judgments made about one group by another, often including negative judgments. This is perhaps the stumbling block for some people, either because they believe that groups should not make such judgments, or they do not like some of the judgments that get made. This is understandable, particularly in light of the English experience of sexism, racism, and class prejudice (Kushnick 1998) but it does not alter the empirical evidence that positive and negative judgments are made at all levels of society, by all sorts of groups about other groups, including victims of devaluation about other victims of devaluation. Given that, by definition, SRV theory only operates in a social context, it is not surprising that the social environment is seen by the theory as being key to the devaluation process, and certainly very powerful in contexts of collective devaluation. As with all the four factors, of course, there are complex interactions and feedback loops between the social environment and other elements, so that, for example, someone brought up to have respect for older people may find themselves in a culture that devalues that group, and therefore be torn between the two judgments, or in a social environment that reinforces the respect that the person was taught as a child, therefore confirming the positive judgment.

What is actually 'observed'

In many situations direct observation of another person or group can much affect the social judgment of them by others, as evidenced by how often people will say 'He was much nicer than I expected' or 'she was much more fun than you'd led me to believe.' But even this effect is acknowledging the power of prior expectations, and in many cases these dominate the judgment, despite what is actually observed. Psychologists have shown a number of instances where prior expectation totally overcomes direct observation, or where direct observation tends to focus on factors largely irrelevant to the overall judgment of the person or group (Fiedler 1996). So, for example, the social and environmental forces surrounding a visit by the Queen, together with one's own upbringing and personal views on the royal family, are unlikely to be greatly affected by the fact of personal observation or even direct contact. Most anecdotal accounts talk of people merely commenting how much 'shorter she is in real life.' It is also an interesting insight into the relevance of direct observation that a great deal of the literature on racism reveals the virulently held views on different racial groups revealed by people who have never met, or even observed, anyone from the ethnic group about whom their opinions are held (Kovel 1988).

Where direct observation and contact does seem to be important, it involves a number of other dimensions. First impressions, again well supported by the psychology literature (Fiedler 1996), are seen to be more powerful, especially those experienced early in life, in informing the expectations that any observer may bring to a future encounter. If impressions were intense, perhaps associated with intense emotions, then that, too, will have a more powerful or long lasting effect. Then again experiences after the initial impressions that strongly reinforce the resultant expectations can be very powerful, though this works both ways, in that experiences that dramatically offer counter judgments to already held views have their own power (Hastie 1980).

Degrees of devaluation

One of the issues in the English experience of SRV that separates it, to some degree at least, from the experience of other countries, is the fact that it has largely remained in the field of learning disability. The origins of all versions of normalization in that field, and the retention in that field, or at least in the broader field of disability, of Scandinavian versions have led to normalization's successor, SRV, being seen as only of interest to learning disability services and academics. Other particular English factors, discussed in chapter 1, include the dominance in the teaching of 'normalisation' of CMHERA, with the name 'mental handicap' in their title, and the perceived impact on services for people with learning disabilities of 'normalisation' ideas. This is despite attempts by CMHERA and some of their associates to broaden the scope of their teaching to other service users especially the field of mental health. The specific reference, in the earliest definitions of SRV in the early eighties, to all groups 'at risk of devaluation' still does not seem, in England, to have moved the theory beyond learning disability, at least as judged from the literature. To this can be added the continued use of the word 'normalisation' or 'ordinary life principles' as synonyms for SRV. This has made it all the more difficult for those teachers and academics who wish to teach and discuss SRV theory in its fullest context, and for critics to claim that SRV does not 'take account of' issues relating to other oppressed groups than people with learning disabilities.

As so often, a look at the detail of SRV theory would argue strongly against this view, particularly as it analyses factors affecting the degree of devaluation of different groups. First of all, and perhaps obviously, as a theory firmly set in a societal context SRV clearly highlights great cultural and societal differences as to what and who is valued and devalued. This is to repeat the argument made earlier in response to the critics who accuse SRV of presupposing a homogeneous society. SRV does not say that there are not certain groups who appear to be devalued in many different societies, or to discount those observers of the international scene who note an increasing coming together of certain value trends in at least the industrialised nations (Kushnick 1998). Nevertheless, the degree of severity of devaluation, and the form it takes, does vary from culture to culture, and within sub-cultures, and those who seek to apply SRV in any given situation should take great care, as has been noted already to 'read' the culture(s) in judging which group will be devalued, and to what degree. With that in mind we can observe a number of factors that, given an astute observation of a society or group's values and expectations, can be seen to influence the likelihood or severity of devaluation.

- How far the values of the dominant group, which the devalued group are perceived to be violating, are deemed important or precious. If these are what the dominant group have at the very core of their identity, then perceived offence against them will strongly increase the likelihood and severity of devaluation. Religious values, in some countries, are primary examples of this, though less in the English experience in recent years in comparison to some more abstract notion of 'Englishness', offence against which feeds into the devaluation inherent in the racism and xenophobia still widely prevalent in English society.

- The number of values that the devalued group is perceived to have violated will affect the degree of devaluation. This, as we shall see, has resulted in the severe devaluation of people with learning disabilities in many cultures.

- How far the dominant values are perceived to be violated seems to correlate strongly with the degree of devaluation. An example of this is the increasing level of devaluation of older people, in a number of countries including England, as they are perceived increasingly to violate the youth and health oriented values dominant in those countries.

On the other hand, there appear to be a number of factors that act to reduce the degree of devaluation of a group, despite the presence of characteristics that would normally result in their being more severely devalued

- There may be religious or economic reasons for preserving some positive roles for people with devalued characteristics. Many people in England treat science as a religion. It is therefore not surprising that the role of Stephen Hawking as 'eminent scientist' should lessen his devaluation as a disabled person. Similarly, where groups of older people are seen to have economic power, as for example in certain English retirement area such as the south coast resorts, the degree of devaluation meted out to older people may be lessened.

- If a group or an individual is seen to have compensatory qualities that are valued, then the degree of their devaluation will be lessened (see chapter 8). This allows the astute observer to note changing patterns of what is valued and what is devalued at any one point in society. Thus for example, the greater visibility of people with learning disabilities, and their observed ability, in a number of situations, to occupy such valued roles as car driver, householder, worker or marriage partner could be argued to have reduced, albeit in a limited way, the devaluation of people with learning disabilities as a group.

- Having once held valued status before acquiring the devaluing characteristics can reduce the degree of devaluation. Ex-professors with dementia, 'eccentric' members of the aristocracy and celebrities with 'stress' as opposed to mental illness are all examples of this factor, though even here the fluid nature of societal values makes constant monitoring necessary.

- The degree of perceived permanence of the devalued condition is important in ascertaining the likely degree of devaluation. Examples of this go back a long way, particularly in the perceived difference between mental illness and learning disability. There has always been a distinction made in terms of the likelihood of recovery, even if other social policies have confused the two groups, and this was even embodied in law, where the lands of an 'idiot' were dealt with differently, and less favourably than those of a 'madman', precisely because the latter's devaluing characteristics, i.e. their 'madness', was thought to be less permanent (Race (1995).

- If a group or individual is felt to have positive connections to a person or group valued by the observer, then their devaluation may be lessened. This is shown, though with other implications, in the attachments to certain groups by 'celebrities' of one sort or another. Whilst this often maintains the 'charity' image of some groups, those celebrities who actually pay attention to the issue, as could be argued is the case with 'Red Nose Day' and its relationship with the disabled community, have managed to at least affect the degree of devaluation of certain groups.

- The connections between the observer and the devalued individual or group can affect the degree of devaluation. If the observer has positive connections to the devalued individual or group then the effect of the other influences on their social judgment is likely to be less, and therefore their devaluation less also. This is particularly relevant to parents of disabled people, especially those with learning disabilities, but can work both ways. There can be few more powerful advocates against the devaluation of disabled people than their parents, and yet of course it is that very power that can also contribute strongly to their devaluation. Those in favour of the abortion of people with disabilities regard as a trump card such statements from parents as 'if I'd known Charlie would turn out like this I would have had him aborted', and this can powerfully counteract the positive views of parents of disabled children. Nevertheless, a positive connection between the observer and the devalued person or group is still a factor in determining the degree of devaluation

Who gets devalued

In the next chapter, many examples will be given of groups of people who are, or have been, devalued in English society. By now, however, readers will be aware of the dangers of being too specific as to particular groups, given the variation in cultures and sub-cultures, and in what attributes get valued or devalued at any particular point in a society's history. To close this chapter on devaluation we will look at two categorisations that SRV theory has enumerated in terms of, first, what appear to be universal characteristics for which people are highly likely to be severely socially devalued and second, signs by which it may be deduced that a group is socially devalued.

The first categorisation lists five characteristics, which can occur individually or, more powerfully, in combination. Again, we urge the reader not to be diverted by whether they themselves share the devaluing perceptions or whether they think it to be right that people hold these perceptions, but to look analytically at English society, and powerful groups and dominant values within that society to see if the analysis fits.

First of all, then, and supported by findings from psychology (e.g. Stroebe and Jones 1996) people who do not look or act like what society expects from 'real' or 'full' human beings, are likely to be severely devalued. History abounds in societies defining who is, or who is not 'human'. That devaluation results is also very clear from history, with the treatment of slaves only being one of many examples. It is important too, as will be covered at length in the chapter on imagery, to note that SRV places great importance on the image of what constitutes humanness as well as the reality of behaviour and personal attributes.

Second, and also well documented in the literature, is the devaluing power of real or perceived failure to reciprocate relationships. It is very important to us to know, or at least be able to perceive, the reaction of another individual to our attentions. If we cannot do this then our reaction is either to assume that the individual is feeling what we ourselves think we would feel in this situation or that they have 'no feelings' and therefore fall foul of the first point above, as sentience is an element of many people's definitions of humanness. Either way, the lack of reciprocity of relationships also falls foul of the increasingly held value that people will not do 'something for nothing' so that acting to help someone who cannot acknowledge that help, or who acknowledges it differently from expectations, as in the case of autism, is hard for carers. Hence the view that such people are 'not worth' helping, which leads to some of the severest forms of devaluation.

People and groups who are perceived to be routinely and deliberately acting in contradiction, or even in direct opposition, to the major values of a society are the third instance of those likely to be severely devalued. Treatment of 'travellers' particularly those identified as 'new age' travellers, is an example of such a group, who are seen as deliberately defying the work ethic, the 'traditional family', and other widely held values in English society. Homophobia is another, though changing attitudes to homosexuality in various influential groups, such as the media, may be changing the severity of devaluation in this case.

Fourth, and going to one of the primary human instincts discussed earlier, being seen as a serious danger greatly increases the likelihood of severe devaluation. The treatment of people with AIDS, and the devaluation of people with mental health problems on the basis of several of well publicised cases of violent murder by former hospital patients provide two relevant examples.

More controversial, at least in how it is linked to highly charged debates on abortion and euthanasia, is the observation that severe devaluation is likely to result when individuals or groups are seen as disproportionately burdensome, demanding, or an obstacle to other people's desired ends. Though the protagonists are actually arguing at the level of higher order values, their debates are often expressed in utilitarian terms, invoking the 'costs' of caring for certain groups of people, especially the 'costs' to the carers. That the carers are disproportionately women also adds fuel to the controversy, but again we would ask readers to look at groups who are talked of in these terms, and observe the correlation with their devaluation. Finally, as we have alluded to already, being perceived as having combinations of the above characteristics is strongly linked to severe devaluation

Signs of devaluation

This chapter has been deliberately set at a high level of generality, in part because a full exposition of the ideas in an English context and in the light of English critiques is vital to an understanding of the English experience of SRV, and in part because devaluation, and the universality of it, is crucial to SRV as a social science theory. This chapter therefore closes as it began, with observations that, according to SRV, are universal signs that a group is socially devalued. It could be said to be an overview of the detail of the experiences of devaluation that will be given in the next chapter, but should be examined in its own right, in light of readers' own knowledge of devalued groups.

The first, and most obvious, sign appears if we look at which groups in society are consistently treated less well than clearly valued members of that society. Readers will have their own views, but in English society I would suggest a number. Disabled people, people in receipt of benefits, people from ethnic minority groups and single parents are four that immediately come to mind. Though some would raise the issue here of the degree of devaluation across the group as a whole and the consistency with which women are treated 'less well,' there is, of course much evidence of devaluation in the lives of women, and much of the analysis which follows of life experiences would be recognised by many women, as it would by gay people.

The second sign of a group's devaluation is its being systematically put at a distance from the rest of society, or at least significant sectors of it. This is revealed in a number of ways, from mere 'social distancing' being practised by valued groups in society, through physical distance being created via the gathering together of valued and devalued groups in different locations, to the enforced separation of devalued groups through various means, usually involving enforced congregation as well as segregation. Housing policies, the creation of 'exclusive' residential areas, as well as the more obvious institutionalisation of various devalued groups provide evidence to support this observation.

Thirdly, the systematic association, or 'juxtaposition' to use a term common in SRV, of one group with other devalued groups, both in terms of a physical and/or a symbolic association is another sign that such a group is itself devalued. More will be said on this later, but immediate examples of 'service campuses' where people with learning disabilities, people with mental health problems and elderly people are served on the same site, or even simple things like job titles which denote the postholder is responsible for a whole range of 'service users,' who may really have very different needs, illustrate the point.

Fourthly, any other systematic association with a group of any of the whole range of images suggestive of negative difference is a powerful indicator that the group is devalued. Appeals for charity, portrayals in the media, classification of the group as 'suffering from' whatever identity they happen to possess and many more images of negative difference all are a sure sign.

Finally, and to some extent ironically, given the avowed beneficent intent of it, scientific research on any particular group, or at least a much higher likelihood of being the subject of such research, is a good sign that a group is devalued. The disability movement in England has made much of this phenomenon, to the extent that research that is not designed and carried out by, or at least with, disabled people is viewed as 'unethical' (Moore, Beazley and Maelzer 1998). In SRV terms, the need for such a stance is a sure sign of the continuing devaluation of disabled people.

Conclusion

Devaluation is at the heart of SRV, as it was of normalization, but unlike 'normalisation,' at least in England, the analysis of SRV looks at devaluation from a high level of generality in terms of how it is applied, and to whom. This chapter has sought to show that devaluation is a universal phenomenon, that it applies both to individuals and groups and that it varies across cultures and sub-cultures. This variation is both of degree, and of the sort of groups who get devalued, though a number of common features can be postulated that seem to operate on a universal basis. We have also tried to demonstrate that devaluation can be observed empirically and thus SRV theory can be subject to the normal scientific tests of refutability via empirical evidence. Having said that, the issues of values raised by SRV, like normalization before it, are most important, and will be returned to as we continue to go into the English experience.

3

Experiences of devaluation: 'The wounds'—Part one

Introduction

Just as devaluation was at the heart of normalization, and was then developed and incorporated into SRV, so too the detailed exposition of the experiences of devalued people was first formulated in normalization, but expanded and developed in SRV, particularly the key element of the impact of devalued roles. In the early seventies Wolfensberger began using the term 'wounds' to describe these experiences, with reference to the usage by Jean Vanier, founder of the L'Arche movement, Vanier (1971). The description and detailed analysis of the 'wounding' process became incorporated as a key part of normalization, and then SRV theory presentations, and the reaction to it has been one of the key decision points for those involved with vulnerable people, in terms of whether they, first of all, acknowledge the validity of the analysis and, second, find it sufficiently offensive to their personal value position on what ought to happen to fellow human beings to do something about it. What they then actually do about it has often involved looking to SRV to provide a 'solution' to devaluation, indeed some have seen it as the only solution. SRV theory, however, though it offers perhaps the most systematic analysis of devaluation and some important strategies for countering it, does not claim to be the 'solution' to devaluation. It also, therefore, does not prescribe at which level those who are moved to oppose devaluation should address their efforts, though again SRV offers strategies from individual to societal level for doing so. Nor does SRV take a 'stance' on issues such as race relations, feminism, human rights or religion, all of which have particular explanations for the 'why' of devaluation, with concomitant positions for its 'solution' (Wolfensberger 1995b).

It is important, therefore, in trying to understand the depth of wounding experiences, for readers to look first at the validity of the analysis before

Table 3.1
The most common experiences, or 'wounds of devalued people

1. Impairment - physical and/or functional

Leading to....

2. Relegation to low social status
3. Rejection, perhaps by family, neighbours, community, society
4. Cast into one or more devalued roles

4.1 As non-human	*4.2 As menaces, or objects of dread*
4.3 As waste, rubbish	*4.4 As trivium, or objects of ridicule*
4.5 As objects of pity	*4.6 As objects, or burden of charity*
4.7 As children	*4.8 As holy innocents*
4.9 As sick, or diseased	*4.10 In various death related roles*

Which in turn usually results in...

5. Symbolic Stigmatising - reinforcing the devalued perception
6. Jeopardy of being suspected of multiple deviances
7. Distantiation, usually via segregation and congregation

Which commonly is accompanied by...

8. Loss of control, perhaps even of Autonomy and Freedom
9. Discontinuity with the physical environment and objects
10. Social and relationship discontinuity and even abandonment
11. Loss of natural, freely given relationships and substitution of artificial, 'paid for' ones
12. Deindividualization
13. Involuntary material poverty
14. Impoverishment of experience, especially that of the typical, valued world
15. Exclusion from knowledge of and participation in higher order value systems
16. Having one's life 'wasted'
17. Brutalisation - 'Deathmaking'

Which can give rise to the following feelings...

18. Awareness of being a source of anguish to those who love one
19. Awareness of being an alien in the valued world
20. Resentment, even hatred of privileged citizens

Adapted from Wolfensberger (1992b)

looking to their reaction to it. One of the difficulties of the English experience of SRV, (or again more accurately of 'normalisation') has been for those involved with vulnerable people, and the vulnerable people themselves, to tend to look for someone to 'blame' for devaluation, rather than try to understand the devaluation and wounding process where they will find a universe of causes. These next two chapters use the analogy of wounds to try and explain the oppression of devaluation, as do those later chapters dealing with the ten 'themes' of SRV. The themes form a complementary heuristic aimed at providing a more detailed explanation of the process of devaluation and leading to SRV based strategies to address it.

In the analysis of these chapters we shall use the term 'wounds' throughout, partly out of respect to the SRV author's usage, but also because it sums up the whole nature of the experience of devaluation, in the sense of an analogy with a number of different wounds, some not necessarily fatal, but whose relentlessness and combination have a major effect on the life of the person involved. The sheer importance of this issue to SRV theory means that two chapters are necessary, with this one focusing chiefly on devalued role perceptions. It remains for the reader to examine their own experiences in the light of what follows, to see if the wounds that SRV describes as the 'most common' apply in English society today. Table 3.1, adapted from Wolfensberger (1992b) lists the wounds that will be examined.

The rest of this chapter, and the whole of chapter 4, is taken up with a detailed analysis of these experiences and represents a crucial part of the understanding of devaluation to which SRV seeks to respond.

Analysis of the most common wounds

1. Impairment

As we have already noted, issues of language have rarely been absent from discussions of SRV, especially in the English experience. In the field of learning disability, this author has worked through a period where this particular group of people have been called mentally subnormal, mentally retarded, mentally handicapped, developmentally disabled and people with learning difficulties, to name only a few, more official, labels. Ironically, it may well have been the English experience of normalization, combined with the growth of the disability rights movement, that created some of the sensitivity about language to describe people at risk of devaluation. The irony comes when some of the critics of SRV have turned on Wolfensberger's use of language in other contexts to front a more general attack (e.g. Brown and Smith 1992b). This has included attacks on descriptions of people as 'devalued' as somehow increasing their devaluation, rather than being an empirical description of what others in society impose on them (Szivos 1992). In this book language has been used pragmatically, in the sense of trying to find the language most likely to have a common understanding amongst readers, and it is in this sense that the word impairment is used, being an observable feature of an individual or group that affects their ability to deal with the world around them. It says nothing about whether the world around them might be restructured so that the impairment would have a lesser effect, but merely notes the experience of impairment. That impairment can be physical, in the sense of a material bodily impairment, or functional, in the sense of a difficulty experienced by the person or group in functioning in the world in which they live, or, of course both. The former, physical impairment, is more likely to have a common agreement between most observers than the latter, since functional impairment depends much more on the interaction between the individual and their environment.

To describe physical and functional impairment as 'wounds' is not to subscribe to the 'personal tragedy theory' of disability (Oliver 1990), merely to acknowledge the experience of impairment as bringing some discomfort and some difficulty in functioning (Morris 1991). What makes those wounds significant in SRV terms is then how individuals affected by either or both of them are viewed by others, particularly, as we discussed in the previous chapter, in a group context, and what that social judgment then leads to. In current English society there are a number of groups who would be agreed by most people to have either a physical or functional impairment, or both. They would include; people with learning disabilities, people with physical impairments, people with mental health problems and elderly people with dementia.

Beyond these groups there are others, also at risk of devaluation, about whom there would be less agreement as to their functional impairment, but whom a significant number of people regard as having such an impairment. Again, we are not arguing here whether or not such people 'actually' have an impairment, but that they are perceived to have. So, for example, homeless people may be regarded by some as simply being individuals who do not have a home, whereas others would say that there is some functional impairment that has caused them to be homeless. Whatever is the 'correct' view homeless people are significantly at risk of devaluation. What follows as the next wound pushes them and others further on that path.

2. Relegation to low social status

As we noted in the previous chapter, social distinctions between different groups of people is a deeply ingrained feature of English society. Though these have changed over time, the capacity of our society to classify individuals and groups in a stratified way is still very great (Carling 1991), particularly so when it comes to those at the bottom of the classification scale. To the already existing class differential that looked down on 'working class' people (Tawney 1938), the post war meritocratic education system added an intellectual hierarchy to English society (Evans 1985). People who are seen not to be 'able' to function in ways that the majority values are therefore classed, in a whole variety of ways, some extremely subtle, as of lesser status. Many examples can be drawn from all sorts of sources, but readers need only look at their newspapers and television to see the sort of status that people who are poor, people with mental health problems, people with learning disabilities and people who are unemployed are afforded in the popular media. As we will say endlessly, this is not to say anything about the intrinsic worth of these groups, but to note the empirical fact of their being attributed low social status.

3. Rejection, perhaps by family, neighbours, community, society

This wound provides, in many cases, a crucial link between the initial experiences and the much more serious consequences of the succeeding ones. Wolfensberger (1998a) describes such wounds as 'hinge' wounds in that a significant number of others hinge on them. Because of its very personal meaning for individuals, the wound of rejection is also one of the wounds that causes some discomfort in people at SRV theory presentations. Of course it is not an all or nothing process, and all people will have experienced some degree of rejection in the course of their lives, whether it be for a job, in a relationship or some other way in which they are, or see themselves as, socially excluded. For vulnerable people, who may already be thought of as of lower social status, the key difference between their experiences of rejection and those of ordinarily valued people comes in its pervasiveness and the way it tends to be acted out in several different ways. Especially when it comes to groups of people at strong risk, such as disabled people, collective views of communities and society as a whole puts the notion of rejection into many people's minds. So even parents who are strong protectors of their children may have feelings of rejection (Richardson and Ritchie 1989a), and many more, of course, literally reject their offspring by placing them in the care of the service system or, more powerfully, by aborting them before they are born. Neighbours may do no more than avoid certain people, but again more direct rejection can come from this group in terms of petitions, neighbourhood meetings, and even outright abuse of vulnerable people. When it comes to communities, such rejection of vulnerable people tends to be addressed more at the group level, in such ways as demanding particular places for groups to 'go to', usually anywhere but in the community in question. Services, as a number of writers have noted, tend to reflect the values of the societies that fund them, and may in fact be set up to deal with people whom others have rejected (Ryan and Thomas 1987). If they too, or some of their workers, also reject the people they serve, either directly, by passing them round the service system, or indirectly by how they deliver their service, then the wound of rejection cuts deeper. Experiences of many vulnerable groups in the service system give ample evidence of the reality of this aspect of the wound of rejection (Race 1995; McCourt Perring 1993; Sinclair 1987).

One further aspect of rejection leads to the next wound, first described by Wolfensberger in his original work on normalization, but now developed much more fully in SRV theory: the placing of rejected people into one or more social roles that are highly devalued. As we shall see the importance of roles in SRV theory is considerable. Here we merely note the process whereby there is a feedback loop between devalued roles and devalued people, in that rejected and devalued people tend to get put into devalued roles, whilst some people, not previously seen as devalued, become so if they are perceived as occupying devalued roles. These devalued roles are expressed in a variety of ways, and Wolfensberger has identified ten of the most common of them, in the elaboration of the next wound.

4. Cast into one or more devalued roles

Just as devaluation is postulated to be universal, according to SRV theory, so the devalued roles identified in the development of the theory are also said to have operated over many societies and many times. Differences have emerged in different cultures as to the relative frequency of different groups being placed in these roles, and their relative importance, but this book would suggest that the English experience of devaluation contains instances of all of them. Before going into detail, we need to note the ways in which people may be interpreted as occupying particular roles.

As we have mentioned earlier, the importance of roles to SRV is considerable, and warrants a chapter of its own. Included in that chapter, and also featuring in much more detail in some of the ten themes of SRV, is the variety of ways by which role messages may be conveyed. Wolfensberger (1998) uses the word 'media' to describe this range, another word which, unfortunately, has had specific connotations in recent years, referring only to television, radio and newspapers. These public media do have their part to play in devaluation and wounding, as has already been noted, but in terms of the analysis of the 'wounds' of devaluation we will use a broader meaning to the word. We will generally use the structure found in PASSING to classify different ways by which role messages can be communicated or enacted. That is through aspects of settings i.e. the physical environment in which people find themselves; through activities, i.e. what is actually carried out by, with and to people; through language practices, i.e. what is said to and/or about people; and through any other miscellaneous imagery that may be associated with a person or group.

The use of this typology inevitably, as it has in the English experience, provides a huge range of different influences on the social judgment of individuals and groups, each with a higher or lower significance for that social judgment in any particular case. The point of going into this level of detail is not, as some have, to provide a source for endless arguments about how much this or that influence is 'key' to devaluation, or for defensive arguments about this or that process being vital to the needs of an individual, or mandated by law, and therefore being an 'acceptable' influence. Instead, it is to convey, as with the notion of wounds, the myriad ways in which aspects of people's lives, some seemingly trivial, can convey role messages about them and thus add up to a very powerful message overall. It also serves to indicate, at least as far as SRV is concerned, the complexity of devaluation, and the inability of any one 'solution', even strategies as systematic as SRV suggests, to overcome its universality. This is important to bear in mind when looking at the next part of the analysis of wounds, as it is throughout the study of SRV theory as a whole.

Historic devalued roles

4.1. People put into the role of non-human

This can take one of four forms. The first, that of pre-human, or not yet human, has of course been used very commonly of people before they are born. The argument over when life begins has figured strongly in the abortion debate, with a range of opinions from different authors, including the view that, even after birth, people are not yet human until they become 'independent thinkers' (Harris 1985). The relevance of this role to devaluation is, of course, that if one sees someone as non-human, then one can do things that one wouldn't do to a human, including killing them. In this case, the metaphorical wound can become literal, and fatal. The same can apply at the other end of life, when people are classed as no-longer-human, the second of the four forms. Just as the pre-human role has figured in the abortion debate, so has the no-longer-human role in the euthanasia debate, with the same result, in some cases, for those so cast. Thirdly, the sub-human role has been much more widely cast on a number of devalued groups, including people with learning disabilities, enemies in wartime, or even just foreigners. This third variant of the non-human role, the sub-human, has itself had three distinct expressions, and these have been manifested in a whole range of ways. The three expressions are of people as sub-human animals, as vegetables and as objects.

As sub-human - animals

The message that an individual or, more commonly, a group, should be seen as animals is not of course new. Foreigners, those from different or no recognised religions to the dominant group, peasants, working class people and people with learning disabilities have all over the years had at least had themselves referred to in terms likening them to animals. Paul Jenkins (1998) in his SRV training materials uses the following quotation.

> These 'Ocean Men' are tall beasts with deep sunken eyes and beak-like noses... although undoubtedly men they seem to possess none of the social faculties of men. The most bestial of peasants is far more human.. It is quite possible that they are susceptible to training, and could with patience be taught the modes of conduct proper to a human being.. (Confucian scholar describing Jesuit priests in the sixteenth century, cited in Hogg and Vaughan [1995, p279])

Similarity between that language, and that used in various textbooks on 'mental deficiency' that would have formed part of the training of those in charge of learning disability services in the seventies and eighties shows how pervasive the 'sub-human' role is, and how powerfully it can affect social judgments of vulnerable groups. 'many of these defectives are utterly helpless, repulsive in appearance and revolting in manners' (Tredgold 1956, p142).

In our breakdown of how role interpretations are conveyed, the aspects of settings that convey the role of animal are equally deep rooted. Though now closing, many of the institutional settings of recent times had powerful messages of animality. Some implied a lack of human sensibilities and sensitivities, such as lack of privacy, mass bathing and sleeping facilities, bars on windows etc. Others implied that people lacked ordinary human sense or judgment, and thus set door handles at levels only staff could reach or otherwise structured the environment to be totally in the control of staff. Still more aspects of institutional settings gave messages that people would, inevitably, behave in a primitive, animal-like or violent way, such as heavy immovable furniture and televisions mounted on high wall brackets. Even in what was claimed to be a 'radical alternative' to institutional living, a 'group home' (Race & Race 1979), the living room carpet was made of a material only used elsewhere in the reception area of Heathrow Airport. The expectation of wear caused by twelve people in comparison to millions again speaks powerfully of animal behaviour. Equally powerful are environmental features which convey the message that people need protection against themselves, such as 'soft edges' to walls or furniture, no locks on doors to individual's rooms (a feature of many so-called 'successor' environments to institutions) and various forms of 'no-go' areas' such as kitchens. Similarly, features that suggest that the outside world, or staff, need protection from people's behaviour, such as fences with tops that slope inwards, or extensive separation of staff facilities, all suggest the likelihood of animaline, unpredictable behaviour. Finally, miscellaneous imagery that is present in many settings can also suggest the animal role. The use of animal imagery in pictures, logos on setting walls, the presence of things called 'sluices,' and the siting of certain settings next to, or near those associated with animals, such as abattoirs, are only a few of the many examples that could be cited. One of the difficulties in writing about SRV theory in a book of this kind is the lack of a pictorial facility to show the host of examples of such imagery present in service settings, which is a powerful feature of SRV presentations. Even this, however, has sometimes been criticised as invalid because some examples are old, or not from the audience's region or country, which again shows the sensitivity of the issue, and the strong desire not to see examples from one's own environment. From personal experience, however, having been involved for the past five years in a degree course where students are placed in a variety of service settings, their own, often naive, description of the physical setting of their service consistently reveals examples of features conveying messages about the service users. Not all are of service users as animals but, as we shall see, there are other common role perceptions conveyed that are similarly devaluing. Whilst such environmental features have undoubtedly improved (perhaps one of the results of 'normalisation' teaching in the early eighties), a number of new, purpose built, facilities for certain groups also exhibit some of the features described above. Again the point is not what any one of the influences on role perception, or any one of the devalued roles, or even any one of the wounds has on a person or group, but the combined effect of any number of these elements.

We have mentioned language already, and the third medium suggestive of the animal role comes from activities which are carried out with or sometimes simply 'done to' people. As with settings, there have been some changes in the messages conveyed by work with different groups of people, such that the use of cattle prods or other forms of so-called 'aversive therapy' have largely been taken out of service activities. More subtle associations with animals have continued, however, including the growth of various forms of 'pet therapy' especially with older people. This is not to deny the comfort and companionship that a pet can bring to anyone, but merely to point out the, often unconscious, message that goes with the systematic, and service controlled, association of vulnerable people and animals.

Finally there are various miscellaneous associations of devalued people and animals. These tend to occur randomly in different cultures, and so the English experience will depend much on the reader's own local examples. The use of cartoon or television animal characters to raise funds for charity, such as 'Pudsey Bear', a teddy bear with a bandaged head, for 'Children in Need', is one perhaps more widespread example.

As subhuman - vegetables or plant life

There are many examples of people being interpreted as vegetables, and again from language will probably come the reader's first experiences of this. 'Persistent vegetative state', a medical description that first came to prominence with the condition of football supporter Tony Bland, who was crushed alongside many others at the Hillsborough disaster (Airedale NHS Trust v Bland 1993), has been the subject of much controversy. The simple use of the term 'vegetative' in connection with someone with severe brain damage can, and does, then rub off on those with less severe brain damage, or even those only assumed to have brain damage. The term 'vegetable' has also passed into common usage for people in a coma, or as an insult for people assumed to be of low intelligence. A common joke about any particular group one wishes to class as 'stupid' goes as follows. A football manager goes into a restaurant with his team. The waiter asks what he will have. 'A steak' is the reply. 'And the vegetables?' says the waiter. 'They'll have the same.' (English humour is, of course, like English services and English devaluation, very much a reflection of the values of society, and it is no surprise that a good deal of it is based on 'put downs' of people or groups who aspire to be above their station, either in the intellectual or class hierarchy).

Setting aspects that convey messages of people as vegetables are rarer than some of the other sub-human roles, and they are often similar to the 'people as objects' role which follows. Nevertheless the notion that people are 'plants' insensitive to heat or cold has resulted in some settings paying little attention to the temperature. Similarly the association, via organised activities of people with 'nature' via 'gardening therapy' or work in garden centres is also becoming less frequent, or the negative image is considered, in the latter case, to be worth it in a trade-off with the competency aspects of employment. Nevertheless, the role ascription of certain people as vegetables by such activities is still there, as it is in the use of vegetables with human attributes in advertisements such as for frozen peas, where the negative human aspects of the cartoon peas (untidiness, ugliness, a 'stupid' sounding voice) are put alongside their negative aspects as peas, so they do not get into the 'select' brand. Other miscellaneous imagery associating people with vegetables or plants comes in the use, by educational services, especially for disabled children, of images of flowers 'blossoming' in the sun, to give the (positive?) message that the educational service will help the children to grow like the flowers.

As subhuman - objects

With this subgrouping language is again likely to be the reader's main experience of interpretation of people as objects, i.e. not humans with thoughts and feelings, but objects. This is particularly the case when considering the so-called 'medical model' of services (Oliver 1996). The disabled people's movement are amongst a number of groups who have objected to being referred to by the medical classification of their impairment, especially in the collective objective voice, as in 'the paraplegics' or 'the spastics' (Barton 1996) This has led to all sorts of language games, some of which actually seek to deny the presence of an impairment, others to emphasise that people are 'people with' whatever impairment, rather than 'being' the impairment, which object defining language suggests. SRV, in pointing out the power of language to define people's devalued roles, does not seek to deny the presence of an impairment, but does acknowledge the devaluing effect of language that equates people with objects. This goes beyond just objectifying people by their impairments, and also includes such things as simply calling people 'objects' or the categorization of individuals by where they live. People with learning disabilities involved with the Sheffield Development Project mentioned in chapter 1(Heron and Myers 1983), were classed as 'hospital people,' 'hospital hostel people' and 'hostel people,' even if they did not actually live in those forms of care, but were thought to be of that 'type'.

Another form of casting people as objects is through activities that treat people as commodities. Anyone who has been involved in the hospital closure programme will be familiar with the sort of 'trading' in people purely as numbers of commodities with prices attached (Booth et.al. 1990). Advertisements for the sale of residential establishments, particularly since the rapid expansion of the private sector in the late eighties and early nineties, will often note that 'residents are included' much as one would sell a business 'with stock'. This has occasionally been literally true where the setting of the service is a converted warehouse, thereby increasing the notion of people being 'objects in storage.'

Finally, there is the perception of certain groups as 'other' or alien, i.e. non-human but not sub-human. Language, especially since the advent of horror and science fiction movies such as 'Alien' and its sequels, has been applied to real people to imply that some impairment or deformity is not just part of human variation but has some external, even demonic influence. An incident in a children's playground on holiday illustrates how this is reaching the minds of ever younger people. On seeing my youngest son, who has Down's syndrome, a fellow eight year old remarked, 'Are you from outer space?' The design of some modern institutions for people with learning disabilities has also provided a setting example, albeit anecdotal. These buildings, officially 'assessment and rehabilitation centres' with 'high-tech' equipment and 'modern' design, for which architects have won awards, have the appearance of space ships, and are known locally by such names as 'Tardis' or 'Enterprise.' Activities involving transplantation of body parts, or some implications of genetic engineering, also feed into a growing confusion as to who is human and who is 'other.' The role ascription of the first cloned human will be an interesting variant on this theme.

4.2 People put into the role of menaces, or objects of dread

This second of the common role perceptions has considerable overlaps with the first, especially the 'sub-human animal' role discussed above, and draws on the observable human tendency to see difference as dangerous. Its manifestations therefore go beyond just the danger perceived in potential 'animal like' behaviour and on to wider, more incoherent fears of the simple 'menace' of strangers. As with all devalued roles, such perceptions operate at all levels, from the individual to the collective. Historically the individual stranger is the stuff of many novels, and the reaction to them of a settled community is predictably hostile. Foreigners, members of different religious or racial groups, people with criminal records and people with mental impairments are particularly likely to be cast in this role, which seems strongly resistant to being affected by the greater awareness of different cultures and countries available through more information and more opportunities for direct experience through travel (Kushnick 1998). The role perception also seems to operate, at the collective level, in the development, from some very real dangerous experiences with individuals, to apply the menace role to the group as a whole. The current move towards the setting up of 'secure units' for discharged patients from psychiatric hospitals owes much to a few highly publicised cases, as discussed above.

Language, particularly in the public media, is one powerful way in which the menace role is cast. The popular perception of 'care in the community' has been severely influenced by journalistic accounts of 'ex-patients on the loose' and our attitudes to foreigners inflamed by stereotypical images, mostly relating to antagonistic situations. Within the service world, language also continues the menace role. What would 'secure units' be but for people who are a danger? What would a 'challenging behaviour unit' be but for challenging people. The problem is that such language then spreads to other users of the service system, who may get so labelled even if they merely argue with staff, or express wishes for other arrangements than are currently on offer. 'Here comes trouble' is a phrase one hears very commonly in service settings, and it is often said in an affectionate or humorous way. Underneath the humour, however is the unconscious expression of the person as a menace. Similarly, though they couch their words more carefully these days than when Enoch Powell delivered his 'rivers of blood' speech in the sixties (Kushnick 1998) pronouncements by politicians on immigration policy often contain code words of menace, such as 'swamping' or 'an invasion.'

Settings in which vulnerable people are served also contain many features suggestive of menace, from the most obvious bars and fences on most of the old (and some of the new) institutions, through elaborate, and often high-tech locks and security devices in a whole range of services, not just for those officially classed as 'dangerous', to the more subtle use of facilities such as 'observation windows' or discrete security cameras. As before such facilities may be said, or even legally mandated to be 'necessary' or 'in people's best interest' but this does not diminish their power in conveying the role of menace.

Activities, too, can serve to reinforce the role. The most telling feature in recent years has been the rapid growth in so-called 'defense' training in services of various sorts, but many other examples, such as electronic tagging, removal of shoes from people, and the use of plastic cutlery, can be found. Some of these become public, with committees of enquiry and moralising in the media (e.g. Levy & Kahan 1991) but these are really only extreme examples of activities based on the perception that people are menaces, to be 'kept in check.'

Other miscellaneous imagery confirms the role perception. Staff walking around with massive bunches of keys, staff being allocated 'danger money' in the form of extra pay to work with certain groups, separate, uniformed 'security staff' at various residential establishments all reinforces in the public mind the notion of whole groups of people, some of whom may in reality be so impaired that they are physically helpless, as menaces.

Though we have spent less time on the analysis of devalued people being interpreted as menaces than on the non-human role, this should not be taken to imply that this role has a less important effect on devalued people. At the societal level, and in a broader sense of the 'menace' than just direct physical threat, many devalued groups are directly affected by being seen as a danger to the lifestyles and 'self-actualisation' of others. Elderly or disabled people are seen therefore as a direct threat to their relatives, by taking away their time and resources, and to society, by taking an increasing proportion of the nation's wealth for the provision of services. Often these two threats are in tension with one another, in that carers, especially women, have been relied on by the State to provide unpaid care, whilst at the same time an increase in the level of taxation necessary to provide at least numerically adequate services is said to be reducing people's standard of living, so that they couldn't make use of the time that would be freed up by such a move. Whatever one's position on the issue of welfare services, which of course is an issue of values, the assumption behind both solutions is that elderly and disabled people are a menace to the 'quality of life' of the rest of the population. As groups, therefore, this goes beyond the 'burden of charity' role described later and into the realms of menace. Newspaper columns talk of the 'threat' of an ageing population.

4.3 People put into the role of waste, rubbish

In the material world, when an object is rejected, as being no longer any use, or even just out of date or out of fashion, then it is typically regarded as waste, as something one can throw away. Some results of rejection of people, the wound described earlier, can lead to their being placed in the role of waste material, of rubbish, even of human waste material, i.e.

excrement. Like most of the Western world, English society has increasingly become a 'throw-away' society (Gabriel and Lang 1995). Conservation efforts have met with some success, but England is far from leading the world in preserving resources. In such a society it is scarcely surprising that those people whom society rejects should be placed in the role of waste material. Language is again the connection that most readers will make first. References to 'cleaning the streets' of homeless people or young people is, of course a direct parallel with waste disposal, and other language used about certain groups, such as elderly people being 'past their sell-by date' or street people being the 'debris' of society confirms the waste material role. Increasingly, as well as being seen in many cases as 'pre-human,' as we have discussed earlier, aborted babies are referred to in terms of 'waste material' or 'medical waste.' We also see the increasing use of the American term 'wasting people' as in killing them. Excremental language as insults to people is also a very old form of abuse in English society, which scarcely needs elaboration here.

Settings that perpetuate the waste role may be more subtle, but many residential services have been housed in buildings that have either been condemned, or are running close to the end of their useful lives. Buildings sited next to rubbish dumps or other run down areas of towns are also fairly common, very often because they are on 'council land', and some of the other functions of buildings on the same site have been removed from local government control, leaving one or more derelict buildings. This is particularly so since the eighties and it is ironic, but not really surprising given other events of that time, that the 'wasting' of local government carried out by the Thatcher administrations should have also contributed to the casting of devalued people into the waste role.

Activities that regard people as waste are intensely controversial, particularly when the notion of being 'deserving' or 'undeserving', a feature of English welfare policy for centuries, is brought into the argument. This is not the case with more basic wasting of human beings, such as in abortion, but in other areas, activities such as homeless people sleeping in cardboard boxes, in rubbish skips, or simply wearing rubbish sacks gets explained away by reference to people 'choosing' to be homeless, or otherwise deserving their homeless state. From an SRV perspective, the fact of being cast into a devalued role, in this case one of discarded rubbish, is the issue, with the notion of deserts only relevant to the degree that the more a society thinks people's devalued state is their own fault, the more powerfully are the wounds likely to be applied. One only has to add the great frequency with which discarded items are used to raise money for various devalued groups to complete the basic itinerary of activities associating people with rubbish.

Miscellaneous imagery of people as waste again comes from the advertising industry, in its reproduction, often in cartoon form, of germs with human faces that are swept away by this or that cleaner or toothpaste, and various suggestions of 'wasting' people who are a nuisance, or are even, as in one case, obviously 'lower class' lottery winners creating a noise in an exclusive pool. The 'butler' figure simply releases a shark to 'dispose' of them.

4.4 People put into the role of trivium, an object of ridicule

We assume by now that the reader will have begun to look more perceptively into aspects of life for vulnerable groups, especially those aspects controlled by the service system. For the next role ascription, however, especially when it comes to language, English society, and the English 'sense of humour' is rife with examples from everyday life which portray people as trivial, unimportant and, much more frequently, objects of ridicule. Paradoxically, the so-called 'reserve' of English people has been attributed to an almost pathological fear of doing or saying the 'wrong thing' and thus being made to 'look ridiculous', and it may be the frequency with which our humour does this that causes such fears (Palmer 1994). We will return to the object of ridicule part shortly, but note first the indicators that tell us to regard someone or some group as unimportant or trivial. If this view is held then what we say about or to a person is unimportant, since they are unimportant, and whatever feelings they might have on the matter are disregarded. In language, therefore we can talk to them as if they were not there, use any sort of insulting language to or about them, because they have no feelings to hurt, or what they have are not worth bothering about. 'Does he take sugar' the BBC radio programme on disability issues, uses as its title a situation familiar to many disabled people, where they are present, but are talked about and have decisions made for them, as if they were not there. The same, of course, applies in settings, where facilities may be arranged as if the people living there are irrelevant, or without them being consulted, and activities, where people may be given food that they do not like, or be taken to places that they do not wish to visit, as if their views and feelings are trivial.

When this extends to those influences that put people in the role of object of ridicule then, as we mentioned earlier, the English experience is full of examples. The notion of the court jester or 'fool' has deep roots in English and many other cultures, although it is rarely noted that this could be a valued role in that the person was allowed to say things to the king that others dare not, and in fact was seen as having a different sort of 'wisdom' i.e. a moral wisdom. The 'fool', therefore, was seen as being able to reveal the 'truth' and keep the high and mighty from becoming too prideful. In Wolfensberger's view (1998b) it is only in relatively recent time that 'foolishness' has been almost totally associated with 'stupidity' and thus devalued as part of the 'object of ridicule' role. Similarly the tradition of the 'village idiot', tolerated and even loved at some points for being a source of 'innocent fun' or 'unworldly wisdom', has nowadays become a powerful source of devaluation.

Language abounds with confirmation of this role. There are so many English words for 'stupid' and so many jokes about the ridiculousness of all sorts of groups; foreigners, elderly people, people with learning disabilities. Tories make jokes about 'common' people, working class comedians make jokes about 'snobs' and so it goes on. When this is allied to service settings for vulnerable people, however, the humour has a sharp edge to it. The prevalence of clowns or clown images in all sorts of services, on posters in residential homes, or in the decor of homes for people with learning disabilities shows how deep and yet unconscious this imagery is.

Activities in all sorts of services consistently reinforce the ridicule role, such as when specific individuals are encouraged, or even taught, to do their 'party piece' for visitors, even if it is something totally inappropriate. 'Fancy Dress' activities, where elderly people dress as clowns or give imitations of singers or television stars is another example of this role. It is scarcely surprising that this goes on, since many otherwise valued people can be persuaded to make fools of themselves on television in the name of 'fun' (and usually some material reward) and those who question the impact of such activities in service settings are accused of having 'no sense of humour.'

It is humour, in fact, which also contributes to other miscellaneous imagery of people as objects of ridicule. Stereotypes of 'stupid' rural dwellers, of 'ludicrously vain' older women, of 'vacuous bimbos' and many others all contribute, when applied to vulnerable people, to making them the object of ridicule. In fact a third aspect of this role is its tendency to persuade people to assume the joker role. When it is reinforced by attention, it has been very common for some people to repeat their 'party piece' even when there are no visitors, sometimes ad nauseam. It becomes so much a part of their identity that they continue, without any reinforcement, to play the role

4.5 People put into the role of object of pity

This role has many parallels with the 'personal tragedy' part of the social theory of disability (Abberley 1987). The key point is that the person or group is seen as 'suffering' from their situation, and thus people act to relieve that suffering, out of pity. The person or group is not seen as being responsible for their condition, hence the tendency for the role to be applied to various disabled groups, or to 'innocent' children, who are not therefore held accountable for their behaviour or for demands their 'condition' might make. Often such pity is enhanced by the feeling that people's condition is an 'accident of fate' which could befall anyone. In language, this role is daily reinforced by descriptions of people 'suffering from' physical conditions, such as Down's syndrome, epilepsy or many others, regardless of whether the person is actually 'suffering' or is in perfectly good general health. Appeal activities that rely on the presentation of suffering people or actually use devalued people themselves again reinforce the pity role, as do various setting features that emphasise the motivation of the staff is out of pity, especially those with religious overtones. Other activities that influence the pity role are those which emphasise their desire to bring a 'little happiness' to suffering people, usually by taking them on 'experiences of a lifetime' to such places as Disneyworld

4.6 People put into the role of object, or burden, of charity

This role has some ambiguities to it, at least in the sense that it may be thought to be a valuing thing to give help, or charity, to a fellow human being. When people are, however, treated as passive and helpless recipients of such feelings and actions, often by emphasising their 'plight' and defining their whole lives by this 'tragedy' then this serves to reinforce their devaluation. Matters are worse, at least in terms of the perceptions of others, if people are seen as the burden of charity, i.e. as causes of effort, hardship, or even suffering in others who 'have' to look after them. So the charity is given grudgingly. The expression 'as cold as charity' well conveys the implications of such an attitude. Other examples of language are strongly linked to the 'pity' role described above, with a host of expressions, such as 'poor', 'brave' and 'needy' being used to describe recipients of services, which themselves are often delivered by organisations called 'charities'. Settings, especially those run by charities, abound with indications that those who use the servants are the 'fortunate' recipients of charitable giving by others. Plaques, notices, even individual beds 'donated by ....' leave the observer in no doubt as to the relative status of the 'givers' and the 'takers'. Similarly activities in a great many services, and in campaigns for them, rarely fail to indicate people as objects of charity, either through emphasising the 'desperate' nature of their appeal, or the 'relief' offered by the service. The Christmas card business often compounds this role, by mixing up all sorts of groups as beneficiaries, so that in the end one is not giving to help any one group, but a general concept called 'charity'. People who use services thus get mixed up with animals, church buildings and environmental preservation groups as 'charity cases' and the whole thing is reinforced by the fact that, since the recipients are unknown to the donors, they cannot reciprocate, thus offending against on of the key values discussed in the previous chapter

4.7 People put into the role of children

For people with learning disabilities in particular, but also for some physically impaired and elderly people, being regarded, and then treated, as a child is perhaps one of the major wounds of their devaluation. As with rejection, probably all people at some times in their lives have been treated as if they were much younger than they are, some even 'reliving their childhood' for pleasure. It becomes a significant contribution to wounding however, when such attribution is applied relentlessly, often with the trappings of 'scientific measurement' and affects powerfully the identity of a person or group.

Language from common discourse, such as parents telling older children not to 'behave like a baby or I'll treat you like one' speaks strongly of the value humans place on growing up, with all the benefits of independence and freedom of choice that implies. Speaking of, or classing someone as a child when they are not therefore transgresses that value most strongly and, as we have seen in chapter 2, along with strong transgression comes strong devaluation. The whole concept of 'mental age', whereby a person is defined by their performance on tests standardised for certain ages, still dominates popular, and even some academic, discussion of people with learning disabilities. The notion of elderly people as in their 'second childhood' is reinforced by the language and tone of voice used to address many such people in the service world. People used all their lives to being addressed by strangers as 'Mr. Jones' will be cheerfully addressed as 'Bert' by staff who may hardly have met them. Feminists and other women have long complained at mature, especially elderly women being addressed as 'girls' (which is the more galling when done by men, combining the patronising male superior role with the child role). That so many examples of language exist that place people in the child role may be a reflection of its pervasiveness.

Settings, especially again those for people with learning disabilities, have struggled to remove associations of their service users with childishness (Booth et. al 1990) but many still, through pictures on the walls, through the overall decor, through the overprotective devices in the name of safety and through frequent physical associations of children's and adults' services on the same site, convey a picture of people who are younger than they really are. Special schools, by frequently taking children from the age of two to nineteen, give out an impression far more like a primary school than a secondary school, thus devaluing the age perception of the older pupils.

Activities, too, abound with examples of the child role. This is not just in services for people with learning disabilities, though it is at its most common there, but there is a widespread quantity of so-called 'recreation' or 'therapy' in services for adults with physical impairments or who are elderly which, in reality, are little more than childish games. Even the hours that services such as day services open are more akin to 'school hours' than adult working hours.

If to this is added the miscellaneous imagery, particularly of old age, that is present in the advertising media that implies older people are really 'in their second childhood' then the severity of this wound is revealed.

4.8 People put into the role of holy innocent

Perhaps less common a role now in Western countries, including England, that have largely rejected their religious heritage is the notion that a person or group is somehow 'innocent' or 'holy and innocent', somehow specially touched by God. It is usually applied to children or people with some mental disorder and gives the person so attributed a rather ambiguous role. Just as one version of the object of charity could see the person served as valued, in that they had elicited help from a fellow human, so 'holy innocents' may be treated with reverence or at least in a special way. Unfortunately this usually goes alongside a desire to protect their innocence, since they are seen as not really having the discretion to do bad things possessed by those not blessed. Along with this, such people are often not expected to develop in the same way as 'mere mortals' and therefore not much effort is put into helping them do so. Thus they remain in this rather unworldly state, in some ways benignly treated, but metaphorically being put in a glass case.

4.9 People put into the role of being sick or diseased

In this role interpretation SRV shares many of the same insights as the social theory of disability and its critique of the 'medical model' of services (Oliver 1990; Abberley 1989). In looking at the whole range of conditions of people that have been cast as 'diseases' or 'disorders', however, SRV goes further than the social theory to postulate that society doesn't just create a 'disabled identity' out of a real impairment, it also creates the impairments as well. Then 'experts' and 'professionals' who 'diagnose' these 'disorders' can also create their own service empires around the 'treatment' of such people. The medical profession has been the most heavily criticised for imposing this role, but as McKnight (1995) and many others have pointed out (Barton 1996) the whole professionalised service system has a powerful interest in classifying people as being in 'need' of their services. This, as Wolfensberger (1996a) has noted, outside of an SRV context, also owes much to the post-Enlightenment view of the perfectibility of human beings through the power of human reasoning, as expressed through the rise of science and medicine to their position of dominance in today's society. The idea of the human as a 'machine' that could be 'fixed' goes back as far as that period, and even in these postmodernist times, work on genetics, on organ replacement and other aspects of medicine have convinced a great many people that science and medicine have the 'answer' to human afflictions. This is not, of course, to deny the great strides in the address of many diseases that medicine has made, but merely to point out that the 'medical model' of 'diagnosis and treatment' has been taken far more broadly than genuine cases of illness.

Language, as before, abounds in examples of placing people in the sick role. Scarcely a day goes by without some condition, previously thought to be part of the normal human range of behaviour, being called a 'disorder.' Human tragedies, once dealt with by friends and families of survivors, with greater or lesser success, now routinely are met with by calls for 'counselling', which has an equally mixed record of success.

The almost total domination of services for disabled people by medical, and medical associated, professions, is an example of activities that perpetuate the sick role. Even where such services have to do with non-medical issues, such as housing, the association with medicine is still maintained, often in a controlling or decision making way. To get a visa to enter the USA, my sister-in-law, who has Down's syndrome required a letter from her doctor, not to say that she was healthy and free from infection, but that she was not a danger to herself or others.

Settings also, in many cases, promote the sick role. From the most obvious example of people who are not ill living in something called a hospital to the more subtle messages created by ordinary houses being run by NHS trusts, certain groups, especially people with learning disabilities and elderly people, are portrayed as sick.

What goes with the sick role, of course, is what goes with the role of patient when one is genuinely sick, i.e. submission to the expertise of the professional, a lack of demand that one attempts to sort out the situation oneself, and a sense of hostility when one does not 'take one's medicine'. As this is written proposals to alter mental health legislation to require people to take their prescribed psychotropic medication on release from hospital are being considered by the government, as if this will be the solution to all crime by 'disordered' people. Mental Health, of course, is a field where, above all, there is much dispute about what constitutes 'sickness' and yet one which grows daily in its domination by technological and pharmacological medicine, a great deal of which produces literal wounds on those taking it, in terms of the sometimes fatal side effects (Brandon 1991). The sick role leads on, inevitably to the next, that of people being dead or dying.

4.10 People put into death related roles

'One Foot in the Grave' is a popular television series about an older person who reacts strongly against society's placement of him in the dying role, and therefore the language is used in an ironic way. The fact that it can be so used, however, is reflective of the prevalence of the placement of elderly people into the dying role. Of course, we can all be said to be dying, in the sense that there will always be a finite time before we die, but language in this case has the effect of producing an identity that is perceived to be much nearer the point of death than may ultimately be the case. Just as the child role is at its strongest in services for people with learning disabilities, the dead or dying role is strongest in services for elderly people. Names of such services, particularly of individual residential establishments, abound with imagery of death or dying, or that people are at the 'end of the road'. 'Sunset Home' and 'St. Peter's Gate' (one example of which really exists) are two examples.

Setting locations also abound with death related imagery. The frequency of the siting of elderly person's homes next to graveyards is something which continues to amaze people at SRV theory presentations, though they then very quickly come out with their own examples. So, too, is the frequency with which settings are literally at the 'end of the road' or at a 'dead end'

Activities that place people in the dead or dying role again occur most often in settings for elderly people, though many other segregated residential establishments for all sorts of other groups can, and do, practice such activities (Abrahams et.al. 1996). Things such as stripping people of most, or all of their assets, or encouraging relatives to take them 'before its too late', can go alongside the withdrawal of many personal or social contacts, and sometimes the de facto withdrawal of certain legal identities such as bank accounts, can all be portrayed as very practical actions that are 'facing up to reality.' The message they convey, however, and one which spreads to other residents whose life expectancy may be very different, is of people 'waiting for death'.

Finally, miscellaneous imagery seems to increasingly convey the message that certain devalued groups are dead or dying. An old favourite is the frequency with which advertisements for certain human services, especially elderly and nursing homes, appear on the obituary pages of newspapers.

Final points on devaluing role perceptions

As we noted earlier, the importance of roles to SRV theory is significant, and more detailed explication of this will be given in chapter 5. To conclude our description of the wound which comes when people or groups are cast into these common role identities, it is important, first of all, to remind the reader that, like the wounds themselves, it is the pervasiveness of the role ascriptions which does the most damage. Arguing at length about the relatively low frequency of any particular role in English society, or that the importance of one particular role is greater than another would be to fail to look at the picture overall, or to see the connections and reinforcements between the different roles. Equally, to advocate that society should simply 'stop' casting people into these roles is also missing the point. The universality of devaluation, and the almost infinite number of roles into which people may get cast, both positive and negative, means that, even if one could get society to 'stop' casting people into the roles analysed above, others would replace them, though not necessarily for the

Table 3.2
Association between common social identities and devalued roles

	1	2	3	4	5	6	7	8	9	10	11
Learning Disability	+	+	+	+	+	+	+	+	+	+	+
Mental Disorder	+		+	+	+	+	+	+	+	+	+
Old Age			+	+	+	+		+	+	+	
Alcohol Misuse			+		+	+	+			+	
Poverty	+		+	+		+	+				
Racial Minority	+		+	+	+				+		
Criminal Offences	+		+				+			+	
Epilepsy			+			+	+			+	
DrugAddiction			+	+		+	+			+	
Deafness						+	+				
Blindness						+	+				
Illiteracy						+	+				
Unborn		+	+	+							
Political Dissidence			+							+	

Key
1. Sub-human
2. Other non-human
3. Menace/dread
4. Waste/discard
5. Ridicule/trivia
6. Pity
7. Charity/burden
8. Holy innocent
9. Age-demeaned
10. Sick
11. Dead/dying

same people. What we have described are therefore those roles which SRV theory has observed to be the most common, and invited the reader to apply them to English society, and to examine the meaning that they convey to significant numbers of people in that society. We also invite the reader to consider whether the groups of people most commonly observed across a number of Western societies and presented in Table 3.2 above, which is adapted with permission from Training Institute materials are those to whom they are applied in English society . The Table presents observations of which groups are most likely to be cast into which roles. A final point to be considered alongside this Table is that, as would be expected, devalued people may be cast into a succession of devalued roles or into more than one role at a time.

The rest of the wounds listed in Table 3.1 which then follow from these common roles will be discussed in chapter 4.

4

Experiences of devalued people: 'The wounds'—Part two

Introduction

In Part One of our analysis of the common experiences, or 'wounds' as they are referred to in SRV theory, we looked at the notion of wounds as a series of damaging events or processes in the lives of particular individuals or groups vulnerable to social devaluation. Each wound in itself may or may not be a very powerful contributor to devaluation, but in combination they can amount to a life defining devalued identity. The previous chapter dwelt at some length on one particular wound, that of individuals or groups being cast into one or more common and historically observable devalued roles. This was given special attention because of the part that roles play in SRV theory and in its analysis of devaluation. It is important, however, for the reader to recall that this particular wound followed from the initial wounds of impairment, either functional, physical or both, leading to the next wound of relegation to low social status, which in turn led to the wound of rejection.

That so-called 'hinge' wound led us on to our detailed analysis of the common devalued roles. The 'hinge', however also leads to other wounds and it is necessary to add a note about the relationship between the wounds before going into further detail of them.

Inevitably, in an attempt at a logical exposition of SRV theory, ideas are presented sequentially, and as we have already noted some of the wounds tend naturally to follow one from another. Such is the complexity of devaluation, however, that a sequential presentation may give a false sense of linearity to the process, with one wound appearing to be dependent on the one preceding. SRV theory should not be read in this way. We have already noted that feedback loops and connections exist between many of the wounds, as they do between the common devaluing roles, and it is in the sense of a system of experiences, each having some connection with the others but not being a precondition for another's existence, that we would like the reader to examine the wounds. In the further analysis of this chapter, therefore, we hope that readers will try to make the connections back to the previous chapter, as well as forward to what follows. The shorter space devoted to some of the remaining wounds should not be taken as a sign of their lesser importance. In some cases, it will be because of the depth of chapter 3 that no lengthy explication will be necessary here once connections are made. In others, though a wound may not have the variety of sources of manifestation, it nonetheless will still have its part to play. A good example of both of these qualifications comes in the next wound, that of symbolic stigmatising, or 'marking' of people into their devalued status.

Symbolic stigmatising: Reinforcing the devalued perception

Given the importance of perception in the devaluation process, it will not come as a surprise that anything that reinforces negative perceptions in peoples' minds is an important devaluing wound. As the chapters on imagery and on role circularity will elaborate, one of the key ways in which a perception can be reinforced is if the object of the perception is attached to, or surrounded by, symbolic images that confirm the perception as 'correct'. What seems to happen very often with devalued and vulnerable people is that, as part of the response of society to impairment, and especially as expressed through human services, they are in fact surrounded by symbols and imagery that 'mark them out' as being different in ways that are devalued. Wolfensberger uses the analogy of 'branding,' an historic means by which different groups or individuals have been literally 'marked' by burning a symbol onto their body, and also draws the parallel of the equally historical notion of 'stigmata', the marks of the cross, as marking out individuals as different from their fellows. That the latter marking has evolved from a means of people being valued to a reason for devaluation, and to a word, in 'stigma,' that is used commonly in English to mean a sign that a person is associated with a 'bad' event or group could be said to be itself symbolic of the change in societal values and resultant devaluation of certain groups, but would take rather more space than this book to elaborate. (for much greater elaboration of historical developments, readers are recommended to discover and attend events given by Wolfensberger's Training Institute, especially two entitled 'A History of Human Services' and 'The Historic Notion of Two Intelligences')

'Stigma' is also, however, a word with a specifically academic meaning in the sociology of deviance and in texts on social policy, with Goffman's (1963) work of that title being perhaps the best known of the former, and Pinker (1971) being the English academic most associated with the latter. The subtitle of Goffman's work, *The management of spoiled identity* not only gives the key to its links with SRV theory, but also provides one of the key sources of criticism of SRV, dealt with at length in the next chapter and in the analysis of the theme of the 'conservatism corollary' in chapter 10. This criticism is based on agreement that a devalued identity is imposed on individuals by society but then has SRV suggesting that to 'cope' in society people should have to 'manage' that identity, i.e. accept it but manipulate its presentation to gain acceptability, thereby not challenging the status quo (Hattersley 1991; Brown 1994). All that will be said here on the issue is that, in looking at the wound of symbolic stigmatising, SRV is saying nothing about whether societies and groups ought to be doing such 'branding', or whether others in society ought not to respond to it by reinforcing devalued perceptions of people, but merely that the evidence seems to suggest that they do.

The way in which such symbolic stigmatising is carried out has, like the transmission of role perceptions, a range of forms. The media we cited in role transmission, of language, settings, activities and miscellaneous imagery is useful here, though we can add the social environment, service structured groupings of people, and personal appearance to the list of ways in which people can be 'marked' as having a devalued identity.

The important point with stigmatising is that, like devaluation itself, it is from individual and group perceptions of difference, and reaction to it, that such stigmatising comes. So, again, SRV is not saying that individuals and groups 'have' a stigma, in the sense of it being an intrinsic part of their identity with which they were born, but that it is imposed on them.

A lot of the symbolic stigmatising of people therefore either reinforces a devalued identity, including most importantly a devalued role, or helps to create the devalued identity. In this context SRV draws on broader social science from the field of semiotics, the study of signs (Blonsky 1985), with symbols being seen as one form of sign. If symbols are constantly associated with a person or group, such as in the language used to or about them, then the associations drawn by others with those symbols, such as the association of the word 'dependence' or 'dependent' with a person or group who are a drain on others, will become, in effect, the stigmata that that person or group will have imposed on them.

Similarly if the symbolic association of a physical setting is with a school, for example, because of the size of the building, or its architectural design, and yet the building is for adults, such as a day centre for elderly people, then the stigma of elderly people being in their 'second childhood' will be carried by those attending that centre. Activities that have symbolic associations, such as children's games or 'art and craft' work can, if they are a constant part of people's lives, again give the stigma of childishness, or reinforce it if it is already there. Being surrounded by large numbers of people with a devalued identity, such as occurs in the way some services group those who use them, also gives a symbolic meaning to observers concerning the identity of any and all members of the group. The social environment, especially if it is structured and controlled by services, can also be a source of 'marking' in that if one is artificially placed in a 'special needs' social circle, where social interactions are only with people with that identity, then one will be perceived by others as having the 'mark' of the group. This should not be taken to imply, as some critics of SRV have averred (Szivos 1992) that SRV 'says' that no devalued or vulnerable people should ever associate with one another. Apart from the fact that, as already noted, Wolfensberger (1995a) has made clear that SRV does not mandate any action, but merely points up the likely consequences of particular actions, the notion of symbolic stigmatisation is used to describe the effects of some social environments, especially those artificially created by services, in reinforcing a devalued identity. What is then done about it is a different issue.

The same applies to personal presentation of people or groups. Stereotyped appearances of devalued people or groups can clearly be seen to act as a mark of their devaluation. The dressing of adults with learning disabilities in childish clothes and the dishevelled appearance of many people of the streets are just two examples. The fact that there may be reasons for such an appearance, including the most heavily used reason, that they 'chose' to look like this, does not stop such an appearance from being seen as a symbolic mark of devaluation.

Again, what is done about this is a separate issue, as it is from the observation of other miscellaneous imagery surrounding a person or group being a source of symbolic stigmatisation. So, as we noted in the previous chapter, being a recipient of charity, and having that charity promote its work by appeals to people's sense of pity, is to also run the risk of such imagery pushing one into a devalued role, or of having that role reinforced. It is ironic that, following the massive expansion of the independent sector, including charities, in the eighties many of them were involved in management exercises on their 'brand image' or 're-branding,' little realising that they were also thereby 're-branding' those who use their services.

Jeopardy of being suspected of multiple deviances

Though dealt with briefly here, this next wound can, by itself, cause much harm. In connection with other wounds, however, especially that of being cast into one of the common devaluing roles, it can add to the harm of one devalued identity the harm of others. An obvious example of this, in the English experience, is the still prevalent confusion in people's minds of learning disabilities and mental health problems. This has resulted in the whole community care initiative being tainted by the perceived 'menace' of ex-psychiatric patients, despite the fact that 'community care' applies to a whole range of groups.

How services are structured is also a reflection of the 'multiple jeopardy' wound, the implication being that if service users have 'similar needs' then they can be served effectively by generic services. Though it may make perfect organisational sense to structure services in this way, the result is to convey to the outside world that most or all users of services are equally 'in need' and thus perpetuate their devaluation by combining all or some of the separate wounds that each group attracts.

Distantiation, usually via segregation and also congregation

This is another wound named by Wolfensberger as a 'hinge' wound, as others hinge on it, and it results from a number of others. As a natural consequence of the wound of rejection, it is highly likely that those who wish to reject a person or group should also wish to put them at a distance. That this has been carried out at individual, group and even societal level by segregating the devalued parties, often in ways which congregate them with large numbers of others of the devalued class, is evidenced by even a cursory study of societies and their history, and English society is no exception. Segregation was, of course one of the key features of the eugenics movement of the late nineteenth and early twentieth century which formed the basis of the Mental Deficiency Act, 1913 and the wide expansion of institutions in the twenties and thirties (Race 1995), though this was only a more recent example of a much older historical strategy. Wolfensberger (1969; 1972), in pointing out these roots and in highlighting segregation and congregation as key aspects addressed by normalization gave, as we pointed out in chapter 1, great impetus to the growing anti-institution movement in the field of learning disabilities. From the non-service world the apartheid policies of the previous South African government give a similar perspective. Those who have drawn on this and other insights to form the broad set of views that fall under the heading of the 'inclusion movement' are also, almost by definition, responding to segregation (Hegarty 1993).

It is therefore crucial to our understanding of wounds to realise the prevalence and power of segregative and congregative practices in human services, and also to note that, despite the community care policy and the closure of some institutions, such practices are still widespread (Sinson 1993). Justifications for segregating people from their fellow citizens may have changed from those put forward by the eugenicists, but the underlying impetus still remains (Cox and Pearson 1995). As a wounding experience then, being put apart, with varying degrees of remoteness, from community life, very often in congregation with a number of people with the same devalued identity, is a present reality for a great many groups. Elderly people, people with learning disabilities, other disabled people, people with mental health problems, homeless people, some single mothers and smaller, but no less significant groups such as asylum seekers are all living testimony to the widespread manifestation of this wound.

The effects of segregation and congregation in terms of the wounds already mentioned should be fairly clear. Rejection, whether deliberate or otherwise, is surely going to be perceived by observers and by segregated people themselves. The likelihood of people in segregated and congregated environments being cast into one or more of the common devalued roles by all the different media noted in the previous chapter, is also high, as is the attachment of the stigma of devaluation, and the confirmation of people's low social status. We would ask the reader to step outside of any work roles and just think in terms of their awareness of popular perceptions of such places to try and appreciate the effect of this wound.

That is just in terms of wounds already mentioned, which deal with the creation and reinforcement of a devalued identity which is then responded to by segregation and congregation, but as well as reinforcing that identity segregated and congregated services have been foremost in pursuing practices that form the basis of the wounds which follow.

Loss of control, perhaps even autonomy and freedom

Though an important wound in SRV's analysis of devaluation, it is ironic and instructive that the perceived or actual loss of control over one's life, often expressed as lack of 'choice', should have become a key, if not the key, source of attack on human services by a number of groups, including some of those who are critics of SRV (e.g. Szivos & Travers 1988; Baldwin & Stowers 1987). Again it stems from practices in segregated and congregated institutions, documented over thirty years ago by those academics, mentioned in chapter 1, who constituted an embryonic anti-institution movement. Morris (1969, p187) uses the words 'custodial role', and King, Raynes & Tizard (1971, p4 et. seq.) the word 'regimentation,' to describe the situation where individuals and groups, usually placed in the institution against their will, were herded about from ward to day room, with mass practices of feeding, washing and many other activities that took from people any sense of personal control. Goffman's (1961) word for it was the symbolic 'stripping' of people of assets and autonomy as they entered the institution.

In the thirty years since then, the anti-institution movement, the normalization movement, and growing self-determination movements have all campaigned, using the lack of control as a key plank in their argument, for greater control, or 'choice' by people over their lives. A national enquiry on residential care in the eighties had as its title *A Positive Choice* (Wagner 1988). These examples show how highly valued are autonomy and choice in English society, a feature shared with most of the Western world. As we have noted several times, the more strongly a value is said to be held by a society, the more devaluing is the perceived opposite. The wound, therefore, of loss of control is seen by many to be the most important, and a number see it as impossible for organised services to give people control over their lives. SRV does not enter that particular argument, though we will come back to the point that some critics make that SRV itself is a means of taking control from people (Perrin & Nirje 1985).

Instead, we must first note the many ways that control is taken away from people in general, not specifically people at risk of devaluation, in such things as tax laws, general regulations on behaviour such as speed limits, drink-driving laws, parental controls on children and so on. The two key differences from these restrictions and the wound of loss of control are, first, that the former controls are deemed by most people to be necessary for a society to function and second, that within those controls valued people still have a great deal of autonomy over key areas of life, such as where to live and with whom, what sort of job to try and do, and more mundane choices such as what to wear and what to eat. In the exercise of that control people show varying degrees of competence and generally can face the consequences of those choices. For vulnerable and devalued people, however, it is precisely in those key areas such as where to live and with whom, what to do for a job and how to spend one's time, that loss of control occurs. That it also sometimes occurs in those more mundane areas of life such as what to wear and what to eat is also significant, but simply increasing individual control in those areas should not be seen as a 'solution' to this wound. It is an undeniable fact that, for many people in receipt of services, control over what happens in their lives is not in their hands, and their everyday experience is one of lack of autonomy and freedom.

Discontinuity with the physical environment and objects

A particular feature of institutional care, but also present in a number of other segregated service environments, is the creation of what almost amounts to a 'separate world.' This has been illustrated in studies, again including those which historically began the anti-institutional movement, but also more recent reviews of residential care (Hatton & Emerson 1996).

Both the physical world of place (in terms of familiar objects and locations, the sense of the connectedness of physical cause and effect, such as preparing, cooking and eating a meal) and the world of time (in terms of the association of times of day, week and year with particular events) are both subject to discontinuity. Bedrooms become dormitories, where people come and go, homes become residences, with people again moving from one to the other. Even the move from home to acute hospital, and the return, for elderly people who are otherwise fine has often become a series of sudden discontinuities as a result of current policies on waiting lists and discharges. Inside the service world, details of living are 'taken care of' so that food just comes from a kitchen, never from something one has bought and prepared, beds are made, washing is done, and time goes by with landmarks varying according to staff schedules rather than the natural patterns of the day. So people lose what sense they might once have had of the physical environment of the world beyond their own private 'service land.'

Social and relationship discontinuity and even abandonment

Though discontinuity with the physical world is important, the next wound is perhaps more so, given our needs as human beings for relationship with others. Obviously in segregated and congregated settings, but also in the wider world of services, people and groups at risk of devaluation are likely to have few long lasting relationships, some will have few relationships of any sort, and most go through a succession of people who become their 'friend' or 'key worker' and then move on. *They Keep Going Away* the title of a book by Maureen Oswin from the early eighties (1984) sums up the notion behind this wound. Even since the movement out of hospitals of the eighties, study after study (e.g. Cattermole et.al. 1988; Firth & Rapley 1990; Sinson 1993; Richardson & Ritchie 1989b) confirms the findings that various devalued groups have deep memories of the few relationships that they have had, but equally deep pain from the frequency with which these change. This often then leads to deep insecurity in people's minds that they are worth having a relationship with at all and that, in effect, they have been abandoned. Parents and relatives may literally abandon people, as attempts to find 'home connection' for many people coming out of the long stay hospitals illustrate (Korman & Glennerster 1990). Elderly people, too, frequently experience much reduced, if any, contact with friends and relatives once they enter residential care.

As with some other wounds, readers who hear about relationship discontinuity point to the increasingly mobile population, and the loneliness of many people not in the devalued classes. SRV does not deny this, but as before points to the combination of this wound and the others, which people not in these groups will not necessarily have. In addition, the number of occasions where people in receipt of services have service mandated relationships, which then change as service workers move on to further their careers, also reinforces the sense of a series of individuals moving in and out of people's lives, with no continuity. It also speaks to the next wound, with which it is intimately connected.

Loss of natural, freely given relationships and substitution of artificial, 'paid for' ones

The studies cited in the previous section, especially those dealing with the move from long stay institutions, also revealed the frequency of this wound (Korman and Glennerster 1990, esp. ch.9). That is, not just that there is a succession of discontinuous relationships in people's lives, but that people get to the point where they have few, if any relationships at all other than with people who are paid to be there. Again, some point to modern trends to try to suggest that this is just a feature of modern life, and it is true that the increasing individualism noted by Wolfensberger (1996a) and others has tended to result in many lonely people. As before, however, SRV asks the reader to note the combination of this wound and others, and also how service practices, particularly segregation and congregation, actually increase the chances that the only relationships in people's lives are those with paid service staff. Service records indicate dozens, sometimes hundreds of service workers in the lives of people with learning disabilities, yet on asking about friends, the answer is one, or often none. We must also note the link between this wound and the wounds of rejection and relegation to low social status, with the obvious point that relationships exist in a social context, and it is much harder for a natural relationship to develop when the social context is already giving powerful messages that the person or group is to be at least avoided, if not actually 'put away.'

Deindividualization

On top of the previous four wounds, all of which are particularly exemplified in institutional settings, the experience of being treated as one of a group, as recipient of a service to an undistinguished mass of people, adds to the devaluation process. As with those wounds, it was identified some while ago, named for example as 'block treatment' by King, Raynes & Tizard (1971). Even in more modern services, however, especially those still delivered in a segregated and congregated setting, such as elderly persons' homes, nursing homes and various hospitalised services for people with mental health problems, the sense that individuals are part of a 'category' rather than people in their own right still prevails. A study of ordinary houses, hailed as the solution proposed by 'normalisation' (Sinson 1990) also found many practices where people were treated as a group rather than as individuals. Naming it as 'micro-institutionalisation' the author then goes on to cite normalisation as the 'cause' of the practices, rather than looking into the connections between the various wounds. This would make it very likely that a strong element of deindividualization would result, even in an 'ordinary house', given the combination of relative segregation, the reliance on staff mediated relationships and activities and the staffing levels mandated by an 'economic' cost for care,.

Involuntary material poverty

It is interesting to note that, as we discussed in chapter 1, the origins of normalization were in the Scandinavian countries which, after the war, had some of the most highly developed social security and welfare systems anywhere in the world (Johansen 1986), but it was then developed in the most highly market oriented service system in the world, that of the United States. It is also important to remind the reader here of the point made in chapter 1, that the period when normalization was introduced as an academic idea, in the sixties and seventies, was dominated by similar attempts at state socialism via Labour governments, and its version of the welfare state. Whereas when normalization was introduced via the training route in the eighties, and taken on into the nineties by the development of SRV, England was undergoing the most radical of all reforms of the welfare state and human service organisation brought about by the Thatcher government (Lewis and Glennerster 1996).

This is crucial to our understanding of the English experience of a number of the wounds, not least the wound of involuntary material poverty, in that, in those Scandinavian countries, and others like England with a 'welfare state,' poverty was supposed to have been dealt with. Indeed part of the rhetoric of Thatcherism was that the welfare state was encouraging the poor to idleness, by sustaining them in a state of dependence from which there was little incentive to escape. The notion of what actually constituted poverty became the subject of considerable debate (Walker 1993) and so, in discussing the wound of poverty from the wider global perspective of SRV, the reader should be aware of the English context.

Having said that, the general process by which this particular wound operates still seems to be relevant to the English experience. This process works in two ways in the overall system of devaluing experiences. First, that if a person or group is poor, regardless of other wounds, then the likelihood of devaluation is greater and second, that involuntary poverty can result from a number of the other wounds.

On the first point, the history of poverty and the associated differentials in terms of all sorts of social indicators such as poor health, poor housing and poor education is well documented (Walker 1993). Putting this in SRV terms, poor people have traditionally been of low social status in English society; have, in many cases, been segregated into large 'ghetto' housing estates; have far less autonomy than those who are not poor; and are at far greater risk of being cast into a number of the common roles, especially the role of 'danger' or 'burden of charity'. As we noted above, the debate of the Thatcher years did not help, with the old notion of 'deserving' and 'undeserving' poor being successfully revived..

On the second point, the changes in the organisation and financing of human services in the Thatcher years, especially the much greater power of a service 'market' has increased the ability of society to add the wound of poverty to those already wounded (Wistow et. al. 1996). This particularly occurs through the service system. It had always been the case that those in receipt of services, and therefore at least at risk of devaluation, were in danger of having their material assets withdrawn or reduced. People in various institutional settings would often be able to carry all their possessions around in one suitcase. People in residential care, even the supposed alternatives to institutions, would find that nearly all of their benefits went to paying for their care, with just 'pocket money' being handed out for minor items (Lynch & Perry 1992).

With the advent of the social care market methods by which people were stripped of their assets became even more common, sometimes even overtly part of policy. For some years, many elderly people in residential care have had to sell their houses to pay for their care, and the overall policy has not changed with a new government, though the means limits have been raised slightly. This has then meant more pressure from relatives to hand over their 'inheritance' well before the elderly person is in 'need' of residential care, with all sorts of resultant roles thus being cast on to that elderly person, not least of which is then being the recipient of 'charity' from their own relatives (Taylor-Gooby & Lawson 1993).

Finally, with the rapidly expanding use of computerised technology for banking and other financial transactions, those less competent in such matters, typically the vulnerable groups we have already mentioned, will find themselves in much greater financial peril, either of being placed in a class that receives little or no credit, whilst the rest of society lives on that basis, or of being persuaded to enter into too many financial obligations which then get out of hand with disastrous results. Either way, devalued people are at much greater risk of ending up poor, and poor people at much greater risk of ending up devalued. The English experience of the decline of the welfare state that appears to be occurring can only make matters worse.

Impoverishment of experience, especially that of the typical, valued world

As some of the critics of SRV might have said, amending Groucho Marx, 'I wouldn't want to belong to a valued world that wouldn't have me as a member;' the implication being that if this is what the valued world does to people, then they do not want to be part of it. This point will be considered in more depth later, including the fact that most people who say such things do not seem too ready to cast off the benefits of the valued world themselves. It is relevant to state here that by calling impoverishment of experience a wound, SRV assumes that the experiences of the valued world are worth having. Wolfensberger's phrase 'the good things in life' as a primary goal for devalued people that SRV hopes to defend or attain, has been severely misinterpreted as acceptance of our modern obsession with material possessions and processes, so assuming that these are the only 'good things' worth having. A more detailed explanation of this phrase comes in the next chapter. What the wound of impoverishment of experiences is actually about is something much deeper than this. Especially in institutional settings, but also in some highly protective family situations (Richardson & Ritchie 1989a) vulnerable people may go for long periods of time, perhaps lifetimes, without experiencing the infinity of small everyday events that in most people go to make up their 'lifestory'. As well as simply experiencing things, of course, everyday events are a major source of learning, particularly about social situations and relationships. Institutionalised and over-protected people therefore suffer the double effect of this wound, in that they do not get these experiences very often, and when the chance does arise, they find it hard either to cope with, or appreciate the experience. Thus efforts by staff dealing with ex-institutional residents to 'integrate' people into social situations becomes much more difficult, if those residents have never been to a pub before, or travelled on a bus, or even crossed a road. As long ago as 1968, Gunzburg, one of those noted in chapter 1 as being involved in discussions of normalization, wrote a chapter in one of his books entitled, 'A stranger in his own country', about people with learning disabilities, and this conveys the flavour of the wound we are discussing, in that its effects are to render people as helpless as visitors to a foreign country in observing all the myriad of social and other experiences that enable citizens of that country to function. It is also worth noting the peculiarly English dimension of this wound, in that regional and even inter-village variations in behaviour can cause degrees of devaluation of 'strangers', so for the person who has had few experiences at all in common with the rest of their community their risk of behaving in ways that will be perceived negatively is that much greater.

Exclusion from knowledge of and participation in higher order value systems that give meaning and direction to life and provide community

This wound is not just talking about formally organised religions, but the whole series of ways available, in the valued world, to try to answer the questions that have concerned humanity for centuries. It is true that this has tended to be dominated by religions, and in the Church of England there is a built in link between local communities and their churches that reflects a considerable cultural heritage. Even here, however, where one might expect welcoming for certain devalued groups, especially disabled ones, there has been rejection—either outright rejection, or a peculiarly English version of tolerance that lets devalued people know just how noble are those 'putting up with' their presence. Like other countries, too, the Church of England has its share of 'special services' for people with learning disabilities, again emphasising the 'charity' or 'holy innocent' role.

Given the attitude of the majority of English people to organised religion, however, exclusion of people from it would not necessarily be perceived as a particularly bad thing. Church attendances in single percentage figures are only one testament to the apathy, and often outright hostility, to religion in this country, though this is sometimes in contrast to the degree of religious activity amongst ethnic minority groups. This is a broader issue than cannot adequately be dealt with here, but if the general assertion is true, the wound under discussion is doubly telling, since not only are certain groups of people excluded from religion who might benefit from it, but others who are included then receive the opprobrium of the wider society as only being there to ease the conscience of the devalued church. Further, the alternatives to formal religion that are sought by valued people, such as psychotherapy, 'self-actualisation' or the pursuit of various alternative 'religions' such as science, sport, or sexual gratification, also tend to get denied to devalued people, especially if they lack the financial resources that most of these religions demand.

So as well as being prevented from gaining whatever intrinsic benefits there are from the various higher-order value systems, many devalued people miss out on the sense of community or communality that tends to go with pursuit of many of them. In this context, ironically, those disabled groups who have come together and tried to explore the common experience, or 'meaning' of their identity could be said to be pursuing a higher order value system and gaining from the sense of community that their common identity gives them. The potential downside of that process, however, is that some of the communities thus formed, as they have with some women's groups and groups from particular ethnic minorities, see the group as their sole identity and thereby continue or create the wound of segregation from the rest of society.

Having one's life 'wasted'

As we have noted above, some wounds can operate very powerfully on their own, whilst others combine in a systemic way to add to the devaluation of individuals and groups. If the latter is the case, this can result in a further wound, which is that a great majority of someone's waking life can simply ebb away, in effect be wasted. The significance of this wound depends to some extent on one's value position on what constitutes 'development' or 'growth' in a person or group, and will be discussed more fully in the theme of the developmental model, but there would appear to be three key views that contribute to the wasting of people's lives. The first, derived from an acceptance of prevailing views or just held as a personal opinion, is that certain groups of people, such as those with learning disabilities, or the elderly, 'cannot' develop. Expectations of such people to learn or retain even basic self care skills, let alone more esoteric ideas such as appreciation of art or music, are thus very low or non-existent. The second view is that individuals or groups are so unimportant that any effort to develop their abilities is not worth the effort. This view was, and is still in some places, held of school children with learning disabilities, first formally, in the sense that they were officially deemed 'ineducable' before the 1971 Education (Handicapped Children) Act and since then in some of the expectations and performances of the special school system, and resistance to inclusion in mainstream education. Thirdly, and more malevolently, is the view that certain groups should not be given the opportunity to learn and develop. This can stem from the perceived 'needs' of the economy, such as was part of the post war education policy, known as the 'eleven plus' where only a small percentage were selected for the more academic schools, to keep the rest at the 'level' they needed to work in the factories and offices, or from deliberate bias in favour of one group over another, such as the other element of that same policy which kept a fixed percentage of boys passing the eleven plus, even though the overall performance of girls was higher (Evans 1985)

The combination of these three views then results in practices that are all too familiar to people who work in services, and as we have already noted it is through services that many of the devaluing policies are carried out. The sight of many people in different services simply sitting, or lying, or being engaged in activities that present no developmental challenge to them, is one of the clichés of the service world. For some people it may only come later in life, when they enter services for elderly people, Denham (1997), or after an accident that results in a physical impairment, Swain et.al. (1993). For others, life wasting can be life long. Children born with a physical or mental impairment can, almost from birth, be subject to low, or no expectations from their parents, often because those parents themselves are subject to the low expectations of society or their professional advisors. As they grow older more professional advice, often conflicting and often related to vested interests, reinforces the view of dependency and helplessness, again conveying low expectations of development. So all the effort that would have been put into working with the child may be diminished, and they may not even be expected to take their share of common tasks in the house, thus again reducing their opportunities for learning and growth. Then the special school, exempted from the national curriculum, may spend endless hours on simple tasks to occupy the children's time, partially dictated by the congregation of so many devalued children in one place. From here may come the college course, often called 'preparation for living' or some similar title (note the assumption implicit in the title that students haven't done any living yet) and then on to the day service, which may consist of endless days doing 'music therapy' or lying in a 'sensory room'. Or, for those more enlightened centres who are into 'choice,' an hour long morning discussion of what you will 'choose' to do today, followed by an hour doing whatever it is, then preparing for lunch, followed by another discussion of what you are choosing to do in the afternoon, then doing that for an hour before preparing for the journey home. Even those who rail against the 'Protestant work ethic' that they claim underlies day services must surely see the waste of peoples lives that such a lifelong career represents.

For people in institutionalised services, of course, the picture is often much worse. Anyone who has visited nursing homes, residential homes for all sorts of people, and even the small 'ordinary house' alternatives to institutions cannot fail to be struck by the preponderance of life wasting that takes place, with groups or individuals sitting around, staring into space and, in the view of many, 'waiting to die'. This can often lead to that wait being abbreviated, as in the next wound of brutalisation and deathmaking.

Brutalisation - 'Deathmaking'

One significant feature of the English experience of SRV have been the critiques of Wolfensberger's other writings and presentations that have been used, in an argument ad hominem, to criticise SRV (Brown & Smith 1992b). Nowhere is this more true than in what he describes as 'deathmaking' where his observations (e.g. Wolfensberger 1990) have been seen as anti-women (Brown & Smith 1992a), as a religious crusade (Jackson 1994; Jones and Withers 1991), or even as a public purging of childhood experiences (Flaker 1994). Over the years since this material was first presented there appears to be less dispute about the reality of violence and deathmaking in society, though arguments about causes and solutions still abound. It is contended here that Wolfensberger's views on 'deathmaking', which essentially draw people to make moral and values based decisions on their own actions, do not affect the validity or otherwise of SRV. Similarly the place of the death-related role ascription described in chapter 3, while important, indeed often literally vital, to those affected, should not be read, because of Wolfensberger's concern with the higher order issue of deathmaking, as necessarily more important than any of the other historic roles. Its effects, of course, by often hastening the death of those so ascribed reveals the logical conclusion of devaluation as being literally to get rid of the devalued person or group, and being in the dying role can also increase the likelihood of a person or group being put into some of the other historic roles, e.g. sub-human, burden, that have life threatening implications. Nevertheless, it is important for the reader to consider the death or dying role alongside the other historic roles, and with the same analysis. Similarly the consideration of the wound of brutalisation and deathmaking should be as part of the system of devaluing wounds, with its validity judged in that light.

By now the reader will have noticed quite a few ironies occurring in the English experience of normalization and SRV, and a further one comes in thinking about the wound of brutalisation and deathmaking. Some of the same people who were only too ready to use the experiences of the brutal regimes in hospitals, exposed by the various 'scandals' of the sixties and seventies, were the first to criticise as 'impossible' or 'exaggerated', though rarely in print, the connections made by Wolfensberger between this and many other forms of 'deathmaking' carried out on devalued groups and individuals, particularly by the service system. Only now, as more and more examples of abuse, not only in care homes and institutions but also in family homes, are being revealed (e.g. Decalmer and Glendinning 1997) is there beginning to be at least an acceptance of the prevalence of brutalisation of devalued groups. The link with devaluation and deathmaking is still not really being made, still less with officially sanctioned and legitimised deathmaking, such as abortion and war. However, the connections have been made by some of the disabled people's movement (Morris 1991), though even here opinions are not entirely clear cut.

SRV, as opposed to Wolfensberger's other work on the subject, again does not look in depth at the underlying causes, since these are ultimately the underlying causes of devaluation, and those are the subject of a higher order values debate. What SRV does do, with this wound, is to point to the obvious logical consequences of the devaluation and wounding process, and invite the reader to look at the world around, particularly the world of services, and see if the empirical evidence supports this logical outcome. If people are seen as of low social status, are rejected, are seen in the roles of sub-human, or menace, or waste material, what would be more natural than to do things to them that would not be done to valued people, including hastening their death. If people are put at a distance, in segregated and/or congregated settings, with very little or no autonomy and control, where they suffer from discontinuous or no relationships that might act as a protection for them, brutality and even outright killing can, and has taken place undetected, Decalmer and Glendinning (1997). If people are so disconnected from the physical and social world around them, and from experiences and higher order value systems that might give meaning to life, that they are having their lives wasted, what more natural than to shorten that life, to avoid using 'taxpayers' money' to keep such people alive. Even though some of the examples of such behaviour in services has been brought to light, and the perpetrators punished, no bland reassurances that 'things are different now' or that the abuse was merely the result of 'evil individuals' can take away the systemic nature of this logical conclusion to devaluation, and the daily evidence of its continuing practice.

Awareness of being a source of anguish to those who love one

Along with the issues of 'choice' and 'rights' the other key point of contention in the English experience of normalization and then SRV has come over the issue of 'identity,' and whether anyone who is not subject to a devalued identity is able, or should be allowed to, discuss 'what it is like' to be a devalued person. In analysing the wounds of devalued people, and in particular the last three, including this one, which draw on observation of devalued people and groups, SRV is attempting to describe the phenomenology of devaluation, and in effect invite the reader to put themselves empathetically 'in the shoes' of devalued people. Obviously, no-one but an individual themselves can speak precisely of their own experience, but in formulating a theory from a mass of empirical evidence SRV would claim, in common with many other social science theories, to at least be describing an observable reality at the probabilistic level. In deducing, therefore, from personal accounts (Atkinson and Williams 1990) and observable behaviour (Fleming and Kroese 1993) that many devalued people become aware of the wounding process and react to it in certain ways, SRV is not pretending that such reactions happen to everyone, or that it is not possible to react in entirely different ways. So again, looking at the next three wounds is not subscribing to the 'personal tragedy theory' of disability but merely observing what seems to happen in the lives of a significant number of devalued individuals and groups.

The first is most often seen where devalued people are, at least at first, part of a family situation, though it is often reinforced when decisions are made about admission to the care of services. The constant discussion of 'what to do' with a person with learning disabilities, or an elderly relative, the much greater effort needed by families to deal with the maze that is the service system, and the simple weariness that comes just with the work truly needed on behalf of an impaired family member all convey the powerful message that the person is a source of anguish to loved ones. If this is then further reinforced by family's campaigning for more services to 'look after' whatever category of devalued group the person belongs to, or if they apparently reject the person by placing them in services, often with the conviction that the person will be 'better off' there, then the weight on their minds is likely to be considerable. This often leads to people 'blaming themselves' for the anguish that they see being caused, with sometimes disastrous consequences. Many elderly people have been swayed in the euthanasia debate, not by the thought of their own pain, but by the thought of being a 'burden' or a source of pain to their loved ones.

Awareness of being an alien in the valued world; personal insecurity, perhaps dislike of oneself and/or rage

This next wound is broader than the previous one, in that it is concerned with the individual's reaction to the devaluation process as a whole. The messages, of course, are very similar to the messages being given out to the rest of society, that cause and reinforce devaluation. If a person or group are relegated to low social status, they will be as aware of it as other people, perhaps more so. If they are rejected, perhaps by being moved from place to place in the service system, a natural sense of insecurity will be inspired. The whole range of messages assigning people to one or more of the common devalued roles will have the same meaning for many devalued people as they do for the rest of the population. So it goes on; any and all of the wounds not only has an impact on the physical situation of devalued people, but must have a mental impact. Stories abound of people reacting to this awareness by turning in on themselves and trying to change their physical appearance or any other attribute that they think is that part of them that is causing all these wounds. Equally frequent are the accounts of people turning on themselves in rage, to the point of suicide, and certainly self damage (Fleming and Kroese 1993). If you are constantly being told, either literally or through actions and all the other manifestations of devaluation, that you are worthless, that nobody wants to be with you, that you are a drain on others, what again is more natural that you should seek to take out your anger on what you perceive to be the cause of all these bad things, i.e. yourself. What makes this wound even worse then is that such behaviour is not understood as a reaction to devaluation, but one more 'symptom' of your devalued identity.

Resentment, even hatred of privileged citizens

This final wound may be very understandable, in that the combination of all or some of the preceding wounds would tend to lead those on the receiving end to look for oppressors, and to resent the people not so devalued. At the individual level, such resentment can again be the source of further devaluation, in that aggressive or even outright violent behaviour may result, and further casting in the 'dangerous' or 'animal' role be the consequence. With groups of people, some of this may be channelled into radical action in support of changing the situation whereby certain groups are devalued. The difficulty, as with the 'community of identity' discussed under the wound of exclusion from higher order value systems, is that the radical action becomes a source of enmity between various groups in society. As at the extreme edges of feminism and anti-racism, such enmity sees no solution to their own devaluation except through the destruction of the oppressor, which of course, from the point of view of SRV theory, is merely to replace one devalued group with another. More commonly, such radical groups do not seek the total destruction of their oppressors, but some sort of legal change to affect their 'rights' to be treated equally. This has met with limited success, at least in obtaining some degree of sanction against certain kinds of racist, sexist or disablist actions, but in the broader sense of halting devaluation such action has severe limits, not least because, as we have seen, much devaluation has the approval of major sectors of society, being based on widely held values which cannot just be legislated away, with some (such as the abortion of impaired babies) having legal support as well.

So even in groups where some radical action has occurred, the resentment of valued citizens by those who are devalued is likely to continue, and in many cases to take the form of a smouldering anger that is easily perceived as yet more reason for privileged citizens to avoid those concerned.

Conclusion - experiences of devalued people - 'the wounds'

Chapter 2 concluded by claiming to have demonstrated the universality of devaluation and the empirical nature of SRV theory. We have followed this at some length in the next two chapters by looking at the process of devaluation through the common experiences, or 'wounds' of devalued individuals and groups. It is hoped that this lengthy exposition has convinced the reader, both through its own argument and through the reader's examination of that argument in the light of their own experience, that devaluation is taking place through this process, both in society as a whole and particularly in human services. Further, it is important to re-emphasise that, as was claimed for devaluation as a concept, the wounding process operates at all levels, from the individual, through the intermediate social group, to whole sectors of society. Address of devaluation, therefore, which is the purpose of SRV, also needs to take place at all of those levels. The importance SRV attaches to addressing the roles that are held or imposed on people should also have become clear from the previous two chapters and we now go on to look in more detail at ideas from role theory and elsewhere that will form the basis for the strategies to counter devaluation proposed by SRV.

5

Social roles and SRV theory

Introduction

One of the increasing drawbacks of involvement with the academic world, alluded to in chapter 1, is the tendency, as publication has mushroomed, for ever more specialisation and demarcation between disciplines, and for any work more than a few years old, even acknowledged 'classics', to be regarded as 'outdated.' SRV suffers more than most in this respect, in that its roots in normalization and its links with deviancy theory have caused it to be shunned by many in the field of sociology who claim to have 'moved on' from explanatory 'functionalist' theories. Further, as we discussed in chapter 2, the roots of normalization in the field of learning disabilities has made it extremely difficult for academics dealing with other groups to get to hear about SRV. Psychologists have their own range of 'schools' and those involved with learning disabilities, especially behaviourists, have their own ideas about 'theory' and are suspicious of SRV's broad ranging approach (e.g. McGill & Emerson 1992). If to this we add the mixed reaction to American ideas in English universities, it is scarcely surprising that the English academic experience of SRV, as it evolved from normalization, should be patchy and often hostile. Few academics have looked at the much greater importance, placed by Wolfensberger in his reformulation, of role theory to SRV.

Were they to do so, they might find, as Lemay did in examining a considerable number of publications from around the world in preparation for the 1994 International Conference on 'Twenty-five years of Normalization/ SRV' held in Ottawa, that while role theory has also been around for a long time it could be described as the 'nexus between sociology and psychology' (Lemay 1995, p518). Lemay also found that social role theory 'is of great importance to both fields, but few practitioners have gained much practical use from it.' (ibid, p518) What Wolfensberger did, therefore, in recognising the importance of social roles in the devaluation and wounding process was also to seek their utilisation in the combating of devaluation. This was the essential step in the evolution from normalization to SRV, and one which went largely unrecognised at least in academic discussion in England, where the differences are often considered to be nominal.

The key purpose of this chapter, therefore, is to provide an overview of those aspects of role theory that are particularly relevant to SRV, and show how this leads into the strategies proposed by SRV to counter devaluation. This will lead us to the ten themes of SRV, which provide further insights into the devaluation process and SRV's reaction to it.

Background to role theory

As with many social science constructs, particularly those that have been around for some time, the nuances of interpretation and power of predictability of role theory have been the subject of much debate and controversy in the academic world (Hall 1997). SRV does not really enter that debate at the fundamental level but, as with its foundation in devaluation, takes the empirical base of role theory, and the at least probabalistically consistent findings of how social roles operate, to garner what is important to SRV theory.

In this overview, therefore, it is inevitable that the full explication of role theory given in the literature will not be replicated, but only those aspects of particular relevance to SRV. Paul Jenkins, in his SRV training materials (1998) makes a useful distinction between schemas, statuses and roles, though this is not universally accepted by academics. Jenkins quotes Fiske and Taylor (1991, p8) in defining a schema as 'a cognitive structure that represents knowledge about a concept or type of stimulus, including its attributes and relations among those attributes' and thus defines roles in this context as a type of schema that represents knowledge about certain aspects of the behaviour of people. If that definition comes from the field of psychology, then from some schools of sociology comes the notion of status, as being the position in society that people occupy, as defined by that society or key groups thereof (Cuff et.al. 1992). Notice the connection here between that definition and our analysis of how individuals and groups are judged, in that status was noted as one of the key influences on that judgement. As a socially defined phenomenon status can be ascribed simply on the basis of what one is born to, such as one's gender, ethnic or racial identity, or can be the result of what one acquires, such as one's occupation or marital state. Similarly, because it is created by society or at least a sub-set of society, a person often occupies a certain status regardless of their own intentions, according to how society currently defines the position they are in. They may wish that their position had a higher status, or think it ought to, as evidenced by the struggles of feminists to alter the status of women, but at any point in time, regardless of the intentions of its occupants, all social positions have a certain status. Roles are then linked to status by the fact that each status carries a set of rules or norms of expected behaviour, also of course socially defined. Jenkins (1998) notes the possible confusion between roles and status in that sometimes the same word is used for both. So 'wife' for example, is a social position with a certain status, depending on the cultural context, whilst it is also a role, with certain expectations of behaviour, again highly dependant on the social context. It therefore may be helpful to think of roles having some social expectation of behaviour, as in the sense of 'playing a role', which is defined by socially imposed rights and obligations, and that one can 'live up to' that role by fulfilling those rights and obligations, or at least appearing to do so. Status, on the other hand is a social position one occupies, regardless of what one does about it, though if many people consistently act differently to the expectations of the status then the overall value of that status can change, either positively or negatively. Thus the value of the status of the royal family could be said to be changing.

Role domains

Role theory, at least as used in SRV, is therefore an attempt to conceptualise the complex interactions of individuals in a social context in terms of the social expectations of rights, privileges and obligations attached to particular roles. The literature shows a number of ways of classifying roles (Hall 1997), all of which seem to point to the conclusion that though the number of roles available in any society may be vast, they tend to fall into relatively few domains. Wolfensberger (1998a) cites eight common role domains, and also notes that within each, and within particular societies, there are examples of roles that are either positively and negatively valued. Table 5.1 below uses Wolfensberger's framework with this author's choice of examples that are currently positively and negatively valued in English society. Readers are invited to give their own examples, rather than dwell too long on agreement or otherwise with those of the author, since it is the general principle that positive and negative value is attached to certain roles that is at issue. Readers are also reminded of the point, discussed in chapter 2, that devaluation does not have to be carried out by all, or even a majority, of any given society to have a powerful effect, and so the author's judgement of which roles are positively and negatively valued would still be valid whether or not the reader themselves holds positive or negative views on the role in question, provided a sufficiently powerful section of society did so for a significant period of time.

Stereotypes and Roles

From the social psychological literature the notion of stereotyping needs to

Table 5.1

Common Role Domains, with positive and negative examples from English Society

Domain	Positive role examples	Negative role examples
Relationships	mother, father, daughter, son, friend, grandparent, brother, fiancee, sister,	divorcee, bigamist, adulterer, orphan, child abuser, single parent, wife beater
Residence	homeowner, tenant, landowner, good neighbour, good landlord home maintainer	homeless person, tramp, social security tenant, slum landlord, council estate dweller
Economic productivity	employee, employer, trainee breadwinner, careerist, expert, entrepreneur	unemployed, unqualified, dependant, scrounger, dole cheat
Education	professor, academic, graduate, student, teacher	drop-out, special needs, ineducable, illiterate
Leisure, sports	professional sportsman or woman, fan, tourist, explorer, walker, winner	couch potato, bore, loser, whinger, killjoy
Community and civic identity and participation	voter, patriot, party member, taxpayer, community worker, volunteer, fundraiser, charity organiser	immigrant, foreigner, drop-out, traveller
Religion	vicar, priest, rabbi, guru, imam, churchgoer, choir member, organist	Jehovah's Witness, religious zealot
Culture	musician, artist, historian	philistine, vulgarian passive TV watcher

be considered here, as another piece in the jigsaw by which roles can be assigned to people or groups (Condor 1990; Miller 1982). As a way of helping humans to cope with the massive amount of perceptual input we receive it can be adaptive to form what one might call a thumbnail sketch of a person or group. Again the links to the process of social judgement should be clear. If, via this shorthand way of dealing within perceptual inputs, we habitually classify a group by a few common characteristics, and then along with those characteristics we associate certain beliefs or knowledge about that group, again likely to be only partial, then whenever we run across members of that group we are likely to make reference to that association in the form of a stereotype. This enables us to process information more quickly than going through all the detail of the actual information presented and, once formed, stereotypes tend to resist information that goes against what the stereotype would suggest. Of course the stereotypes are often based on very partial information, and are closely connected to prejudice, in the sense of that word that means making a judgement without receiving the full evidence, and prejudice can, as we have seen, play a major part in the devaluation process. This is not to say that stereotyping and its part in role ascription is entirely bad, more that it appears to be a part of how we are able to cope with functioning in a complex society. What is a problem, as far as SRV and devaluation is concerned, is that, at least to judge from the popular media, we seem to be relying more and more on stereotyping and less and less on detailed examination of the attributes of any group, as more and more discourse is carried out in short sound bites and images. The written and visual media, in particular, seem to be constantly looking for stereotypes on which to hang a particular story and in doing so reinforce the casting of people and groups into roles about which the stereotypes already exist, rather than examine the complexities of a particular situation.

Roles and their expectations

The theme of role expectancy and role circularity, dealt with in chapter 7, goes into greater depth on the effect of roles on devaluation, but in this general overview we need only say that, almost by definition, roles carry with them rights or privileges afforded by society and expectations demanded by society. So the role of parent goes with the right to have power over the child, at least to a certain age, and to receive financial and other benefits on the child's behalf, but also carries the responsibility to feed and clothe the child, protect it from harm and generally act in the child's best interests. The role of employee affords those holding it the privileges of a salary, safe working conditions, opportunities for advancement and so on, but also the expectation of turning up for work, of observing the employers codes of conduct etc. Expectations are very powerful in shaping both the behaviour of those holding a role and the rest of society, such that if someone acts contrary to what is expected from their role then others become confused or even hostile. Many experiments have shown the powerful effects that a perceived role can have, even in cases where the role was 'set up' for experimental purposes (Marques 1990) 'Role-playing' as a training or therapeutic technique has been widely used, and one of the key findings of accounts of such techniques is the ease with which people slip into roles which may have attributes totally alien to them, or offend their values, and how quite intensive sessions are necessary at the end of the exercise to get people 'out of role'.

Societies and Roles

As with many social science insights into human behaviour, many people react to the previous analysis of the power of roles with a mixture of discomfort and hostility, as they become aware of the application to themselves of those insights. In particular there is, as with devaluation, a tendency to say that the casting of people into roles is something done by other people, and that it can be legislated or procedured out, at least in its harmful effects. SRV does not say this, but instead notes a number of empirical facts about societies and roles, and invites the reader to set this evidence against their own experience, whether or not this is comfortable or whether they think it 'ought' to happen.

That all societies have roles should be very evident, not least from the number of words that have role associations. Indeed, in many countries, people's names are derived from occupational roles, with 'Carpenter' or 'Smith,' for example, indicating the frequency of those roles in English history. It also seems to be common to most societies that different roles come at different ages, many in fact being assumed at points where some sort of 'rite of passage' is occurring, and that in mature adulthood people hold the greatest number of roles with that number declining somewhat in old age. Nearly all people of any age, however, occupy more than one role at a time and in most societies there are many more roles available than any one individual can fill. The number and type of available roles does vary with societies, however, and seems to depend on the complexity of that society and its nature. In industrialised societies, where certain roles, especially work roles, have become very specialised and demarcated, and the media of information dissemination has become highly sophisticated, then the number of available roles is enormous.

It also seems to be clear, from anthropology as well as other disciplines, that people in all societies become identified, and are given degrees of social status, by the roles they fill, and that this process operates at the societal and sub-societal level, right down to the level of small groups (Hall 1997). In fact the same role occupied by one person or group may have a very different status, depending on which groups are granting that status. So the role of gang leader may have high status to the rest of the gang, and perhaps to rival gangs, but to the wider community and the majority of the society, the status of that role will be rather lower. Further, such studies also suggest that people are aware, at least at the unconscious level, of the power and identity giving function of roles, and therefore do all they can to enter as many roles as possible. Lemay (in press) calls this 'role avidity'

Finally, as was noted in the introduction to this chapter, the wide range of writers on role theory are not in full agreement on how far roles are either permanent, or clear (Marques 1990). Certainly the value given to roles changes over time as well as between societies, as some might argue has happened in the case of the role of schoolteacher in the last twenty years in England, and there are certainly some roles that are somewhat ambiguous in their expectations and their value. An example of this might be current expectations of the role of 'partner' which has gone well beyond its original meaning of one of two people in a business arrangement.

Getting into roles

We noted earlier that the expectations and privileges of social roles come from wider society, or a sub-group thereof. We now look at how people or groups actually get into those roles which society defines. The first way is for the role to be ascribed, with or without the assent of the person or people concerned. The role of son or daughter is clearly ascribed, as revealed by the agonised teenage cry of 'I didn't ask to be your ...' The role of employee is, at least in the first instance, one to which people aspire, but which takes the assent of at least one other person, the employer, and the assent of the wider society that the employer can offer the role. It is also possible for individuals to assume a role, though the role is usually much more embedded if at least a significant proportion of society agrees that the person is occupying it. So someone can assume the role of party leader, even if the party just consists of themselves, but the role will be much more embedded if there is a membership, and the person is elected leader. This embedding of the role, and the prominence it assumes in a person or group's identity, depends on a number of factors, which are discussed below

The prominence of social roles

The first factor which affects how prominent a part of an individual's identity is held by any particular role is the perhaps obvious one of time. The longer anyone spends in a role the more both the person and outside observers will see that role as a key part of their identity.

Second, the more a role is concerned with the major activities of life, the more it will be a prominent part of a person's identity. So roles to do with work or family will tend to be a more prominent part of someone's identity than those to do with their hobbies, although some people, of course, can make some activities that are hobbies to others a major part of their life, in which case, for example, the role of gardener or football supporter may become more prominent than husband or father.

Third, the degree to which an individual or group is seen as embedded in their role, that it is only for them and a few others, also affects the degree of prominence. If there is seen to be a great deal of breadth to the role, with many others as potential candidates for the role, then the prominence for any individual will be that much less.

Fourthly, the degree to which a role is fixed, or entrenched to a person or group, without the possibility of coming out of it, will also affect prominence. If a role is permanent, such as a murderer, then even though it may be disguised, society will still see the person in the role many years after the offence. Roles of strong but not permanent entrenchment, such as a parent, are also very prominent in someone's identity.

Finally, the visibility of a role lends greatly to its prominence. Prince Charles's role as father and widower may be very entrenched, but the public visibility of his role as heir to the throne continues to be the most prominent one in his identity.

Conveyors of role messages

In chapter 3 we looked at some ways, or media, by which people were cast into some of the common historic devalued roles. This was expanded in chapter 4 by further examples, in the wound of 'branding', of how messages about a person or group's wounded status might serve to confirm or reinforce that status. Role theory, through consideration of such things as stereotyping, confirms that the judgements we make, particularly social judgements, are rarely made with deliberate rationality. By abbreviating and classifying the inputs to our perceptions, we are, as noted above, able to deal with the complexities of interactions in society to a greater or lesser extent. Goffman, in his work *Frame Analysis* (1974) talks about 'cues' for behaviour in social situations, which we put alongside a finite number of potential scenarios, to orient ourselves to any particular situation. Most social situations fit these scenarios, so we respond to the cues largely unconsciously. Partly the cues relate to the impression we get of the people in the social situation, and how they are likely to behave, and part of that expectation has to do with the roles we perceive them as holding. Thus a parent entering their child's classroom will pick up from various cues whether what is happening is within the range of expected classroom scenarios, part of which will be a person in that classroom fulfilling our expectations of the role of teacher. Only if the behaviour does not fit expectations, such as the teacher not carrying out what is expected of his or her role, would there be more conscious analysis, and an attempt to put the situation into a different 'frame.'

SRV theory, and the evaluation instrument PASSING, break down the different cues or, in their language, conveyors of expectations, into six categories, which, as noted above, have varying degrees of power in any given situation but combine very powerfully to give out the perception of particular roles being held by individuals in that situation. Table 5.2 below summarises those media, or channels, through which role messages and expectancies are conveyed.

The table is, of course a more detailed version of elements we have used before in the analysis of the common wounds, and more specific examples will be given in chapter 7 on role expectancies. It is also important to repeat the point made earlier that whether the reader likes the empirical observation that messages about people are conveyed in this way is irrelevant to the question of whether they are so conveyed. The sheer amount of money spent by politicians to persuade us of their suitability for the role of government and the means by which they do this should alone be enough to convince all but the most sceptical of the importance and power of these message conveyors. What one then does, as we have noted several times, then depends on one's values as well as one's convictions as to the validity of the analysis.

An important secondary point here is that, just as roles are socially defined, but have their basis in some natural attributes of individuals and groups, so the expectations derived from roles can have a 'natural' basis, i.e. they naturally arise from the role, but those expectations can be enhanced by the association of other attributes with the role which it did not originally possess. A trivial but perhaps familiar example of this are the various 'extras' that are now part of wedding ceremonies, but appear on standard checklists, as if those preparing for the role of bride and groom are merely choosing what to leave out from what is expected rather than opting for all sorts of contrived (and expensive) additions.

Roles and the Development of SRV theory

From the first four chapters it should be clear that, while devaluation and the wounds were an essential part of the analysis of normalization, at least in the form outlined by Wolfensberger and taught in England in the eighties, the depth of that analysis and the strategies to address devaluation were enhanced and reformulated as a result of the importance given to social roles. This is clearly shown in the changing definitions, first of normalization, and then of SRV. If we leave aside the early history of normalization and the Scandinavian definitions, not because they are of no importance but because this discussion is looking to trace the development of Wolfensberger's SRV theory, we can see the first key change is from his 1972 definition of normalization as the 'utilization of means which are as culturally normative as possible, in order to establish and/or maintain personal behaviours and characteristics which are as culturally normative as possible' (Wolfensberger 1972, p28). That change was to take account of a growing awareness, partly through observing how normalization was playing out in practice and partly through academic discussion and debate, that the power of the devaluation process was such, and the part played by social roles was so crucial, that 'culturally normative means' applied 'as much as possible' were insufficient to deal with it. Therefore

Table 5.2
Major Channels through which Role Messages and Expectancies are conveyed

1. Physical environments	a.	Structure, i.e the physical design and features
	b.	Context, i.e the location, proximity to other settings, history and access of a setting.
2. Social context	a.	The people or groups associated with the group or person – in a service context, the people sharing the same service.
	b.	The people or groups physically near the group or person – in a service context this may be service staff, or users of other services located nearby.
3. Activities		Behaviours carried out by, expected or demanded of a person or group, including the nature and timing of those activities.
4. Language	a.	Language directly addressed to a person or group
	b.	Language used indirectly about a person or group
	c.	Names of services and service settings.
	d.	Language and other symbols connected to a person or group by referring to their activities, service processes or other people or groups that they are associated with or near to.
5. Personal presentation	a.	The posture, bodily appearance and expressive movement
	b.	Clothes and other personal attire
	c.	Grooming
	d.	Other distinguishing marks, e.g. tattoos, insignia
	e.	Possessions
6. Miscellaneous		e.g. Source of funding of services

(Adapted from Wolfensberger and Thomas 1983)

in the definition formulated in the late seventies and appearing publicly in 1982, the inclusion of social roles appears. Here, normalization was defined as 'The use, as much as possible, of culturally valued means to enable, enhance and/or maintain valued social roles' (Wolfensberger and Tullman 1982 p132), and in various articles appearing shortly afterwards (e.g. 1984), Wolfensberger outlines the reason, not only for the reconceptualization, but also for the renaming of normalization as SRV.

By 1992, in the second edition of the monograph, *A Brief Introduction to Social Role Valorization,* the definition had become 'the enablement, establishment, enhancement, maintenance, and/or defense of valued social roles for people - particularly those at value risk - by using, as much as possible, culturally valued means.' These two definitions were the most commonly used in the English experience of teaching 'normalisation' and SRV in the late eighties and early nineties, as discussed in chapter 1, and, as mentioned there, may have contributed to English recipients, especially academics receiving the information at second hand, being confused about the differences between 'normalisation' and SRV, and being unaware of later developments in SRV. We hope that by now the depth of analysis should have given readers of this book sufficient idea of the key differences between the two, and it may have had something to do with analysis being made on the basis of short definitions, rather than detailed study, that so much confusion remains.

The second key development, outlined at the 1994 Ottawa conference was the firmer placing of SRV within the realms of social science, so that by then, the definition has become 'the science of the enablement, establishment, enhancement, maintenance, and/or defence of valued social roles for people' (Thomas and Wolfensberger, in press). By 1998, the definition draws on links made between SRV and findings from the wider social science field by redefining it as 'the application of what science has to tell us about the defense or upgrading of the socially perceived value of people's roles' (Wolfensberger 1998a). It should be clear that this book is working to this latest definition but it is hoped that the book as a whole, rather than this section on definitions, will be used in evaluating SRV theory. This examination of definitions is intended, mainly, to emphasise the difference between SRV and normalization (though noting the common root in social devaluation) by highlighting the importance of roles to SRV, and by placing it in the social science domain as a theory to be examined in the same light as other theories. Having said that, all the definitions, both of normalization and SRV, point to action to address devaluation, so SRV's claim to be a social scientific theory does not mean it has become an esoteric abstraction. On the contrary, the strategies which follow have direct application in practice, and sit very clearly alongside, without necessarily being in contradiction to, other guides to action for and with vulnerable people, including those that do not seek a coherent empirical basis. Whether one should follow SRV strategies, in whole or in part, depends, first of all, on one's reaction to devaluation and then to one's reaction to the 'costs' in terms of values, of the various alternative courses of action to address devaluation (Wolfensberger 1995a) What SRV would suggest is covered in broad terms in the next section, and then in more detail in the ten themes which follow.

The goals of SRV

Two of the most consistent criticisms of 'normalisation' i.e. that version of normalization and SRV that has come down through the English experience, are, first, that it colludes in the status quo of an oppressive, capitalist, sexist, racist, and disablist society (Bano et.al. 1993; Brown & Smith

1992a), and second, that SRV is something 'done to' vulnerable people by the valued members of society, either directly or more usually through services (Chappell 1997). In looking at the goals of SRV theory, therefore, it is necessary for the reader to consider their own position on these two issues, in terms of where they see their address of devaluation as lying. If they concur that English society is indeed oppressive, for all the reasons implied above, then this would, first of all, not invalidate the notion of social devaluation, merely give particular explanations for it. If they then consider what actions, if any, would address that oppression, and at what level it could be addressed, various other options would appear. One would be action at the societal level, to somehow persuade English society to stop being oppressive. This option has, of course been attempted by a number of political groups, more or less legitimately, and it could be argued that they have met with some success, if one looks at the oppression of women or ethnic minority groups. It could equally be argued, and has been (Weeks 1994), that such changes as there have been have been largely cosmetic, and the same forces of oppression operate as they have done for centuries. Taking the former line, one would probably be spurred to action to join a political group, again more or less legitimate, whilst taking the latter one might conclude that nothing short of revolution would change things, and the evidence from history of revolutions doing away with oppression, as opposed to replacing one set of oppressors with another, is not encouraging.

SRV, in looking at the universality of devaluation, does not claim to have the complete answer to it. Neither does it deny the oppression exists, but instead points to the process and the results, and looks for strategies to apply what 'science has to tell us' in addressing those results. If the reader then seeks to do something, not everything, about devaluation then SRV offers as a first order, or main, goal the possibility of access for vulnerable people to the good things in life. This will not remove oppression, though as we shall see there are action implications of SRV at all levels of society that do at least attempt to ameliorate oppression, and change some of the prejudices which support it. If every action, however, that might be part of an SRV strategy for a particular person or group has to pass a test of ideological purity as to whether it directly opposes the status quo then the likelihood of much taking place to help anyone is small. If all of our actions in society, including actions by those who have sufficiently colluded with the academic status quo to reach the positions they have, were subject to the same test, then precious little would be done at all. So SRV is asking the reader to consider whether they would like, as an address of devaluation, the possibility of increasing the good things of life for vulnerable people, rather than joining in a insoluable debate about what the good things in life ought to be. Wolfensberger, in many other writings and discussions, invites people to consider the latter question, especially in a much broader critique of existing societal trends than that made by his academic critics (e.g.

Wolfensberger 1996a.), but within SRV theory he is confining himself to the still mammoth goal of attempting to help vulnerable people live the sort of lives that most of us take for granted.

As for the second criticism of 'normalisation', that it is a service imposed helping of people rather than 'what they want', then again the reader needs to go back to their own value position. If they consider the ultimate determinant of their own lives should be 'what they want' then they might first like to look at how successful they have been in achieving that, and at what cost or benefit to their relationships and their place in their immediate and wider society. If they then also consider the role of those who may have been concerned for their welfare, either from a powerful position such as parents, or a less powerful one, such as friends, and how much of the 'things in life' that those people have helped them attain, then they will be in a better position to take a view on those critics cited above. As with the values and trends in society, there has been no more trenchant critic of the abuse of power by the service system than Wolfensberger (e.g. 1991). Nor is there a writer who speaks so frequently of the need for individual, unpaid, personal commitment to vulnerable people (e.g. 1996a). What SRV theory posits, however, is again an acknowledgment of the power of others, especially the service system, to impose their version of reality on vulnerable people and therefore to try and influence those others to interpret that reality in such a way that the good things of life are afforded more readily to vulnerable people. SRV sees unrestrained 'abandonment to choice' as just as likely to reinforce devaluation as abandonment to the service system, with services deciding for individuals and groups what it is that they 'need.' As society and the service system are currently structured, major decisions about people's lives are taken by other people. Anyone hoping, therefore, to address devaluation solely by doing nothing unless it is totally 'chosen' by devalued people will be very inactive. Once again, the nuances of strategies implied by SRV are such that the simple slogan of 'own choice good, anything else bad' just doesn't begin to address the issue.

So, unashamedly therefore, the primary goal of SRV is to attain or regain the good things in life for devalued and vulnerable people and groups, and whilst there is some cultural relativity in the fine details, the English reader is invited to consider what they might wish for themselves under this title. Wolfensberger et. al (1996) list seventeen points, drawn from what they call a 'de facto consensus' of human history, and though space does not permit a full summary here, a list of the headings given in Able 5.3 opposite should give the reader some idea as to whether their views fit that consensus. Incidentally, it may also be closer to considerations as to what the reader thinks, on deeper reflection, are the good things in life, as opposed to a superficial and media led reflection.

Obviously the details of what those headings mean will vary from person to person, and societal group to societal group, but it should be clear from

Table 5.3
The 'good things in life' - the primary goal of SRV for devalued people

Family, or small intimate group	A place to call home
An intermediate but still small-scale social group	Friends
A transcendent belief system	Work, especially meaningful work
Absence of imminent threats of extreme privation	Opportunities and expectations to discover and develop skills, abilities, gifts and talents
To be viewed as a human and treated with respect	To be dealt with honestly
To be treated justly	To be treated as an individual
To have a say in important issues affecting one's life	Access to most of the 'sites of everyday life'
Access to at least many of the activities of human social life	Being able to contribute, and having one's contributions recognised as valuable
Good health	

(adapted from Wolfensberger et. al 1996)

our analysis of devaluation and the wounds that devalued people are strongly at risk of having very few, if any, of them. This is the crux of the argument in support of at least considering SRV as a strategy. People have been, and are being, deprived of some or many of these things which the great majority of us, including those calling loudly for 'individual lifestyles', take for granted. A serious examination of the list reveals the enormity of the task of at least increasing the probability that devalued people and groups will have access to some of them. It also reveals that the pressure of the entire exercise is not on an individual 'fitting into' some sort of middle class lifestyle, but includes collective efforts, an acceptance of interdependance, and the voice of devalued people themselves being heard. As the primary goal of SRV therefore, it is a clear response to an understanding of devaluation, and a desire to do something about it.

In proposing as a second order, or second level, goal the valuation of people's roles, or in the detail of the 1995 definition, the 'enablement, establishment, enhancement, maintenance, and/or defence of valued social roles' SRV is not suggesting, as some critics have claimed, that the good things of life will be attained if and only if valued roles are achieved. There may well be other second order goals to achieve the same primary goal, though one does not hear them formulated as comprehensively. Instead, focus is more often made on one or other of the good things in life as being the goal, in particular 'having one's voice heard' (Chappell 1997). Clearly too, if one could change society so that it did not devalue people then the good things in life would be afforded to everybody, so a secondary goal could be to work politically for such change. Again the probability of success seems to be low, given the lessons of history, but there is nothing in SRV theory to say that wanting and working for a fairer society is an invalid act. All SRV attempts to do is to propose that, if one wishes to counter the effect of devaluation and the wounds, then the power of roles and expectations in the wounding process can be used in that attempt.

SRV then proposes a third order goal as a strategy for achieving the valuation of people's roles, which follows the structure of the PASSING evaluation instrument, in that it suggests that actions to enhance a person or group's image, combined with efforts to enhance a person or group's competencies, will tend to increase this valuation. Such a simple sounding sentence has far reaching implications at all levels of society. So, again, the commonly expressed criticism that SRV is all about 'moulding individuals' to 'fit' into society is inaccurate. Whilst there certainly are efforts that can be made at the individual level, both to enhance an individual's image and competencies, Wolfensberger has always taught, even in the application of normalization, that action is also possible, and may well have a more beneficial effect for groups of people, at the level of primary and secondary social systems and of entire societies (see Wolfensberger 1972, Table 1, p32 for an early published example of this point). Arranging, or working to arrange, the physical and social conditions of a small group for example, so that the image it conveys is of a group of valued citizens, participating in their local communities with valued roles such as householder or worker, can do much to increase the probability that the whole group will be afforded some of the good things of life. Arranging the social and physical conditions of services for, say, elderly people in a locality so that the image of those people does not cast them into the death or dying roles can have major effects on the whole local elderly population. Working towards policies and legislation which would increase the access of disabled people to employment and thereby enhance their image as contributing citizens could have effects on the value afforded to disabled people as a whole.

All of those are examples of action possibilities suggested by SRV mainly to enhance people's image, which as we have seen is crucial to how people are perceived, and therefore what roles they hold, and therefore their vulnerability to devaluation. All are equally important in the context of SRV, at least in the sense that SRV would not suggest stopping work with individuals because society hasn't changed, or not working with a group, because all the individuals in it might not benefit equally.

The same applies to efforts to enhance people's competencies. Arranging the physical and social conditions so that an individual's competencies are likely to be enhanced is, as we shall discuss at length in chapter 8 on the developmental model, a powerful tool in increasing the valued roles played by that individual, but there are efforts that can equally be made at the primary and intermediate social systems to which people belong, and even at the whole society level. Whatever one thinks of the 'lifelong learning' initiative of the current government it has afforded many people and groups the opportunity to increase their competencies in certain areas, and therefore be perceived in more valued roles.

So, with the clear understanding that they can take place at all levels of society, such efforts can therefore take their place in the broader range of strategies for establishing valued roles for people, the secondary goal of SRV. As a generality, one would want both to mould the roles that people or groups might play so that they are seen as positive in the light of the values held by observers and affect the values held by others so as to value, or at least not devalue, characteristics and roles that people or groups already hold. The means to do this are more likely to succeed if they themselves are culturally valued. This means being aware, again at all levels of social organisation, of what is seen as age-appropriate and culture appropriate and appreciating the subtle nuances and changes in those social judgements. As noted above, the most promising means suggested by SRV are image and competency enhancement, and the greater the vulnerability of devaluation the more efforts within those two dimensions will be necessary and, it is suggested, the more crucial is the contribution of SRV. This raises a further point from the English experience, which is the primacy in certain quarters of self-organization of devalued groups and its relation to SRV.

As before, the first point to be made is that SRV only predicts probabalistically the results of actions, it does not dictate actions. Those who hold the value position that devalued groups should not aspire to the image and competency of valued roles in wider society, but instead define their own valued roles from within their 'identity group', will react against others seeking to arrange their physical and social conditions. The consequences of this for the group may well be a sense of solidarity and acceptance, though as part of the wider society they may well aspire to some of the 'good things' that society affords its valued citizens, and these are likely to continue to be denied devalued groups, if their reaction is one of hostility and separateness. This then becomes a matter of deciding which is more important, one's identity as part of an oppressed group, or one's identity within the wider society. This is a matter of values, not theory. What seems to be more problematical is the much greater vulnerability of those devalued people not involved with the self organised groups, who not only are likely to be devalued in the ways already described, but also do not get the sense of solidarity and acceptance of their 'identity group'. In addition they may suffer from the backlash of those potential allies who feel themselves attacked by the more radical groups and therefore withdraw from attempts to counter devaluation.

So, in effect, the goals and strategies of SRV are linked in intention to that part of the Hippocratic Oath which admonishes doctors to 'at least, do no harm' i.e. guard against further devaluation of vulnerable people and then go onto do more positive things for people by enhancing their image and competencies, thus increasing the possibility of a number of valued roles and the 'good things of life' . The ten themes, outlined in chapters 6 to 10 below, give more detail of these strategies, as well as providing more depth to the analysis of devaluation, but the overall approach can be summarised below, under the heading of 'Avenues of SRV'.

Avenues of SRV for enhancing the value of the social roles of individuals and groups

All the avenues described below can be utilised via the basic framework of paying attention to the image and competency aspects of the physical and social settings in which people find themselves. As with the definitions of SRV, this summary should not be taken on its own to judge the validity of SRV in addressing devaluation, since detail of the situations of individuals and groups at risk need to be applied in each case. In particular those considering going down the various avenues summarised below should, first of all, be aware of the particular wounds that apply, or are most likely to apply, to the individual or group concerned. Sensitive thought should be given to the specific risk factors of those concerned, alongside an inventory of the roles they already hold, or have recently held, and thus their current social standing. This should then suggest which, if any, of the avenues below might be explored.

The first avenue is to explore means by which existing roles held by the people concerned can be confirmed as giving value, either through enhancing or enlarging them, or trying to make sure there is no value loss in relation to them.

The second is to be careful to avoid the entry of the people or groups in question into devalued roles, which may be in addition to some devalued roles they already hold.

Third, depending again on careful analysis of the situation of the people concerned, looking at ways to enable them to enter valued roles, possibly for the first time or in addition to some existing valued roles, or as a replacement for valued roles that have been lost.

Fourth, and perhaps most relevant for those severely wounded, are efforts to extricate people or groups from devalued roles, especially those historic common roles described in chapter 3.

Fifth, where there are devalued roles already held, serious and well thought out attempts to reduce the negative power of those roles, or to exchange the devalued roles for less devalued roles. Finally, there is the avenue, called 'social value surrender' by Wolfensberger (1998a), whereby a valued party in a group or partnership situation reduces the 'value gap' between themselves and the devalued by assuming characteristics, parts of roles or complete roles that the devalued person occupies. Wolfensberger (ibid p101) cites the example of children in a class where a child was undergoing chemotherapy and thus having a shaved head all shaving their heads, but also notes the extreme sensitivity with which such strategies should be treated.

Conclusion: Roles and SRV theory

This chapter has attempted to chart the link between the universality of devaluation and the experiences of devalued people, originally formulated in normalization, but expanded and reconceptualised in SRV theory, via the increasing part that social roles are seen to have played in that devaluation. The wider underpinning from role theory has been discussed, to give some backing from social science for this aspect of SRV theory, though as we shall see, it does not rest on this support alone, having other parallels in the social sciences. We have tried to explain the evolution to the current definition which, in the words of Wolfensberger (1998a) represents 'a systematic effort to apply social science in service of the valuation of peoples roles, so that they are more likely to have access to the good life or the good things of life' The fact that the universality of devaluation, and the state of English society, means that any attempts at addressing devaluation in England involves costs of one sort or another has been noted in discussing those critics who would see SRV as 'colluding' with an oppressive society. So, too, in discussing other critics who claim SRV is 'imposed' on people, the costs of those self organising groups who take a totally separatist stance to both their own members and, more particularly, other devalued people, are considered. Ultimately, with both sets of criticisms, the question of what action to take becomes a matter of judgement of those costs by reference to values. We have described, in general terms, the primary, secondary and third order goals of SRV theory, in particular noting the strategy of addressing the impact of the social and physical conditions of people's lives on their social image and competencies, both of which contribute powerfully to their social roles, and thus how they are valued by society. In the ten themes which follow, it will be important for the reader to remember the other key point made in this chapter, which is that SRV strategies, as does devaluation, operate at all levels of society, from the individual through the primary social group to intermediate social systems and entire societies.

6

The ten themes of SRV:

Consciousness and unconsciousness;
symbolism and imagery

Introduction to the ten themes

Readers familiar with earlier written accounts of 'normalisation' by English
authors (Race 1987; Emerson 1992.) and those who have attended all but a
few training events on SRV in England, or who have been on a PASS or
PASSING workshop in this country, will usually have been presented with
seven 'themes' of normalization, or SRV. To this day in some places where
SRV is taught, those seven themes are used to further explain the detail of
devaluation and wounding and to look at how SRV can address it. From
their introduction, the intention has been that these themes, like the notion
of wounds, are an heuristic, that is a construct of ideas that can elaborate
and elucidate a basic theory or concept but which do not in themselves
constitute that theory. Thus they have been used to explain normalization
and then SRV, but are not in themselves essential parts of it. Unfortunately,
either because of their power of explanation, or perhaps because of their
prominence in the teaching process, they have become seen as constituent
parts of SRV rather than a way of explaining it. This has led some writers to
ignore or minimise the essence of normalization and SRV in explaining the
process of devaluation and the wounds, and the specific development of
SRV as a theory with particular emphasis on the importance of roles and the
need to obtain or defend valued social roles for people. They have then
sought to pick out one or two of the seven themes as if they were theories in
their own right, and by attempting to 'disprove' them, have sought to
discredit SRV theory as a whole (Rapley & Baldwin 1995). Even in less
critical and more descriptive writing, the notion of the themes as being
what SRV is 'all about' is still strong, (Emerson 1992).

When, in 1995, the first presentation of SRV using ten themes was made, there was some consternation among people who had adopted the thinking outlined above. Had Wolfensberger 'discovered' three more parts of SRV, like three more chemical elements in the periodic table? The answer of course was that, just as the seven themes were not constituent and separate parts of SRV, but an overlapping and interlocking set of ideas that help to explain it, then three more, or thirty more, elements in this method of explanation would not alter SRV itself, but hopefully explain it a bit better, and perhaps deal with some of the issues which had arisen over the years in both theoretical discussion and practical application. In the English experience, of course, as we noted in chapter 1 and elsewhere, interest in SRV was declining by this time, and there was still confusion about the differences between 'normalisation' and SRV. The introduction of ten themes was therefore, hardly noticed, especially in academic circles. However, since this book is both for readers who have never heard of SRV and those who have been exposed to the various versions of the ideas taught and written about in England, we present the ten themes, in this and subsequent chapters, hopefully as what their author intended them to be, a means to amplify and explain SRV's account of social devaluation and the strategies to address it. Comparisons, for those who have read or heard some of the ideas before, are likely to be less useful to understanding than simply taking the ideas as presented, and connecting them to their place in SRV theory. It will also be useful, we think, for readers to make the connections between these ideas and various elements of social science theory, though we would again warn of the dangers of partialisation of disciplines.

Introduction to the theme of consciousness and unconsciousness

This theme has been around for a long time in both normalization and SRV teaching, but apart from the odd critic seeking to partialise it within the field of psychology (Rapley & Baldwin 1995), it has not, in the English experience been the subject of much critical debate. This may be because of a general acceptance, at the level of popular discourse, of the existence of unconscious processes in human beings, and even in the more aloof world of social science an agreement that something along those lines is occurring, even if there is fearsome debate about causes and intentions. It is therefore not surprising that many different meanings are given to the words 'conscious' and 'unconscious'. These range from the purely physical state of being awake, as opposed to being knocked out or in a drunken stupor, through actions taken 'consciously' (with full awareness of what is going on), or 'unconsciously' (as a result of a learned behaviour done almost automatically but not in the forefront of one's attention [Lewis (1990)], to the more specific psychological meaning usually associated with Freud

(Macmillan 1992). Psychology also makes reference to conscious and unconscious learning, as will be discussed later (Tye 1993).

What first normalization and, in more developed form, SRV has sought to do in this theme is to draw from various social science fields, including psychology, sociology, management and organisational studies, ideas about the prevalence and power of unconscious behaviour in individuals and groups, including formally organised bodies such as human services, and relate them to the underlying issue of devaluation. In using this theme, therefore, as with many others, whilst reference will be made to supporting literature, no attempt will be made to arrive at a definitive conclusion on consciousness per se, merely to support its place in our understanding of devaluation and actions to counter it. Perhaps the key overall point would be made to the reader if they consider just how much of their own personal behaviour is governed by rational, well thought out conscious decision making or by unconscious, habitual reactions to the world around them.

Consciousness in human individuals and groups

As we noted in talking about stereotypes in chapter 3, the quantity and complexity of perceptual input, the amount of material that we have to take in and process, has been vast in all societies and all times, but has grown exponentially in Western industrialised societies as we approach the third millennium. To deal with this vast array of material and still remain sane, let alone behave adaptively, requires many processes of abbreviation and information handling. One of these is to 'shut away' material that is either useless for present purposes, or that may run counter to present action, or that requires a depth of thinking and understanding that is felt to be beyond the individual's capability. Complexity, therefore, tends to produce a reaction in human beings that either shuts it away completely, if no 'solution' or action is required, or looks for a quick and simple 'solution' that deals only partially, and sometimes totally incorrectly, with the underlying realities of a situation. A trivial example of this is the tendency, in a great deal of sport but especially professional football, to hold the team manager totally responsible for what eleven players, with all the complex interactions with another eleven players, achieve on the football field. The many, more serious examples of 'scapegoating' in history, such as immigrants blamed for unemployment, reveal how common this process is amongst groups and even whole societies. This is scarcely surprising, given the complexity of even relatively small social groups and group behaviour. Systems theory, as well as social psychology, lends academic support to this point, though, like much else in social science, it is hotly disputed by the postmodernists (Cooper 1990).

Also from psychology comes support for a second point about the relevance of consciousness. It points to a great deal of perception and learning taking place unconsciously. Thus even relatively focused attention such as might occur in a lecture is reinforced, or sometimes deterred, by unconscious associations with particular events in the listeners' lives or other unconscious memories. Hence two students hearing the same lecture, allowing for differences in intellectual ability, end up learning very different things from it. When this is broadened to the much less structured and much more subtle interplay of inputs and perceptions by which we learn social behaviour, the adaptive need to abbreviate and the vast storehouse of unconscious experiences combine to produce greatly more learning occurring at the unconscious level. Of relevance here to SRV, and dealt with at length in other themes, is so-called learning by association, i.e. the linking in the mind of two events or objects, that just happened to be together at a particular point in time, so as to be able to recall one by recalling the other. Many students 'learn' their notes, not necessarily with understanding, by picturing the place in the folder they occur, or the lecturer's behaviour when they took the notes, or some other association with writing those particular words that they want to recall (Bechtel 1990).

Linked with the point on learning and unconsciousness is the further observation from psychology that there are many things that were once learnt, which have ceased to have an immediate usefulness and therefore have been dropped from conscious memory, but that nevertheless can still have a considerable impact on attitudes and behaviour. Some of this goes into a 'mind-set' about particular people or events and, though it can sometimes be recalled in analysis, most of the time the individual is unaware of the unconscious memory that is affecting their behaviour, (Bechtel 1990)

As well as affecting current behaviour unconsciously, what has also been found with regard to memory is that, over time, memory loss not only puts past events into the unconscious but also tends to distort the past. This not only has an effect on individuals but in groups and larger organisations, in that the 'collective memory' can be seriously distorted by elements lost during the passing on of information, especially if this passing on takes place over a substantial time period. The familiar story of a message being altered through minor alterations as it is passed on is a popular illustration of this phenomenon.

As was mentioned earlier, another reason for the jettisoning of some input into unconsciousness comes when there is a conflict between current actions and consciously expressed ideals or values. As this operates at the unconscious level, there is no question of 'deliberate' hiding away of the expressed ideals, indeed it appears to be part of the human condition that we have such 'noble' ideals on the one hand, and yet have 'human nature' or more animal-like behaviour to deal with on the other. This is uncomfortable for most people, who do not like to acknowledge their baser instincts, and is usually responded to in a number of different ways. One is simply to repress the conflict in their mind and carry on with the action anyway. Another is to carry on with the actions but do so in a more indirect form, as, for example, when married men who would like to indulge in extra-marital affairs confine themselves to viewing pornography. A third is to distort the actions, or at least how they are seen, into something that does not clash with the consciously stated ideals. This occurs especially when there are additional pressures to carry out the actions, such as it being very costly not to do them, either in terms of public prestige, or even more direct costs, such as that one might lose one's job if one did not do them. In this situation the real import of the actions will be pushed into the unconscious, and highly credible reasons, even ones which lend a spurious nobility to the actions, will be put forward. Wolfensberger, in various publications, (e.g. 1992b). uses the word 'detoxification' i.e. 'taking the poison out of' to describe such processes, and it is highly relevant to SRV in that many wounding actions, especially in human services, can be 'detoxified' by reference to such things as 'professional practice' ' good medicine' 'only doing my job' while the effect of the wounds is pushed into unconsciousness.

Consciousness and unconsciousness in social systems and organisations

Naturally, since human social systems and organisations are made up of individual humans, they have the propensity for realising the unconscious behaviour of those individuals added together. This is clear from so much of the effort in management theory over the decades, Martin (1990) being devoted to getting a large group of people, with their own individual unconscious systems, to behave in at least broadly consistent and compatible ways to the collective end, and results in such things as standard operating procedures, checklists and quality control measures that force the conscious attention of employees to certain minimum requirements of the job. That these efforts have largely been unsuccessful is evidenced not only by the ever changing theories to address the issue in the management literature but by the ever increasing quantity and complexity of so-called management information. Not only this, however, but social systems and groups have to deal with the fact that people tend to behave with much less consciousness in groups, and especially large groups, than they do as individuals. Mob behaviour has been widely studied, and has been found to be subject to unconscious feelings of tribalism, of greater security as part of a group and even of greater affection for the abstract group replacing a lack of affection in family and other primary groups (Loizos 1996), all of which can lead to behaviour which, as individuals, mob members would be much less likely to undertake.

Studies of organisational behaviour have also much to say on group unconsciousness, in particular the way in which organisations almost always seem to take on a 'life of their own' with organisational survival becoming the overriding goal, regardless of the original goals and values of the founders of the organisation (Turner 1990) So an organisation set up to deal with homeless children can see its original goals pushed into unconsciousness, as more and more options become available for the organisation to grow and prosper, so that it ends up by sending children off to foreign countries as de facto slaves. This, of course is what occurred in England with a number of the Victorian charitable organisations such as Barnardo's and the Children's Society. Not only were the original goals pushed into unconsciousness or detoxified as being compatible with the actions, but the organisational memory of these events was so successfully repressed that only some seventy years later is some semblance of the truth emerging (Hansard 1998). From general organisational theory the notion of the 'manifest' and 'latent' functions of organisations makes a similar point, in that what is put forward by organisations, usually with highly slick and expensive imagery, as their main function, is very often secondary to their real function (Turner 1990). Since the privatisations of the eighties, for example, many people have seen through the glossy advertising, especially when it comes to the salaries of utility executives, and realised that the water companies main function is not to provide water for the nation, nor the power companies to provide power, but for both to maximise the financial return to shareholders. Of course this is what nearly all private companies have been doing for years, it has just become more obvious when what were previously natural resources and common assets have been usurped in the same way. So, too with human services, again heightened in the English experience since the gradual privatisation of the eighties. Even in the services still provided by the state, the manifest function, to provide some form of care for vulnerable groups that meets their needs, is often in conflict with the latent function of distantiating those people and groups that society devalues, and also of course providing employment for a growing section of the population. The fact that the new independent sector, at least in some cases, is more open about being concerned with the survival and growth of its organisations does not alter the collective unconsciousness in a great many people's minds of the real function of human services. Within human service organisations, too, the 'effect on the organisation' is a very powerful, though not always explicit, reason for condoning or hushing up devaluing or outright harmful practices, as many of the government inquiries into 'scandals' of various sorts have revealed (Martin 1984)

Finally, there is also growing evidence from the management literature that the trend for group decision making, and the various teamwork technologies, rather than realise the potential of all the members to contribute their own rationality and individual values into decisions, has led to conformity and 'the party line' being hallowed over discussion, debate and resolution (Salaman 1996). One only has to consider the current government's obsession with 'party discipline' and their effective use of what were perceived as 'splits' within the previous government, to see the power of the view that any agreement is better than disagreement, even where the disagreements are between two groups with perfectly valid arguments.

Unconsciousness and devaluation

A detailed reading of Chapters 2 to 4 should have given some clues to the reader as to the connection between unconsciousness and devaluation. It will be remembered that the key to devaluation was in the perception of individuals and groups of other individuals and groups. If, therefore, we accept the premise, noted earlier in this chapter and supported by the literature, that a great deal of perception is unconscious, then a great deal of the processing that goes into the social judgments is going to be unconscious. This will be especially true at the collective level where, as we also noted in chapter 2, the most powerful effects of devaluation occur. In presenting SRV theory, therefore, a great deal of the material 'dawns on' people, not in the sense that it is new, but in the sense that it is something that they were aware of, but never really put together in the conscious way that is achieved by SRV.

It is also not surprising that the literature on social reform uses the same notion, in that it talks of 'raising consciousness' of oppression. Friere (1972) used the word 'conscientization' in his writings on revolutionary movements, and it is this sense that SRV can use the notion of unconsciousness to address devaluation, by making people aware of the dynamics that they have pushed into unconsciousness, with or without the help of collective pressures.

If people become aware, through SRV or in other ways, of the fact that social devaluation is largely unconscious, they can also then make the connection between this and the wounding process, and realise how much unconsciousness contributes to wounding. Studies of the Holocaust have made the point that so much of what went on, especially in the 'euthanasie' movement which preceded the extermination of the Jews, went unchallenged because of the unconsciousness of so many people, not just in the sense of ignorance, but in the sense of awareness being repressed into unconsciousness (Lifton 1987).

Using awareness of the issue of unconsciousness as one SRV strategy to counter devaluation

As noted above, SRV theory can help the reader to be aware of the part played by unconsciousness in the devaluation process. Beyond this understanding, however, SRV can suggest a number of ways to use it in combating devaluation and wounding. First of all, of course, individuals and groups seeking to address devaluation will need to attain, and actively practise means of attaining, high consciousness of the reality of the lives of vulnerable people, and the effects on those lives of practices, especially service practices. This will be in the face of many disguises, detoxifications, and even outright lies about what is really going on. Being clear about what is causing devaluation, describing and perceiving the various ways in which it is expressed, and its various effects on individuals and groups is something which, perhaps, was one of the greatest achievements of the 'normalisation' movement in England, but which seems to have been diffused as the debates over community care and the enormous power of the financial and organisational forces released by the previous government came into effect (Hadley & Clough 1996). The need for high consciousness has not gone away, however, and the development of SRV as a social science theory has not altered this need.

Consciousness can be assisted in a number of ways, such as the use of real stories of people's lives being given prominence over abstract 'measurements' of people, in fact generally using relevant close personal experiences to analyse wounding. Critics of SRV might be surprised to see this suggested as part of an SRV strategy, given their assumptions about it being 'imposed' on people rather than listening to them, though in reality that has always been one of the strongest methods proposed by SRV for understanding devaluation. Perhaps they feel that way because SRV does not propose personal experience as the sole strategy for raising consciousness, but also suggests complementary strategies such as much more precise language and concepts to describe service practices, describing in an 'undetoxified' way what is going on in services, having as explicit criteria for judging service quality the notion of the effect on devaluation, and explicitly separating issues of values from issues of empirical reality. Further, since the willingness of service commissioners to reward such consciousness is not likely to be high, support from others in rewarding, at least by a mutual awareness, the practice of high consciousness is another strategy to be employed.

All of this is, of course, likely to be extremely difficult, given the pervasiveness of devaluation and unconsciousness. SRV does not therefore, as we have said on a number of occasions already, claim that devaluation will be overcome, or even that massive increases in consciousness will be achieved, by adoption of these strategies, but it does claim that such strategies are at least part of a conscious and coherent theory to describe devaluation and to address it. The next theme in helping us to do that has many connections to consciousness and unconsciousness, and invites us to consider the part played by symbolism and imagery.

Introduction to the theme of symbolism and imagery

It is perhaps indicative of the power of imagery that presentations, and particularly pictorial slides, showing the messages given out by the whole range of media described earlier, should be one of the things that many people remember from SRV theory events or, in the English experience, from PASS or PASSING workshops. As with unconsciousness, readers of earlier chapters may already have made a number of connections between imagery and devaluation, and this next section is intended to make the connections even more explicit, as well as indicating where SRV might suggest using imagery as a strategy to combat devaluation.

In fact, as a theme of 'normalisation', imagery could be said to have had the most effect on services for people with learning disabilities in England, at least in the sense that a great deal of attention has been paid to aspects of the physical imagery surrounding people, and also in the 'language wars' which have proved such a diversion from real action to combat devaluation of this particular group. As we shall discuss below, symbolism and imagery are a most vital part of how messages about people are conveyed, and hence of devaluation. This is why, as one of the two third order goals of SRV discussed in chapter 5, action to enhance the value of the image of people and groups at risk of devaluation is crucial. A word of warning is necessary here, however, especially in the light of the English experience of 'normalisation'. The connectedness of the various elements of SRV is important, so that efforts in one direction to combat devaluation need to be judged in the light of their effect on other elements and, in some cases, may result in a choice, or even a 'trade off' between SRV strategies. Again perhaps because of its power, but perhaps also because a lot of it involves actions other than direct contact with devalued people, a great deal of effort has been engaged in 'getting the image right' sometimes at the expense of more productive activities at the level of competency. So a finding of the major survey of projects moving people with learning disabilities out of hospital, referred to variously in this book found that while the quality, and also the image, of the physical environments were almost universally superior to hospital settings, the nature of peoples' place in their community was much more problematic (Hatton & Emerson 1996) This implies that the effort on address of competence, especially in relationships and everyday activities that encourage community belonging had received rather less attention, or was much more difficult to achieve despite the efforts of those concerned. So if the reader gets the sense that imagery is the be-all and end-all of SRV then that is far from the author's intention. It is, nevertheless, very important.

Symbolism and imagery in human activities

As we noted in chapter 2, since the early usage of the theme of imagery in normalization, academic study in the field of semiotics, that is the study of signs, has given considerable scientific backing to the importance of imagery in communication (Eco 1977). This has come by semiotics looking at the way information, ideas and even commands can be conveyed, not by elaborate verbal or written representation, but by symbols, movements, tokens or other 'signs'. Imagery, therefore can be thought of as the ideas which are conveyed by representations of things as they are processed by the brain, along with all the other sensory input it receives. As with stereotypes, the use of imagery to deal with the outside world serves the adaptive purpose of short-cutting the elaborate process of taking in all the information presented to us and, also as with stereotypes, it can result in perceptions based on very partial, or incorrect information. In fact common discourse talks about a 'stereotypical image' as being an image which both conveys and confirms stereotypes held about people.

As we have also discussed earlier, an image can be conveyed either directly, i.e. from the thing or person being observed, or by association, i.e. by connecting the image of what is next to, or near, a person or object to that person or object. So a young child in a school uniform would convey the image of a pupil, as would a child without a school uniform but located in a classroom, surrounded by books, other children and being taught by a teacher.

Language is, of course, communication by symbols, especially written language, and the imagery conveyed by language has a big part to play in how we convey messages to one another, including how we convey perceptions, but anthropology and history teach us that symbolic exchange, and the use of imagery to convey messages, predates what we now call language (Pinker 1994) and in some cultures, e.g. Chinese, the written symbols are not a direct representation of what is spoken. It would therefore be expected that a great deal of symbolism is embedded into the collective unconscious of individuals, groups and whole societies. This is not only shown from history, but in the increasingly global power of pictorial imagery worldwide, as television and other media become widespread. Advertising also deals much more intensively with pictorial and symbolic imagery than it does with language (Bignall 1997)

Within the broad range of imagery, personal imagery, i.e. the presentation of the individual by appearance, dress, surroundings and possessions, has also become increasingly important, at least as far as how one is perceived by others is concerned. Whatever one thinks of the phenomenon, many studies have revealed the effect of personal imagery on the perceptions and actions of others, both positive and negative (Bignall 1997) A cursory study of what is seen to be the ideal personal appearance by reference to the images of advertising may be either sobering or depressing, and bear very little resemblance to the appearance of the great majority of real people, but the quantity of money spent on such advertising, and on the products it sells, bears eloquent testimony to its power. All of this has much relevance, of course, to devaluation, and hence to SRV.

Imagery and devaluation

We have seen, in chapter 3, how various media can convey messages about a person or group that results in , and also confirms, a negative social judgment about them. In chapter 5 we expanded this to look at how messages were conveyed about a person or group's social roles. Another way of looking at this is to consider how images associated with a person or group can convey messages about them. These days there are whole careers and organisations built on exactly this premise. The 'image consultants' know that messages can be conveyed by images about a person's social status, social roles, competence and similarity or difference to others. Even an 'age-image' can be created, and certainly many things can, and are done about people's personal appearance to produce an age image different from their chronological age. If all these things can be done to enhance people's image, and to convey positive messages, then clearly imagery can produce the opposite effect. If a person is surrounded by images that are negative, especially if they are already vulnerable to devaluation, then devaluation is the likely result. If existing stereotypes exist about a person or group, then attaching images to them that confirm or expand those stereotypes, especially if this comes through a wide variety of media and occurs frequently or even continually, then this represents a serious risk of deep wounding occurring. Yet this is, of course what we see in so many places in our society, especially in services for certain groups of people. Often totally unconsciously (hence the connection with the first part of this chapter) but in a whole variety of ways, people in receipt of services are surrounded by images that create or confirm them in a devalued identity. The PASSING evaluation instrument uses the same broad headings as we have used earlier, but goes into much greater detail of the aspects of human services that are likely to convey positive or negative images about people. As before SRV acknowledges that there may be perfectly legitimate, and even some legally mandated reasons for aspects of services being as they are, but merely asks the reader to examine the effect of such imagery on already vulnerable people. Table 6.1 below lists the summary headings, with examples for each from the English experience, but again invites readers, rather than contest the particular examples, to look at the images given out by the services with which they are familiar and see what similarities or differences they find. Note also the connection with Table 5.2, in chapter 5.

Addressing devaluation through the theme of Imagery

As with unconsciousness, one of the key parts an understanding of the theme of imagery in SRV plays is simply to demonstrate its power and pervasiveness. Through all the media we have just discussed, a consistent image of a number of vulnerable groups is put forward, which not only adds to devaluation, but in effect teaches and justifies it. The effect of these images in reaching large numbers of people, far larger than those who inhabit the service world, and doing so over many generations, seals the condemnation to clienthood of a large minority of the English population. It also of course, because the image also detoxifies a great deal of the reality, allows a great many people to express their participation in or sponsorship of services in terms of higher ideals. The imagery presented, because it largely operates, as we have said, in the unconscious, ensures that identifying and combating devaluation is very difficult. Even where it is pointed out, devaluing imagery has so many small, constituent aspects that the address of one is either marginalised as trivial 'political correctness,' or is so embedded that people spend vast amounts of energy trying to find an alternative way to express an image differently but cannot alter the underlying attitude. So we still find the most powerful means to confirm people's devalued status in the eyes of society and themselves, to legitimise distantiation and segregation, to invite aggression, brutalisation and even deathmaking, comes from the imagery that surrounds them. The fact that imagery also raises a lot of money for human services only adds to its power. Two English studies illustrate this last point. In one, McGill and Cummings (1990), the authors looked at a number of issues of a British newspaper over a random period. The newspaper they chose, the Guardian, is generally regarded as the most liberal and socially aware of the so-called 'serious' newspapers, yet even here they found widespread images of people with learning disabilities that were consistent with many of the common roles of devaluation, especially the 'diseased organism' and 'eternal child' roles. In the other study, Eayrs and Ellis (1990) looked at charity advertising, again for charities to do with learning disability, and found those images which elicited feelings of guilt, sympathy and pity, resulted in the highest level of fundraising, whereas those which gave images of people with learning disabilities as valued citizens, with rights and responsibilities, drew forth the lowest response.

Faced with the enormity of the power of imagery, then apart from realising its power, which is nevertheless an important first step, what strategies can SRV suggest to address it? First of all, as well as appreciating its power, a clear understanding of the range of media of imagery is important. If this is undertaken with a precise and conscious appraisal of what it is possible to address from these media then a further consideration should be at what level this address takes place. As with all SRV strategies, possibilities exist at all level of social organisation, from the individual to society as a whole. One problem with the English experience is that a great deal of discussion and argument has taken place about what to do at the individual level, much less has been applied at the higher levels, in particular the planning of services in such a way that individual efforts are not totally overwhelmed by service constraints. There have been many more efforts, unfortunately, devoted to stopping things happening that may have a negative effect on people's image than on positive efforts to arrange the physical and, especially, the social environment to maximise the positive imagery and minimise the negative. The structure of Table 6.1, or the PASSING instrument from which it derives, gives a broad checklist of areas to examine for positive changes, but again it is important to do this as part of an exercise involving the other aspects of SRV as well. The enormity of the power of imagery is also such that an examination of where to put one's efforts needs to be tempered with the realisation that devaluation will never be fully eliminated. This can then lead one to a judgment of where the most powerful images are for any particular group or individual and what are one's chances of altering those, thus avoiding spending energy on much less influential images or railing against things that are unlikely to change. All of this, of course, then has to be set against one's personal value position on any proposed action. So if values dictate that no-one should be helped to improve their personal appearance, because they should be accepted 'as they are' then the costs of that inaction to the person's image are predictable, but will be regarded as worth it by people who hold that values position. In that case, action to persuade the wider society that personal appearance is unimportant would be a place to put one's energies.

Overall, then, the key strategies suggested by the theme of imagery are to be aware of its power, its multi-dimensional nature, and its ability to value, as well as devalue people. Then, a discerning look at the level of intervention that is both possible and in accord with one's values, together with conscious thought with regard to the particular individuals and groups at image risk, will bring up a number of possible courses of action.

Table 6.1

Media through which images are conveyed by human services

Characteristics of the Physical Setting

Internal and External Appearance Aspects

• does the setting, both inside and outside stand out from its neighbourhood, or even have a neighbourhood. The experience of our isolated institutions, but also of so-called 'integrated' service settings such as hostels for people with learning disabilities or mental health problems, elderly persons homes or nursing homes continues to convey an image of a distantiated, separate group.

• does the setting, both inside and outside, look like a place where its function would be carried out in the wider society. So, for example, does a residential establishment look like the sort of place where valued people live. Here, the notion of the 'culturally valued analogue' i.e. what most people in the culture would use, comes in, as in does in other places in SRV. The issue is that an image that conveys that people using the service are a part of the mainstream of the culture or sub-culture is far more likely to resist devaluing perceptions than one which stands out as different, especially where the service is for very vulnerable people. So, again, residential homes that look like prisons, day services for adults that take place in settings that look like schools, all add to the image of a distantiated, devalued group being in attendance.

• does the setting, both inside and outside, look as if conscious efforts have been made to create and maintain the beauty of the environment, not by some arbitrary standard of beauty, but just a sense that the people there have an appreciation of basic cleanliness, upkeep and sensitivity to the changing seasons in how the setting is maintained. As noted above, this is an area where a great deal has been done since the eighties in changing the beauty of environments from their former institutional drabness, with uniform decoration and redecoration, to appealing places to be, at least from an aesthetic sense.

Physical Features

• are there other physical features of the building that convey images about those who use it, such as signs proclaiming that this is the 'Royal Hospital and Home for Incurables' (even if that is abbreviated to RHHI), or other features such as bars on windows or a battery of security cameras around the walls.

Location/Proximity

• what is the setting adjacent to, and what images are conveyed by the neighbouring environment, especially other service settings. We have already mentioned the frequency of elderly persons homes being sited next to graveyards, and the multi-purpose 'campus' of services to all sorts of different users of services. At the first ever PASSING workshop in England, a team visited a day service for people with learning disabilities which was next to a 'drop-in' centre for people with mental health problems, a hostel for people with learning disabilities and a prison. This was known locally as the 'mad, bad end of town'

History

• what is the history of the building and its location, and what images come from that history. In England the legacy of the workhouse is still strong, at least to people who are now elderly, yet a great many services have been set up in old workhouses, or in their grounds. One service for elderly people visited by the author was cited just outside the old city gate of a medieval town. The gate was one of those that was barred to outsiders during the plague years, and between it and the home was a large hollow, that nearly all the residents, and of course local people, knew was the place where hundreds of plague victims, barred from entry to the city were buried in mass graves.

Groupings with Other People

Other users of the service
- what image is conveyed by the way the service groups together the people who use it. This is not just a matter of size of grouping, though the mass practices of former institutional times and the current trend in many services for ten, twenty or even more people of one service 'category' together does produce an image that people are all the same, with, usually, the impression that the most visible or noticeable people make being attached to the whole group. Beyond size, however, the tendency for people with very disparate needs to be grouped together again tends to project the image of the more needy on to the less needy.

Staff
- what images are conveyed by the staff of the service, both personally and professionally. It important here to remind readers that this Table is listing sources of imagery that are attached to people at risk of devaluation, not indicating what should be done about this. So in noting, as an example, a real situation that happened to a student in a service for people who were defined as having 'challenging behaviour' where the entire staff of the establishment were 'into' body-piercing, tattoos and leatherwear, we are asking the reader to consider the image that might be transferred to service users, not saying what should be done about it. Staff qualifications and experience, if known by observers, or if deduced from such things as uniforms, also have their image effects, as in the case of staff who are qualified as nurses. It may well be that a medical image is appropriate for the service setting, but equally there are cases where the devaluing effects of putting people into the sick role when they are not sick can be exacerbated by a nursing identity in staff. Again, what is done about this is another matter.

Others, especially users of other services.
- what images are conveyed by other groups or individuals that the service places alongside its users. These images may be positive, as when a person with a learning disability is placed in an integrated college course, and the image of the majority of students will pass to that person, or negative, as when groups from different services from all over a locality are brought together in something like a 'multi-purpose day centre'. Whilst there may be other benefits of such a move, the image created by these widely differing groups again tends towards the 'lowest common denominator' of a devalued identity.

Personal Imagery

Appearance
- what images are conveyed by the personal appearance of the people who use

the service. We have dwelt at length on this issue earlier in this chapter and will not go into more detail here, except to remind readers that it would be a very different world, possibly a more desirable one, if people's personal appearance did not count in the impression that others hold of them, but it does not seem very likely to be realised in the near future.

Possessions
- what images are created by the possessions held by vulnerable people. Again this has been covered earlier , and again the direction of English society, especially after the rampant materialism of the eighties, points to an increase in the weight given to possessions as a judgment of people. Certainly the advertising industry is rife with image associations of possessions and high social value.

Autonomy and rights
- as an issue of image, autonomy and rights have not had nearly as much discussion as has the premise that vulnerable groups 'have' or 'ought to have' the same autonomy and rights as other citizens. That is not the issue here, though it is relevant to point to differences between the rhetoric of rights as a value position and the actual possession of rights as citizens that even valued people have. This is especially true in countries such as England with no written constitution, and therefore very few enforceable rights. Autonomy and the exercise of what are perceived to be rights is, however, highly valued in English society, and therefore as an image issue, the perceived ability of people to exercise some control over their lives is something which gives them value, just as the perceived lack of autonomy in some services, especially institutional settings, reinforces devaluation.

Language

Personal names and labels
- what images are conveyed by the way in which vulnerable people are talked to and about? This subject has been a matter of enormous debate, with some people becoming extremely angry at the use of one particular term used by a speaker or writer, whilst others get equally angry at the use of an alternative. In our earlier discussion, we spoke of the 'language wars' which various groups conducted in the eighties, sometimes getting to the point where no communication was possible between people who were ostensibly on the 'same side' as far as devalued people were concerned. Disability has been especially prone to such debates, and whilst this may point to the power of language in devaluation, it may also reflect a frustration at not being to make massive changes in the devaluation process that has led to an obsession with controlling language. There are, of course many examples of language giving images to people or groups that add to their devaluation. 'Mentally subnormal', 'geriatric', 'schizophrenic' are all examples of medical or legal terminology that have come under criticism, but it is probably the use of more personally abusive terms or nicknames that has a greater devaluing effect.

Service names and Labels
- what images are conveyed by the names and labels used by services? In the

English experience, state services dominated until the eighties, though of course there were still many charities and voluntary organisations. Even within the state sector, however, the logos associated with any service give out a variety of images, and the charities, if nothing else, give out an image of charity. With the increase in the independent sector in the eighties, names and logos designed to appeal to the funders rather than the public appeared, again varying in the image they conveyed. The Royal Society for Mentally Handicapped Children and Adults, now known by the word Mencap, has gone through a number of name changes over the years, reflecting popular imagery about the group they represent, people with learning disabilities, though not the bulk of their members who are parents of people with learning disabilities. So from being a society for 'backward children' in the fifties, they moved on to a society for 'mentally handicapped children.' Then acknowledging that their work also covered adults, the words 'and adults' was added to the 'mentally handicapped children.' Royal patronage, which of course has its own image issues in England, then followed, with the society moving from a 'National' to a 'Royal' one. Finally, with the burgeoning of logos and acronyms in the eighties, and a 'relaunch' in the nineties to reflect the Society's new role as a major service provider rather than pressure group, the 'Mencap' label was adopted. The reader is left to ponder on the effect of these changes on the image of people with learning disabilities.

Setting and location Names
- what images are conveyed by the name of the service setting, or the location in which it is placed? One of the most interesting things about covering this subject in workshops is the number and range of image associations from the names of services and their settings. This should not surprise us of course, given that, at least initially, locations and buildings were often named according to purpose, and many of those original purposes now have devalued image associations. So the number of times 'Spital Hill' or 'spital lane' appears in the address of services reflects their origins or locations in hospitals, very often isolation hospitals for TB or leprosy. Most of this is now largely unconscious, however, so the owners of the elderly persons home located outside the old city gate that was mentioned earlier in the table thought nothing of naming the home after the name of the gate, not perhaps realising other images associated with the name 'St. Peter's Gate.' Despite all the impact of the eighties on names, unconsciousness still prevails, as demonstrated by a recent proposal in a Midlands county to open a home for people with so-called challenging behaviour at a place called 'Loggerheads'.

(Table devised from headings in Wolfensberger and Thomas 1983)

7

The ten themes of SRV:

Mindsets and expectancies; The power of role
expectancies and role circularity

Introduction to the theme of mindsets and expectancies

In the development of SRV theory leading up to the 1994 Ottawa Conference
mentioned earlier, a number of different emphases emerged, where issues
that had been part of one or a number of the seven themes used to help
explain SRV were considered to be of sufficient significance to be taught as
themes in their own right. This is the case with the theme of mindsets and
expectancies. As we shall see from the second part of the chapter, some of
this theme was dealt with in the more specific issue of role expectancies,
and some in the later theme of the developmental model, where various
mindsets about certain groups of people and their potential for growth and
development are challenged. In addition, as we shall see, unconsciousness
plays a significant part in the creation and preservation of mindsets. So, like
all the themes, interactions and overlaps with one another can be found,
but in developing this theme there is also a broader reference to social
science, in particular social psychology, to lend weight to the notion that
mindsets and expectancies can impact very powerfully on vulnerable
people, and increase the probability of devaluation and wounding.

Human beings and mindsets

As frequently is the case in SRV theory, we can draw on observations from
social science about human behaviour, particularly processes of the mind,
in general terms and then relate this to the process of devaluation. In
general terms, then, studies from psychologists and others have come up
with the notion of a mindset being a sort of conceptual model that enables

human beings to interpret the world in a way that is acceptable to them (Abrams & Hogg 1990). It is another of the adaptive processes that we seem to possess to deal with the array of input that our complex world presents to us, but it also relates to the more esoteric questions asked by philosophers about whether there is such a thing as objective truth, or whether all we perceive is filtered through a complex and individual set of values, beliefs and mindsets. Kuhn, in his much quoted work on paradigms (1970) also talks about a way of placing boundaries around our thinking to accord with what is the 'accepted wisdom' which only alters when there is sufficient evidence or new ways of looking at a situation that produces a 'paradigm shift.'

One of the key issues in the creation of mindsets is that they have to do with deep seated beliefs, that are often not susceptible to alteration by 'the facts' because by their very nature many of those beliefs are not verifiable by 'the facts' and, of course, what are considered to be 'facts' i.e. objective reality, are themselves dependent on underlying beliefs about how the world works, or should work. So, for example, the mind set of an atheist materialist would interpret the 'fact' of a famine in Africa very differently from a Christian, both in terms of the underlying cause, possible actions in response, and motivations for those actions.

Mindsets therefore are made up of a combination of beliefs and observations of the world and therefore a series of expectations about what should happen in any situation. With regard to fellow human beings the basis for mindsets can be expectations from factual identity, such as age or gender, and ascribed identity, such as perceived competence or occupational status. The link with roles should be clear here, and will be discussed at length in the next theme. Mindsets about people are thus only a subset of mindsets about the world in general, by which our thinking on social, political, religious and other issues can be strongly influenced.

Expectancies, therefore, can be thought of as what we perceive as likely to happen in any given set of circumstances, and can be generated by our more global mindsets. So someone with a mindset that people are basically honest would have a different expectancy, if they left their wallet in a pub, than someone who had a mindset that people are only as honest as they have to be. This is, again, a probabilistic basis for expectancy, but such is the power of mindsets that even if the wallet were returned to the latter person, or was not returned to the former, the chances of that changing their mindset would be fairly low. Given that expectancies present one with a 'likely' outcome, that is an outcome with a high probability in terms of one's mindset, then any action taken is going to be strongly influenced by that expectancy. Included in this, of course is the pursuit of 'evidence' to confirm the mindset and interpretation of phenomena to reinforce the mindset. SRV training events cite the first century physician Galen, who described the human anatomy as being laid out in a certain way, which was then taught to trainee physicians for centuries, including a considerable period of time after dissection and other investigations had demonstrated that a number of the organs described by Galen didn't exist. Such was the power of the mindset of medical students and their teachers that Galen was the absolute authority on anatomy that they would even point to the non-existent organs as if they were there. David Schwartz, someone involved with a great amount of SRV implementation in the USA, tells the story of an immigrant to a particular area of America who wanted to grow grapes of a certain variety. The mindset of the local farmers was that this was impossible, and they cited all sorts of 'factual' or 'scientific' reasons why this was so. With a different mindset the immigrant persevered, and eventually achieved the 'impossible' by growing grapes successfully (Schwartz 1992). So mindsets do not just affect individuals expectancies, they can affect whole groups of people and become, in some cases, accepted as 'facts' by a whole field of study.

Mindsets, expectancies and devaluation

Many studies of educational settings have illustrated the effect of gender on the expectations of teachers, and this is also extended to pupils expectations of themselves, especially in choice of subject (Riddell 1992) That this is slowly changing is revealed by the increasingly better performance of girls than boys where more equal opportunities, and thus expectancies, have begun to take effect (ibid.). Thus, on a large scale, the power of mind sets to operate both positively and negatively is demonstrated. SRV, in dealing with those most at risk of devaluation, notes the effect of a negative mindset and thus low expectancies in relation to such individuals and groups. This is not just in human services, though its effects may be greatest there, but also in the creation of mindsets with regard to certain groups that are held by the public at large. Consider, for example, the mindset that is expressed by the medical and scientific community with regard to physically and mentally impaired people, and how that is transmitted to parents, and prospective parents. This mindset, as reported by parents in countless studies (e.g. Wertheimer 1981; Sloper & Turner 1993) produces expectancies that are predominantly negative, to the point where many parents decide to abort a potentially impaired child. Paul Williams reports (1993), on the extreme difficulty he has had in obtaining any form of funding to produce a book or leaflet giving a positive account, with positive expectancies, for parents of children with Down's syndrome. A similar phenomenon seemed to have grown, at least in the early stages of discussion around both so-called and real examples of Altzheimer's disease, with powerfully negative mindsets being set up for many elderly people and their relatives which then interpreted many of the normative signs of old age as 'symptoms,' very often resulting in premature institutionalisation for the person concerned (Sidell 1995). A more recent book, showing the power of an alternative mindset to this disease, has come from the husband of the writer Iris Murdoch (Bayley 1998), and the very public discussion of his book is, incidentally, one more example of someone with a positive role perception influencing societal views on a potentially devaluing impairment.

Like many of the other processes we have discussed, a great deal of the formation of mindsets, and certainly very many of the resulting expectancies, takes place at the unconscious level. Just as many of those teachers of the sixties and seventies would have been appalled at the thought that they had different expectations for girls and boys, so very few people in the medical world would be prepared to admit openly that they think impaired children would be better off dead, and instead shelter themselves in the detoxifications of 'parental choice' or 'scientific objectivity.' Nevertheless, the power of that particular mindset is responsible for the deaths of many thousands of impaired children each year.

Beyond the mindsets surrounding the birth of a child, negative expectancies of certain groups continue throughout their lives, and with negative expectancies comes, very often, low effort on the part of those involved with individuals or groups. Two particular mindsets dominate this process. One is that individuals or groups are less capable than they really are. This leads, as the disability movement has pointed out (Barnes 1990) to dependence on others to do the things that the individual or group is considered incapable of, which often then spreads to other areas of their lives, including those which they were originally acknowledged to be capable of, so that their lives become totally defined by dependence. The mindset is reinforced both by ignorance of what people are actually capable of, because they do not get to try, and by the other effects of the wounding process 'confirming' the lack of capability as people's lives become more and more identified with their disability. The parallel situation in schools, where low expectation becomes its own self-fulfilling prophecy, has already been alluded to.

The second key mindset in relation to vulnerable people occurs where others, either consciously or unconsciously, do not want the vulnerable people to experience certain valued things in life. This mindset is usually based on generalisations and stereotypes about certain groups, and is strongly linked to notions of who 'deserves' certain things or who will 'benefit' from them. It is then put into effect by those others promoting expectancies about the person or group that are designed to prevent them receiving this or that experience, sometimes to the point where those expectancies assume the nature of 'facts.' Expectancies of the likely results of inclusion of children with disabilities put out by some members of the teaching profession, especially those with a vested interest in the continuation of segregated education, would fall into this category, with the imprimatur of 'good educational practice' to act as a powerful detoxification (Norwich 1990).

So low expectancies coming from negative mindsets create a feedback loop, with the prejudices about what certain people can be or do leading to low expectancies and therefore low demands on people. The low demands on people to develop then result in few opportunities being provided for growth, and therefore few experiences that will assist people's growth. This then results in further poor performance or delayed development, which further reinforces the prejudices and negative mindsets about such people.

Strategies to address negative mindsets and expectancies

As with the first two themes, awareness of the power of the phenomenon is both the beginning of a means to address it and also a sobering insight into the enormity of what is happening. Mindsets, by their very nature, are difficult to alter, and expectancies, as we have seen, tend to have the effect of embedding the mindsets more deeply. Nevertheless, SRV can make some suggestions. First, to try and discern whether the mindset is predominantly based on ignorance or on malevolence. As has been demonstrated in anti-racist training (Hall 1997), much can be achieved just by filling in gaps in people's knowledge about a particular individual or group. Negative material about certain groups can be countered by positive examples of achievement and of valued positions being held by people from that group.

More problematic is the situation where there is at least some degree of malevolence, as well as ignorance, in the mindset, since this is also likely to be largely unconscious. As we said in chapter 2, some of the reasons for the universality of devaluation seem to be built into human nature, including the feelings in all of us of malevolence to at least some other people or groups. Action to deal with such mindsets can only really take place within the individual mind, and it is perhaps again through individual experiences of devalued people, perhaps helped by awareness of issues covered by the later theme of interpersonal identification, that such individual changes may come. Certainly there is much evidence from history that 'forcing' people to change their behaviour may have a short term effect but rarely gets down to the level of mindsets and expectancies (Kushnick 1998).

Further strategies suggested by SRV will be discussed later, as we move on from the general processes described in this theme to the particular dynamics that revolve around roles and role expectancies.

Introduction to the theme of role expectancies and role circularity

Taking the foregoing theme, together with the account of role theory in chapter 5, the place of roles in the process of devaluation should be fairly clear. In chapter 5, the association with certain roles of privileges and responsibilities was outlined. Those privileges and responsibilities create strong expectations, both among those holding the roles and others, as to appropriate behaviour. This leads to, and is reinforced by, some very powerful mindsets being held about the holders of certain roles. One only has to think of the mindsets about such roles as 'husband', 'wife', 'son', 'daughter' to realise the wide range of expectations that stem from them. Observance of those expectations is a matter of degree, and SRV has always seen the relationship as probabilistic, rather than deterministic. Critics of SRV as a theory who have picked up this theme as saying that there is a linear or deterministic relationship between role expectancies and role performance have again missed the point, and their 'evidence' to try and deny the theoretical base of SRV does, in fact, reflect the much greater complexity acknowledged by SRV in this theme than a simple automatic role performance following from a uniform role expectancy (Rapley & Baldwin 1995) It is clear, however, that there is much conformity to role expectancies, and that at least a significant proportion of social psychological and sociological literature lends support to SRV's use of role expectancies as a crucial factor in influencing devaluation (Cuff et.al. 1992; Woodward 1997; Abrams & Hogg 1990).

Role circularity and devaluation

This section is more a reprise than a detailed analysis of the process of role circularity in devaluation, since the ground has already been traced out in earlier chapters. If a person or group of people are placed into a certain role, particularly if it is one of the common devaluing roles described in chapter 3, then this will have occurred because of some real or perceived impairment in physical or social functioning that leads those observing that person or group to attach that role. Along with the specific behaviours or perceived impairments that cause the individual or group to be placed in the devalued role, the role itself raises additional expectations, which often leads those with some influence on the situation of vulnerable people, especially from human services, to arrange the environment in accordance with those expectations, even though the link between expectations and the arrangements may be entirely unconscious. This results in the role expectancies being channeled through a variety of media, which were covered in detail in Chapters 5 and 6, and will just be listed here. The physical and social environment itself contains many messages about people in it, often, as we have covered in the theme of imagery, at the symbolic level. People or groups associated with those at risk also convey powerful role expectancies amongst their messages, as do the activities and behaviours arranged with or demanded of vulnerable people. Language used, to and about people, their personal presentation, and miscellaneous imagery associated with them, especially in human services, completes the picture of the many ways by which role expectancies are conveyed. Small wonder, then, that there is a high probability that these expectancies will have a powerful impact on role performance. This role performance will then be highly likely to confirm, in the eyes of others and of the people or groups themselves, their devalued status, and thus reinforce the original role perception, completing the circularity. The parallel with the feedback loop discussed in the theme of mindsets and expectancies should be readily apparent.

In trying to arrive at strategies to address the power of role expectancy and role circularity, therefore, SRV again notes that, whilst there is a rich source of possibilities to be derived from the role circularity process, its power and operation over many years also places a number of obstacles in the path of those seeking such strategies. Firstly, and this should be clear from chapters 3 and 4, the continuing imposition of devalued roles on individuals and groups as part of the wounding process serves as a direct benefit to other, usually more powerful, individuals and groups. From the simple case of the rich getting richer by keeping the poor poorer, through the power of professionals to maintain a high standard of living by keeping their definitions of 'clients' and their needs within the confines of a 'qualified' circle, to the more individual case of families benefiting financially by having one of their members defined in one or more of the devalued roles, there is benefit to someone else in vulnerable people being placed in devalued roles. This then provides, usually at an unconscious and therefore harder to address level, powerful incentives against revaluing peoples roles or placing them in more valued roles. Similarly, the intensity and length of time that the various role expectancies have been placed on devalued people, together with the range of channels described above, which are particularly prevalent in human services, means that attempts to do something about it can seem an impossible task. Two examples illustrate the difficulty. On a PASSING workshop which included, as part of one of the workshop groups, a person with Down's syndrome, a day centre for people with learning disabilities was visited. Rather than assuming the fairly valued role of workshop participant, this person was subject to being ordered about and told to get on with his work, as if he were in the role of service user, despite his having never been to the centre before and despite the centre being told to expect 'strangers from a local course.' Similarly, parents, mainly mothers, of a group of adults with learning disabilities, found themselves being placed firmly in the role of service user simply by travelling to an outing with their offspring in a 'Variety Club Sunshine Minibus' which buses have long associations with the charity role, especially in the learning disability field.

Even more seriously, as in the case of babies diagnosed as impaired before birth and certain elderly people, people can have ultimately destructive roles placed upon them, such that doing something about their particular cases becomes a matter of life saving, rather than role valorizing, again a daunting task given the mindsets of many people on the issues of abortion and euthanasia.

Finally, obstacles to a strategy of using role circularity can come from individuals and groups themselves, either because they have become so embedded in the devalued role that it has almost become a means of security for them or because they are exposed to conflicting role demands. Either case poses problems for addressing the devalued roles, both from the pragmatic notion of doing something which 'works' and also from the value position commonly held by people in services that the 'choice' of vulnerable people should be paramount In acknowledging these issues, especially the latter case of role conflict, SRV again addresses those critics (e.g. Rapley & Baldwin 1995) who accuse it of being one-dimensional and deterministic in the application of role circularity.

Using role expectancies and role circularity to address devaluation

Despite the obstacles described above, such is the power of role expectancies and role circularity in the devaluation of vulnerable people and groups several strategies can be derived from SRV theory to address such devaluation. In broad terms these would range from prevention, in the sense of being aware of the risks of particular individuals or groups being cast into particular devalued role circularities and helping people to avoid this, through escape, in the sense of helping people break out of the devalued role circularities in which they find themselves, to positive action, in the sense of helping people to enter positive role circularities and then confirming them in the positive roles.

To do this involves, first of all, a conscious awareness of the various media by which role expectancies are channeled, and goes along with the general SRV strategy of striving to achieve consciousness of the effects of what one is doing. Second, again involving a detailed and discerning analysis of and with individuals and groups and their social situation, to try and discover which positive social roles are near enough to that situation to be reachable and which also capitalise on that person or group's abilities, gifts, interests and wishes. This obviously involves getting to know the person or group well, and doing so will also open up the possibility of using their 'role avidity' as an incentive to move into positive roles.

Where the analysis with individuals or groups reveals issues of competency limiting the number of positive roles available, a further strategy would be to emphasise, in the mind of the people themselves and others, those fewer positive roles that are available, including the celebration of positive roles once held. This is especially relevant in the case of elderly people, for whom the normal processes of aging may restrict the availability of certain very active roles.

In new social situations, such as when people are moved from one environment to another, the opportunity for positive roles is strong, in that expectancies will not be so built up, and may currently be ambiguous. In this case the preparation for the new situation can be such that positive role demands and role models are in place from the beginning, so that a positive role circularity can be set up.

Another strategy, which again addresses some of the critics of SRV who talk about it 'imposing' on people (e.g. Baldwin 1985), is one where the positive aspects of various roles that may be available in any given situation are shared between valued and devalued people and groups. This means, usually either the giving up of some positive roles by valued people, so that the vulnerable participants can assume them, or a clarification and emphasis on the positive aspects of roles held by everyone in the situation. The implications of this, especially in some residential services are quite profound and may require considerable humility on the part of staff.

Finally, as described above, the conscious and discerning examination with individuals and groups will also give a clear indication of their vulnerability to particular wounds, and a clear understanding of the extent of the wounds they already have. In looking to help people into more positive roles therefore, such an analysis will reveal the danger of certain actions, which otherwise might seem positive, to result in further wounding. Avoiding or amending such actions would then be applying the 'conservatism corollary' of SRV, about which more will be said in the last theme of chapter 10.

8

The ten themes of SRV:

The developmental model and personal
competency enhancement; Relevance, potency
and model coherency

Introduction to the theme of the developmental model

Thus far the themes of SRV that we have covered have focused on those
elements of human behaviour that contribute to the devaluation of
individuals and groups in society. They served to further elaborate and
complement the analysis of devaluation and wounding discussed in chapters
2 to 4. This then provided a general overarching set of considerations
which, taken with the contribution of role theory, lead to the beginnings of
SRV's strategies for addressing devaluation, to carry out its first, second and
third order goals as described in chapter 5. The large scale of the issues of
unconsciousness, imagery, mindsets and expectancies, and role
expectancies and circularity, and their contribution to devaluation, may
have left the reader a little pessimistic about the strategies for revaluation,
or positive valuation, suggested so far. This would be a realistic, though as
yet incomplete, reaction to what has been presented, though also one
perhaps based on an assumption that SRV has the 'solution' to devaluation
up its sleeve. In the four themes covered so far, we stressed the power of
awareness, or consciousness, of those processes both suggesting some
strategies for address of devaluation but also giving a realisation of the
enormity and complexity of the processes and dynamics that support it.
Those strategies were outlined, and broadly involved a use of the dynamics
which cause devaluation to attempt to reverse it. In the themes which
follow the emphasis shifts, to some extent, to look at strategies by which we
might contribute positively to attempts to create and enhance valued roles
for people, and ways in which planning of approaches to doing this might

be aided and judged. As with all the themes, however, those which follow should not be taken in isolation, but considered in interaction with, and perhaps in tension with, implications of the others.

In looking at this next theme, therefore, and looking at the assumptions behind what SRV describes as the Developmental Model, we should not assume, as some English critics have (Szivos 1992) that SRV is saying that vulnerable people have to pass through a series of developmental hoops before they are 'allowed' to be part of society, or that by simply enhancing their personal competencies devalued people will cease to be devalued. This is just as limited a view as those other critics (Hogg 1995) who claim that SRV is all about producing a valued image, regardless of peoples' experiences. A re-reading of the chapters on wounds should persuade the neutral reader of the invalidity of that claim.

Nevertheless, as one of the two second order goals of SRV, the notion that arranging the physical and social environment so that vulnerable people have a greater chance of developing their personal competencies is an important strategy in SRV theory, and the next theme looks at the basis for such a strategy in general terms, then going into some more specific issues to do with implementation.

The developmental model

As we shall see in the next theme of Model Coherency, the field of human behaviour, and also the academic study of it in social science, uses the construct of 'models' as a way of describing a more complex phenomenon in a generalised way. So we have economic models that simulate the complex interactions of the economic behaviour of societies in terms of a number of key variables; planning models that look to guide the course of action of organisations based on observations and speculations about the likely outcomes of those actions, again on a limited number of variables. Models are all based on a set of assumptions about a phenomenon, some of which are based on empirical data and some on mindsets. As we noted in the theme of the same name, mindsets are influenced by empiricism but depend more on beliefs and values. The relation of models to reality is therefore in large part dependent on the validity of their assumptions; hence economic models rest on the validity of the notion that humans respond to economic forces in certain ways, something which has not always been the case, leading to some notable 'off-target' forecasts that have bedevilled governments relying on them (Burda and Wyplosz 1997). Like economic models, the developmental model proposed by SRV is based on certain assumptions about human beings, and is dependent on their validity. The assumptions have considerable backing from several sources, including psychology, in particular industrial psychology (Russell 1996; Foss &

Knudsen 1996) and they are two. First, that human beings achieve greater well-being through conscious engagement in activities than through passive, often unconscious or inactive, reception and soaking up of external input or, more basically, simple idleness. This does not, of course, just refer to physical activity. By reading thus far, for example, it is assumed the reader will have been consciously and actively engaged with the material, rather than simply letting it wash over them, so activity means mental as well as physical, and involves all the senses and emotions at various times.

It follows from this that it would be desirable for individual humans to develop their capacity for such active engagement, what could be called their growth potential. The second assumption of the developmental model is therefore that, for most human beings, especially those at risk of devaluation, their growth potential is considerably greater than is realized by others and themselves, than is expected by many social roles and human services, and than is apparent by simply looking at an individual at one particular point in time. Only by a conscious and discerning optimisation of the social conditions of a persons life will even a major part of their growth potential be realised and such is the complexity of human existence that the ability, let alone the will, to do this is rarely achieved. Negative predictions, therefore, of a person's growth, based on their personal attributes or lack of them, or on their economic and social environment, tend to succeed in the majority of cases but mainly because they become self-fulfilling. There are always a minority of cases where, either through individual refusal to accept them, or by alternative beliefs being brought into the situation, people develop far beyond the original predictions. The history of the so-called 'eleven plus' examination, whereby 80 to 90 per cent of eleven year olds were predicted to be unable to grow academically beyond a certain point, based on what was essentially an IQ test, is a prime example of the waste of a generation that supports the second assumption (Evans 1985) – one which is still playing out its effects on English society today.

The implications of these two assumptions are a primary example of the relevance of SRV to a whole range of people and the whole range of human services, both formal and informal, especially those working with vulnerable groups. It suggests that strategies to enhance people's competencies (in the fullest sense of that word, as we shall explain) ought to be a crucial part of the task of human services and that looking for and pursuing the possibilities for growth in people is a task which can never be complete. Therefore in planning activities and arrangements for combating devaluation, a powerful set of expectations of growth for people is a vital ingredient, and in human services could be said to be desirable as a major aim, second only to the preservation of life, in those services' plans for their activities. Further elaboration of the reasons for this position are considered below.

The importance of personal competency

If the first assumption of the developmental model is held to be valid, then there would be intrinsic value in personal competency enhancement as part of our natural human growth. Given the concern in SRV for how people are judged by others as a key influence on their lives, then the fact that in Western societies, including England, personal competency is highly culturally valued would lead us to see it as a means to address devaluation. It has, for example, been one of the primary ways in which sexism has been challenged for women to demonstrate that the stereotype of the 'scatterbrained' i.e. incompetent, female is a false one. Further on the same issue, people who are seen as competent are also far more likely to have other differences that would have been negatively valued, overlooked, or at least held to be less important. So even what is, or is held to be, a functional impairment can be overcome or reduced in its impact by the presence in the person of a degree of competency, thus helping to prevent isolation and lack of experiences and giving greater opportunity for social interaction and the development of individual competencies in those areas.

SRV's concern for the importance of social roles gives a further dimension to the importance of competency enhancement. One of the key expectancies of many valued roles is competency to carry out the role, and one of the surest ways to embed a person or group in valued roles is for them to demonstrate ability in the various competencies demanded by those roles. Indeed, even if certain competencies were once possessed and are now diminished or non-existent, an individual or group can often still retain current value from them.

Ironically, in many services for vulnerable groups, there is an explicit commitment to competency enhancement; indeed many services use words like 'training' or 'assessment' as part of their titles. In addition, many professional qualifications for such services include exposure to technologies that 'develop' people. Ramon (1988) provides an interesting analysis of the number of social work skills, as taught in qualification training, which can be applied to 'normalisation work.' Even some English behavioural psychologists, usually critical of SRV as either being 'over theoretical' or 'unscientific' or both, have seen areas of agreement in using their techniques for behaviour change in the process of revaluing people, though unfortunately the possibilities of expansion on this theme are lost in a dispute about which discipline has the longest 'pedigree' in empirical research (see: Emerson and McGill 1989a; a response by Baldwin [1989]; and Emerson and McGill's rejoinder [1989b]) There is, therefore, at least the possibility that competency enhancement can be part of a service strategy and that there will be staff to carry it out. It may take a broader definition of competency than that used by some services and it is important to realise that it only has a place in wider strategies to combat devaluation.

Implementing the developmental model

There are several ways in which services based on the developmental model might be implemented, among which strategies suggested by SRV seem to be as systematic and comprehensive as any others. In broad terms, and allowing for the fact that SRV, by definition, is dealing with people or groups at least at risk of devaluation and wounding, and often already severely wounded, the first part of the strategy would be to try and influence both the physical and social environment to reduce restrictions on the growth potential of the people in question. As we have said, growth can occur in a variety of ways, not just by the acquisition of physical skills, and our observations of the wounding process in chapters 3 and 4 showed how many of the experiences of everyday life, all potential areas for competency development, are denied to devalued people. Areas such as communication, confidence, and expression of individuality cannot be easily acquired in a distantiated, segregated setting, where the opportunities to practice such competencies are severely limited. Similarly, services which use bodily impairments as a reason for denying access by people to opportunities to acquire or exercise their competencies perpetuate their devaluation, whereas those which reduce those obstacles and/or apply prosthetic help to people to grow in competency are making a key contribution to revaluation. This fits, of course, with current notions of 'empowerment' (Ramcharan et.al. 1997) and again addresses those critics of 'normalisation' that put the two ideas in opposition, (ibid, ch 13). SRV strategies would not, however, put all their eggs in the empowerment basket, at least if that means, as it seems to in some cases, 'abandonment to choice'.

As we also saw in chapter 4, the wounding process can have a devastating effect on the motivation of individuals and groups, who may see themselves as worthless, incapable and resign themselves to the role of dependent. Positive efforts at motivation, therefore, are a key part of implementing the developmental model, especially with people who have been severely wounded or who are at the early stages of growth.

The above strategies are largely about reducing obstacles to growth, either potential or existing ones, but SRV suggests that they be supplemented with various efforts aimed at enhancing growth, especially in the physical and social functioning of individuals or groups at risk. Once again the range of competencies to which these efforts can be applied is enormous, from bodily integrity and health, through basic self-help skills to the development of intellectual ability, skills, habits and disciplines. Here, of course, we are into the broad field of teaching and learning, and the range of technologies on offer is vast. The education literature is full of ways in which opportunities can be provided for people, though unfortunately, as in many other fields of study, educational academics are often more concerned about the competition between these methods than in their broad application. Following the second assumption of the developmental model, however, opportunities are rarely made available to the people who need them most, let alone the majority of even valued people. SRV's strategy is to try and capitalise as much as possible on all that is known about developmental growth and apply it to people with real or perceived impairments. Generally the literature supports a number of rules of thumb with regard to the development of competencies in people, particularly those with impairments. A consistent view is that the earlier developmental input is begun, the more effective it is likely to be (Weinert & Scheider 1995) and a corollary of this is that the sooner after the onset of an impairment measures are taken the greater their likely impact. Further, the gains to be made, at least in percentage or 'value added' terms are normally greatest when efforts are made with severely impaired people than mildly impaired ones. It is important here to remind readers that, as with all strategies of SRV, application can be made not just at the individual level, but at the level of groupings, collectivities of larger size and even whole societies. Therefore the abolition of the eleven plus, whatever were the faults of the education system put in place to accommodate this change, did say to a whole generation of children that they were not cut off from expectation of academic development at the age of eleven. Other implications of the multilevel nature of SRV strategy are also supported by the literature (Watts & Olsen 1994) in that where groups of 'delinquent' children are placed in environments where a feeling of security and worth can be achieved, development is possible even for those who are seriously devalued. The same, of course applies to individuals, as does the finding that the degree of structure most likely to produce development is the least restrictive, though this is not implying that there should be no structure (Traxson 1994). Educationalists in England have, of course, disagreed passionately on this issue as applied to general education, but most are agreed on the need not to dismiss peoples' developmental potential. Applying this to services beyond the confines of education suggests that aggressive pursuit of better ways to realise the potential growth of individuals at risk will, eventually, produce better ways to do it, provided the broad notion of growth is utilised, and narrow professional restrictions are not imposed.

As with the other strategies of SRV then, implementation of the developmental model relies on a conscious, discerning effort with individuals and groups, this time to ascertain their growth potential. It may be that, as radical critics of SRV have claimed, certain groups may need to learn 'to pursue collective action as a group' before doing anything else (Szivos 1992, p128). This would be one possible conclusion from the above conscious discerning effort, though there may be others. However, like the efforts at discerning valued social roles for people, many factors have to be taken into account, and a realistic and comprehensive judgement has to be made of both the likely success of measures, and their impact on values held by all parties concerned. So whilst the values of those critics might suggest that collective action was the most pressing, the values of others, including perhaps the people themselves, might be to learn something that might help them become less devalued. Unrealistic assumptions of bodily or mental competence are just as harmful if they result in setting people up to fail as those which result in no effort being made, though SRV would suggest that the assumption should always be on the positive side. The PASSING tool lists a number of issues which services will have to take into account in deliberating on efforts to develop people's competence, once the initial effort has been made. These include issues to do with interpersonal interactions, individualisation of efforts, and issues to do with autonomy and rights. Socio-sexual identity, and issues of age and culture appropriateness in development and growth in this area are also included as are many aspects of the physical environment that are likely to enhance or impede growth, e.g. the ease of access, the availability of resources in the immediate physical setting. Aids and adaptations to support people individually also need to be taken into account, as do the issues of grouping of people to maximise opportunities for learning and growth. Finally, services would expect that efforts to work with people to realise their developmental potential would be both intensive and efficient in their use of time.

Overall, in fact, the developmental model provides a major strategy by which services can address devaluation which is in keeping with much of, at least ideal, service practice. Implementation of that alone would, in many cases, require much more time and effort than is currently allocated in many services. SRV asks for more, however, and the next theme broadens the strategies available to services to plan and evaluate what they are doing, taking into account the full range of the issues of SRV that we have covered so far.

Introduction to the theme of relevance, potency and model coherency

In the earlier evaluation instrument PASS (Wolfensberger & Glenn 1975), there is a rating called model coherency, which attempts to bring together and examine the fit between a service's identity, its resources and its activities, the needs of those using the service, and what a service would look like that met similar needs in the valued population. This was taught extensively in the English experience of 'normalisation' training described in chapter 1. Since the development of PASSING, and the reconceptualization of normalization as SRV, further work has also been carried out on the notion of model coherency, to the extent that a specific workshop called Model Coherency Impact has been developed by Wolfensberger's Training Institute. This has been little used in this country, and since the theme of Relevance, Potency and Model Coherency is also on of the three 'new' themes introduced in 1995, there has been little analysis of it in the literature in England. O'Brien (in press) places model coherency alongside his own formulation of Accomplishments and other frameworks such as Personal Futures Planning (O'Brien & Lovett 1993) as means by which services can try and create a response to devaluation based on the sort of detailed analysis of individual needs described above, though with full reference to image issues as well as those of competency. Regardless of details, those systems all look to a comprehensive coverage of the various elements that impact on the users of a service, and making judgements about the power of that impact for good or bad in terms of devaluation.

SRV's theme of model coherency therefore continues the use of the construct of a model, in the sense that it represents reality by performance on key variables, which are dependent on the assumptions behind the model. So the contents and processes of the model all stem from the assumptions, and if these fit together then the model is said to be coherent. Thus, for example, the assumptions behind a medical model is that there will be people who are sick with a known condition, that there will be others who will attempt to alleviate that sickness, and that physical resources will be made available that will assist in the alleviation. There will also be technical processes carried out by the people alleviating the sickness that they are trained and competent to use, and those processes will be carried out on people in consultation with them, but ultimately in the control of the experts. It is also assumed that the sick people go along with these processes, on the basis that they wish to be relieved of their sickness. If, then, a medical facility is staffed by trained doctors and other professionals who cure or alleviate the majority of the illnesses they deal with by carrying out tried and tested processes, then that facility could be said to have model coherency. If, on the other hand, the staff were untrained, or were treating non-existent illnesses, or were applying techniques that had not been tested, or were doing so on unwilling patients, then varying degrees of incoherency would be said to exist. In services for vulnerable people, examining the assumptions, contents and processes of various service models can be a powerful means of determining the contribution of those services to devaluation or their attempts to address it. Equally, the process of model coherency impact can be used to design the contents and processes of services with and for individuals and groups, once there is clarity and agreement on the assumptions behind those services.

Relevance and potency in model coherency assessment

Since the key element of analysis of model coherency is the address of individual or group needs, there are two key questions to be applied to all the elements of a service. First, what is the match between the needs the service is addressing and the major or most pressing needs of the individual or group? This is what is termed relevance. Second, is what is being done to meet the perceived needs likely to be most powerful in so doing, and is it being done with intense and efficient use of the resources applied? This is referred to as potency. In a great many human services, incoherency is caused by efforts that are either not really relevant, in that they address only secondary or even no real needs of their users, or they lack potency, in that they only touch the surface in dealing with those needs. Some services, of course, can lack both relevance and potency. If we follow the overall goals of SRV in addressing needs generated by devaluation, by paying attention to the image and competencies of those using the service, we can use the concepts of relevance and potency to design new services or to look at how well services are performing. Before that we must look in more detail at a concept of SRV, referred to briefly earlier, the Culturally Valued Analogue.

Importance of the Culturally Valued Analogue

One of the more irritating criticisms of the English experience SRV occurs when some of the terms it uses (and has always explained, in for example the PASSING manual) are picked out in isolation and used to justify a charge of obscurantism or 'jargon.' Part of the causes of such criticisms may be more understandable if the terms are introduced at a workshop, and then passed on secondhand without the sort of definitions that would be expected from academic publication, which of course has been a major part of the English experience. Nevertheless, academics would perhaps be expected to consult the available published material, and had they done so, would find as adequate a definition of unfamiliar terms as would be found in published accounts of most other social scientific theory. 'Disjointed incrementalism', 'infallible *Weltanschauung*', 'ontological verisimilitude' may be terms that trip off the tongue of academics of some disciplines as readily as 'culturally valued analogue' does for those involved with SRV theory, but all would be just as unfamiliar to the general public. That they need explanation in an exposition of whatever theories they are associated with is not normally a reason to criticise those theories, in fact they would be more subject to criticism if they did not explain unfamiliar terms. The concept of the culturally valued analogue, therefore, needs to be explained as part of an attempt to explicate SRV theory, and it is hoped that the explanation, rather than the need for it, will be subject to critique.

It will come as no surprise to readers who have got thus far, that the concept is rooted in the social judgement of societies and sub-groups of those societies on certain phenomena. In terms of human services these phenomena can be broken down into the functions, activities and settings of such services. Each of these can be said to have an analogue, or similar phenomenon, in the valued, non-service world, covering a range of life functions from the broad (e.g residence, work, education) to the very specific (e.g. cooking, manual labour, mathematical tasks). So it is possible to build up a picture of what would be valued in the wider culture by combining the components into a total analogue. This can therefore be compared with the components of any given service, which will give us some idea of the value attached to the service. So, for example, most people would be able to describe the elements, in terms of the function, the activities that go on there and the setting, of the phenomenon of 'home'. This would not be totally uniform, but there would be sufficient agreement that we could provide a picture of what the valued world thought of in terms of that concept to provide the components of a culturally valued analogue to a residential service.

Within the broad components of functions, activities and settings we can ask more detailed questions of each. So we can ask about a service, either formal or informal; what is its function, how is that function carried out, with whom and by whom. When and where is the function carried out, and how is it described, in terms of language and imagery. Those same questions can be asked of the culturally valued analogue and a comparison made. In the analysis which follows, therefore, it is hoped that the use of the term culturally valued analogue (or CVA as we shall now refer to it) will be clear. Having explained the term, SRV does not, again, take a 'stance' on whether it is 'right' for CVAs to exist, merely pointing out that they do. That they can be used to devalue people whose lives or services do not fit into many CVAs is a function of societal devaluation, not SRV. To describe the use by SRV of the CVA as an 'inherently stigmatising' feature of the SRV 'model' (Ramcharan et.al. 1997, p246), is the academic equivalent of shooting the messenger. SRV suggests that, amongst other strategies, services and situations that are coherent with the CVA will probably result in valuation, and those that are not in devaluation. It does not say 'everyone with learning disabilities should attain the CVA' (ibid, p246) nor of competency, that this is only 'to be found in fully paid employment.' Instead, as we shall see below, a much more subtle and detailed analysis of both competency and image elements of people's lives, and their connection to the CVA(s) is necessary.

Model coherency impact

To adopt a strategy using model coherency then, as with the various attempts to counter devaluation described in earlier themes, we begin with a conscious, precise and detailed analysis of the people involved and their life situation This can only be achieved by observation and spending time with people. In terms of a given service, therefore, that analysis begins with an answer to the question who are the people being served. There are three dimensions to such an answer. The first may be said to be factual at least in terms of things that are readily observable. So the users of a service can be described in terms of basic facts such as their ages, the age range, the balance of the sexes, the particular factual devalued conditions and impairments, and the shared histories of people. To this can be added the images that the people project, along with what ethnic or cultural identities that they possess. The second dimension is more impressionistic, and it uses the terms that we have covered in earlier chapters. Who are the people existentially, in the sense of their life experiences, their wounds, and their identities as perceived in the wider world. Thirdly, what has been the impact of these experiences on the people using the service.

Having obtained a detailed answer to the question 'who are the people' model coherency then proceeds to ask the question 'what are their needs' This is not answered in the way, previously common in the service world and still to be found in many places, where 'needs' were defined in terms of 'needed' amounts of whatever services were available. Instead model coherency, along with other processes that have been adopted more recently in services answers the question more fundamentally. So 'somewhere to live' would be a major need, rather than 'a place in a residential home.' For most people in receipt of services, needs can be ranked in terms of urgency, and a CVA can be conceptualised by which those needs are met in the valued community. This may involve more than one CVA, since services very often attempt to meet combinations of life needs that are separated in the wider world. For the CVA, or for each CVA, we can ask what is the content, what are the elements that make it up and what are the processes, how is the content rendered? We can ask the same question for the service concerned, bearing in mind its purview, that is the range and scope of the function in people's lives for which the service is responsible, or claims to be responsible.

We are then in a position to identify the detail of the needs, contents and processes that should be met within the purview of the service, using the CVA as our benchmark, and therefore look at the congruencies of those elements. Where there are incongruencies, or incoherencies, this opens our questioning to possible ideas for lessening the incoherencies by addressing the various elements concerned, or for designing a service that would minimise the potential incoherencies. This should be done in the light of the likely or actual impact of the various coherencies and incoherencies on the recipients of the service and what might happen were these to change.

In the course of this process we are likely to discern or review the assumptions behind the service model being examined, and it may be at this level that address is needed. This will be particularly so if it is hard to find a CVA, since this usually means that the service is carrying out a function that valued people in society would not aspire to, and suggests conscious or unconscious devaluing intentions on the part of service providers. Such things as prisons, shelters for refugees or homeless people are generated from assumptions by society that there is a specific class or subgroup of society that 'need' a particular service model. SRV's response to this issue is to suggest a different strategy than the one it would suggest for services that only have incoherent elements, and for which movement towards a CVA can be found.

Relevance, potency and model coherency are thus elements of a powerful analysis of services and service systems and illustrates the ability of SRV to have an impact at all levels of social organisation. It does not, in itself, propose a service model for any particular group of people, despite misconceptions in the English experience, amongst others that Tyne (1992) points out, that 'normalisation' was all about ordinary housing for people with learning disabilities. Instead, it gives, especially at the level of service planning, a useful tool to develop services which can begin to address devaluation and wounding. One of the key elements of efforts in this direction comes from contact and relationships with other people, particularly those who are valued in society, and thus have stronger defences against devaluation. The remaining themes bring out a number of aspects of this element of SRV strategy.

9

The ten themes of SRV:

Interpersonal identification;
The power of imitation

Introduction to the theme of Interpersonal Identification

Central to a number of the English critics of 'normalisation' has been the
issue of 'identity.' This is usually based on the supposition that
'normalisation' is a 'change strategy' of 'assimilation' of devalued groups
into the wider society rather than a 'political' strategy of groups realising
their collective identity as 'oppressed groups' and challenging the status
quo by banding together in contradiction to the place in which society puts
them as individuals. 'The commitment to pursue valued lifestyles will never
seriously challenge the status quo or hide the fact that service users are not
in control of their own lives' (Brown & Smith 1989, p112)

As with so many of the English academic critiques of the late eighties,
the reference to 'valued lifestyles' rather than valued roles, and the emphasis
on self-determination, reveals the lack of full discussion of SRV theory as it
developed from normalization and the ideological nature of much of the
criticisms. This has been discussed in chapter 1 and elsewhere, and on one
level it is only necessary to repeat the comment made many times that
whatever strategy one adopts depends on one's values and beliefs. SRV
theory merely points out the likely effects of different strategies. In talking
about the importance of devalued people fostering a sense of identity with
the valued community, and of the valued community fostering a sense of
their common identity with devalued people as fellow human beings,
which is the essence of the theme of interpersonal identity, SRV again tries
to derive a strategy that looks to observation of how individuals and
societies operate, and suggests how this might be utilised to assist in the
revaluation of vulnerable groups. Ideological commitment to a separate
'group identity' or 'collective and communal interventions' will override

such a strategy if that is the value position of the parties concerned. Whether it will be successful in achieving a society that 'values difference' is as questionable empirically as a belief that SRV strategies will achieve a society that values common humanity. On the evidence of the universality of devaluation discussed in chapter 2 neither sort of society has ever been, or is likely to be, achieved. One is then left with a choice of dealing with society as it is, whilst at the same time trying to influence its development, or trying to set up 'communities of the oppressed' which have had very variable effects on devalued groups, sometimes serving to reinforce their devalued status by the confirmation of stereotypical judgments made in ignorance. This is not to deny the real benefits of groups coming together out of a sense of mutual experience, or of a political strategy that seeks to advance the cause of any particular group through demonstrations of solidarity; it is to acknowledge the potential damage of a totally separatist position. Ironically, the 'identity' argument has also been used to try and justify segregated services. In an article critical of 'the normalization movement' Angers (1992) argues that attempts to rehabilitate people with mental health problems through the use of the 'natural community' are mistaken because they fail to take account of the 'identity' of people with mental illness that has been rejected by the natural community. He then proposes a 'clubhouse model' of community, i.e. a segregated community of ex-psychiatric patients 'created' around their identities. 'Until the natural community can offer this dimension for its citizens, and especially those with mental illness, there will always be a need for an appropriate created community' (ibid. p122). In judging the more detailed strategy of the theme of interpersonal identification, therefore, readers may like to reflect on the power of an identity to result just as much in devaluation for its holder as it can in valuation.

Contact and communication: The basis of interpersonal identification

The underlying strategy of interpersonal identification is based on the assumption that if different individuals and groups, particularly if the differences of some of them are devalued, can make contact and communicate with one another, then they will discover sufficient elements of their common humanity to begin to identify with one another. On the whole people who identify with one another will want good things to happen to each other, to be with each other more, to be influenced by each other's opinion, even to be more like one another. This idea has roots in many attempts at ending stereotyping of various sorts (Weeks 1994) and of course has rarely run smoothly, given the relative power positions of different groups about which stereotypical judgments are made. SRV acknowledges these issues, in fact in describing the intensity of wounding it probably emphasises more than many analyses the harmful effects of distantiation of people from one another. Fostering a sense of interpersonal identity between devalued and valued groups and individuals is therefore not an easy task, and needs to be linked to all the other SRV strategies.

It is certainly not an attempt to 'force' valued people to come into contact with devalued people, since that will only reinforce the sense of differentness, and the strategy relies on both parties increasingly wanting to be in contact with one another. As with many of the other themes, such a strategy requires a detailed and sensitive analysis with devalued people and groups to establish the context for such contacts that will be most in harmony with the individual or group's needs, wishes, and identities. Their social situation and the particular cultural or community expectations about social interactions also need careful consideration to provide the details of specific actions within the sub-strategies SRV proposes.

Sub-strategies for promoting interpersonal identification

The most obvious point about getting two parties to make contact and communicate with one another is that they must have the opportunity to do so, and in circumstances that will make the contact last more than a brief period. The presence, in ordinary, valued society of devalued people would therefore have to be a prerequisite, and not just in terms of where they live, but in the variety of physical settings where opportunities for interaction occur. And, just as valued citizens have a notion of acceptable appearance and behaviour in different settings, so too does attention need to be paid to appearance and behaviour of devalued people in different settings. We will go into more detail of this issue in the final theme of the conservatism corollary, where we will remind readers once more of the reality of the importance of image and competence perception on devaluation, regardless of how one feels about it.

So the frequency of an individual or group's presence in social settings, and the appropriateness of their appearance and behaviour increases the 'approachability' of both parties to the attempt at interpersonal identification. It is just as important that the more valued individual or group should be approachable to the devalued person or group as the other way around, an issue which is often forgotten in attempts at relationship building. So attention needs to be paid to ensuring that, as far as possible, the initial contact between two parties is experienced as positive. Schwartz (1997) talks of a shared common task as being one way to equalise the status of two parties, as opposed to simply 'bringing people together' and hoping the contact will be made.

As much as possible the aim should be for both parties to experience seeing the world through the other's eyes, which can occur in a variety of forms. It can occur through the written or electronic media, where interpretations of what life is like for people can be powerfully portrayed. More important in the great majority of cases, however, is the use of the great wealth of ordinary experiences of life that exist in the everyday community, and provide many opportunities for contact to be made. It will not just happen automatically , however, and therefore effort, especially by staff in the case of human services, needs to be put into capitalising on the opportunities and creating others. The aim, and it has been borne out in practice, is to create empathy on the part of valued people with devalued people, and to foster each individual or group's sense of responsibility for each other. Given the nature of devaluation, and wider societal developments, this is an increasingly difficult task.

Introduction to the theme of Imitation

In the previous chapter we talked about the various techniques for helping people to achieve their developmental potential, and how the whole area of teaching and learning has an enormous variety of means proposed for effectively doing just that, though among academic educationalists there are often sharp disagreements as to which is the most effective. What educational psychologists are in less disagreement about is what has sometimes been called 'social learning' (Russell 1996), that is learning about behaviour in social situations by observing what is done by others in the social situation and imitating or copying that behaviour. This is one important feature of the power of imitation that is relevant to SRV, in that by its nature it is concerned with perceptions of behaviour that take place in a social context, but the issue of imitation is much broader than this and can have effects at all the levels that SRV is concerned with, from individuals right through to whole societies.

In fact, there is general agreement amongst psychologists that imitation is built into human nature (Hobson 1993). Studies of child development put learning by imitation as one of the most primitive, and therefore most deeply embedded mechanisms for learning that human beings have at their disposal (Reddy 1991). It of course requires at least two parties to the process; the learner, who may be an individual or larger group of people, and an individual or group who is performing the behaviour to be imitated, which we can call a model. Note that this is distinct from the use of model as a schema, as in 'the developmental model' but uses the word as a noun coming from the verb 'to model' or demonstrate, the behaviour to be imitated. Paul Jenkins, in his training materials (1998) makes the distinction between two types of modelling. 'Acquisition modelling' occurs when the actual process of learning is demonstrated, so that the model is, in fact learning at the same time as the imitator. The other type, 'Performance modelling' occurs when the model demonstrates the desired performance itself, which is then imitated by the learner. In either case for effective imitation to occur, some sort of link is necessary between the learner and the model, in order for the learner to be motivated to imitate. We will return to more details of this process later, but two wider points needs to be made here concerning imitation. The first is that imitation goes on so frequently, and in so many contexts, that a good deal of it is, by necessity, unconscious. Indeed, as with imagery, humans on the one hand do not like to admit that they imitate, preferring the illusion of themselves as totally independent actors, but there is overwhelming evidence of its power. Readers are invited to consider just how many of the skills they possess, and how much of their everyday behaviour, was learnt from imitating others. As children, role-playing is just one means of making sense of the adult world, and learning what is appropriate and inappropriate behaviour, and a great deal of what happens in children's games is a clear instance of imitation setting the rules for behaviour in a given role.

This leads us to the second general point, that imitation is neutral as to the sort of behaviour and skills imitated. If the conditions for imitation that we will elaborate below exist, then imitation is highly likely to occur, regardless of the behaviour concerned. This is, of course, one of the great arguments for integration, that we will discuss in the next theme, or certainly against segregation and congregation of devalued people together, where far more modelling goes on in many cases of devalued behaviour than valued.

So imitation, whilst it can be extremely adaptive, which is of course why it is so powerful and so enduring a learning mechanism, can also serve to reinforce certain devalued identities and behaviours. To use the power of imitation to address devaluation therefore, one must be aware of this power and seek to create situations where that power is used to develop valued skills and behaviours.

The Imitation Process

In the introduction above we used the words 'learner' and 'model' in the singular, though we did note that they could be any number of people. This again shows the applicability of SRV across the range of societal levels and in the description of the process which follows the reader is invited to consider how the different elements relate to the different levels. Its power over even whole societies, however, is shown by the recent situation in the United States where one of the reasons why a President was in danger of being thrown out of office was that his behaviour was said by his accusers to represent an 'inappropriate model' for the rest of society.

Looking at the imitation process from the beginning, therefore, there needs to be a model who can and does perform the desired behaviours. This does not necessarily imply an 'expert' in those behaviours since, as we have seen, it may be the behaviour of learning itself that is modelled. What is needed, in addition to a model who can perform the desired behaviours, is a model who has some characteristics that the learner admires, or likes, or aspires to. This is most obvious in the intimate setting of a family or relationship grouping, where children admire their parents, teenagers their peers, but it also applies in wider contexts such as groupings based on beliefs, political allegiances or a shared identity from ethnicity, gender or even oppression. The greater the number of characteristics of the model that the learner admires, of course, the greater is the likelihood of imitation. This, again is why far more of what we learn comes from people we ourselves want to be with as opposed to appointed 'teachers' who may have few characteristics that we admire, and who themselves may have very stereotyped mindsets about the roles of certain pupils (Riddell 1992), a fact that has bedevilled the teaching profession for many years, though many people can point to one or two professional teachers that have had a significant effect on their lives.

Given the existence of the model, the process next depends on certain conditions being in place with regard to the learner. First, that they have, at least to some degree, the capacity to imitate. Given the deep rooted nature of imitation, there are few behaviours that it is not possible to imitate in a very primitive fashion, but using imitation as a strategy can also be in tension with other elements of SRV. Where the imitation is a mere caricature, as sometimes occurs when devalued people are 'forced' to stand up on a public platform when they do not any capacity for it, then this can serve to reinforce devaluation. Where people do have this capacity, of course, such public speaking can be one of the most powerful addresses of devaluation, so the issue should not be taken as all or nothing. The point is, especially where very wounded people are concerned, that care should be taken not to attempt to get someone to imitate behaviours they are incapable of carrying out. Second, the learner must have the opportunity to imitate, since without this immense frustration can occur. Third, the learner needs to be aware of the environment in which the imitation is likely to occur, including their own and others behaviours in that environment, and fourth, the learner needs to be open and susceptible to learning new things or altering the way they do things at present. This again can be a problem for extremely wounded people, or for people for whom a devalued role, with associated devalued behaviour, may be the only one they possess. Many things are still possible, however, as evidenced by the many means of communication possible with even the most impaired people, and this seems to occur when the final link is in place; that the learner does, in fact, positively identify with, admire, or even love the model. Note the link here with the previous theme of interpersonal identification.

Even with a model and a learner in place some of the following factors should be present to make imitation more likely. First of all, the model or models need to be present in large enough numbers, or for a significant proportion of the time, so that their behaviour commands the attention of the learner, rather than competing opportunities to imitate, . The behaviour being modelled also should be performed often enough while the learner is present and attending. This requires considerable efforts of consciousness on the part of staff, where they are the models, sometimes to the point of exaggerating the desired behaviour over what comes naturally. For more remote models, especially those whose presence is only via the media, this aspect of modelling is, of course much less controllable, but efforts can again be made by those close to the devalued person or group to help them observe the remote model's behaviour as often as possible. This can be backed up, as it also can in the case of more direct modelling, by a sensitively timed prompt to the learner to imitate, where this is appropriate, and by reinforcement of the learner as the imitation gets closer to the desired behaviours. Reinforcement of the models also helps with the frequency and appropriateness of good modelling. Finally, 'rehearsal' of the imitated behaviour, perhaps even to the point of 'overlearning' can serve to imbed it in the repertoire of the learner.

All of the foregoing sounds consciously planned and premeditated, to the point of 'naturalness' being lacking in the behaviours. To the reserved and egalitarian English ear it may smack of the sort of demonstrations of 'etiquette' which maiden aunts gave to their impressionable young nieces in Victorian novels. Such a perception may again be at the heart of the English critics of 'normalisation' as 'imposing' one set of behaviours over another (Bayley 1991) and in spelling it out in systematic fashion we may have lost some of the myriad of social behaviours appropriate to particular settings that are learnt by all of us in imitating others. But that is, in fact, what we do. There are models, as we have defined them, and we as social humans are the learners. The factors that we suggested for devalued people to have the best chance of imitating only mirror our own tendency to be more frequently with role models we admire, to observe and take more notice of their behaviour than others, and to be reinforced by our increasing closeness to them as our behaviour approximates to theirs, or to the range of behaviours of which they approve. To attend an academic conference one observes just as much imitation going on as in a service setting which has consciously adopted imitation as an element in their developmental strategy. Yet it seems, as we noted in the introduction, that making people conscious of a process which they largely carry out unconsciously provokes a number of reactions, some of which cause individuals or groups to reject its use in combatting devaluation. These will be examined in more detail below.

Reactions to the power of imitation

The English experience of learning, especially the learning that takes place within formal education systems, has been mixed, to say the least, and it remains a topic likely to raise the temperature in social discourse. Educational practice, however, and certainly the public notion of what constitutes a 'good teacher' still largely clings to a model based on the power of the individual teacher to somehow get over to the learner what they think the learner should know. The learner is then tested in a formal way, and the amount of learning judged on those tests. So the learning recognised most strongly by our society is that which can be accredited in some way. In proposing that far more important learning takes place informally, particularly of socially adaptive behaviours, SRV is at the same time challenging a good deal of the English educational establishment but also pointing to the particular nature of devaluation in this country, in that the skills and behaviours learnt by imitation are largely those whose absence contributes to devaluation, whereas those learnt by 'listening to the teacher' tend to add value, by 'academic achievement' to an already valued group. So the fact that my son with Downs syndrome attends an ordinary school would, from an SRV perspective, be likely to help him to acquire skills and behaviours in dealing with other people, in working as part of a group, in developing the same disciplines of work habits as his peers. The fact that it probably also contributes to his being able to read and write, and develop in some of the basic academic subjects, would also be important to SRV, but again one of the main reasons he is able to do this is what we referred to earlier as 'acquisition modelling' i.e. imitating others in their performance of learning. SRV would also point to other benefits described in the ten themes, especially role expectancy. Justifications for him attending a segregated Special School, such as that he would receive a 'higher staff ratio' and more 'individual attention' are therefore in almost complete opposition to, or fail to recognise, the power of imitation. Not only do such justifications assume the 'specialist teacher' has a much greater influence over his learning than imitation of his peers, but it also places academic learning on a higher level than the learning of social behaviour, since his models for that at a Special School would be similarly devalued children, exhibiting largely devalued behaviour. To a vulnerable person, such as somebody with Down's syndrome, the risk of devaluation resulting from poor social behaviour is far greater than his chances of valuation based on academic criteria alone. Further, there may also be a more unconscious reasoning behind segregated education for devalued children, namely the belief that they somehow learn 'differently' from other children and will thus benefit from this 'specialist' teaching. It is certainly true that there are elements of the learning of children with learning disabilities that are different, for example what the educationalists call 'transference' (Norwich 1990), but there is very little evidence to suggest that the power of imitation works less well in such people. If anything the evidence suggests it is a more prominent learning mechanism than the understanding and using of intellectual concepts and constructs.

There are many other reasons for the existence of segregation in the English education system, but the damage done to the possibilities of the power of imitation for vulnerable people provides a good reason for rejection of that idea. Ironically, imitation has also been applied in a much wider service sphere, to justify continued segregation of various groups. This view acknowledges the power of imitation but rejects its use because of a fear that too many 'wrong' things will be learnt. Part of the problem that SRV has, particularly in diffident England, is that people seem to assume that it is calling for perfection in its models, and that no-one wishes to set themselves up as such for fear of their 'Achilles heel' being discovered. This is then compounded by their observation of others as being even worse models and so use of the power of imitation is rejected. The irony comes in the fact that such a view can not only fail to make use of a powerful strategy for addressing devaluation, it can also compound it, by placing the person or group for whom imitation is not used in the position of 'eternal child' or 'holy innocent' in that they are seen as they passive receptor of all bad models and thus need to be protected from them. As noted above, this argument is then used to justify segregation, though it flies in the face of evidence that imitation and modelling occurs in all settings, so unless one were to keep an individual or group entirely separate as individuals one from another then some modelling will go on.

The positive strategy that SRV suggests for imitation is therefore to recognise that it will operate everywhere and maximise the opportunity for valued behaviours to be modelled. By being at an ordinary school and living in an ordinary family my son has learnt to swear, to have arguments, even to hit people. He is also gradually learning, equally by imitation, that there are places where those behaviours will not be tolerated, and that his friends get away with them by being selective in where and when they occur. So SRV acknowledges that society is made up of models of both good and bad behaviour, and helping vulnerable people to combat devaluation includes developing their sense of which is which.

A related argument which reacts with rejection to the use of imitation is also connected to the identity issue, which we have discussed above. This suggests that the idea that there are more or less 'acceptable' behaviours in any given social situation is inherently wrong, and that people 'ought to be accepted as they are' or that the 'person not the role' should be valued (Elks 1994). Many people might agree with this proposition on the level of values, though as we have noted before this does not prevent many who hold those views from ascertaining, by observation, what is 'acceptable' behaviour in their own circles and conforming to it, or of having their own hierarchy of 'acceptance'. A good illustration of this occurred recently on a professional social work training course, where an ex-patient of a 'mental deficiency' institution, who had been homosexually abused by staff, was describing his experiences to students and made disparaging remarks about homosexuals. The upshot was, that despite staff running the course strongly advocating the value position above, they could not find it in themselves to value, or even accept this person 'as he was' and did not employ him as a presenter again, because their views on 'homophobia' outweighed their views on 'acceptance'. So even if one would like our society to be one in which behaviour was not judged positively or negatively, but just seen as different, the empirical fact of the matter is that we do not live in such a society. Imitation, therefore is likely to be a powerful tool in gaining acceptance of more 'different' behaviours by helping individuals and groups to judge which of these is acceptable in which contexts, and to act accordingly.

The 'accept people as they are' argument has also led to a reaction to imitation when it comes to presenting good models, or more especially when it raises consciousness of negative models. So when staff of services are asked to consider the effect of their appearance as being models of how to present oneself in a given situation, there is often a hostile response. This, again, is partly a reaction to the notion that there should be more or less acceptable appearance, and partly a response to a sense of implied criticism of their appearance, but it is also a reaction to the uncovering of the unconscious assumption that the devalued group is not 'worth' one having a positive appearance for. Yet for many users of services, especially elderly people, the maintenance of a good appearance is a very important attribute, but one which can be very quickly unlearnt, if the behaviour they are imitating is that appearance 'doesn't matter.' Like all SRV strategies, of course, the use of imitation requires a high degree of consciousness of the individual or group concerned, of their particular vulnerabilities and values, and of one's own values. So unsubtle application of imitation can use its power in such a way as to increase devaluation, as we noted in our discussion of the wounding process, when talking about the imitation of behaviours that then get so over-reinforced that they get the person a reputation for their 'party piece' and they become the object of ridicule. Equally, unsubtle use of an admired model can result in the learner becoming totally fixated on that person to the virtual exclusion of all others, even to the point where the same desired behaviours will not be imitated if anyone but the fixated model performs them, or at least other, equally desirable behaviours will not be imitated because the fixated model is not the one carrying them out. We see here, again, the link with interpersonal identification being made possible for a wide range of valued and devalued people, to avoid such problems of applying imitation. Finally, an imitation strategy should not rule out other learning forms. As we discussed in the developmental model, there are many ways to improve people's competency, and though there may arguments about the efficacy of some of them, many more are tried and tested. So whilst a strategy using imitation would want to do a number of things, such as ensuring good models were present in vulnerable people's lives in as many ways as possible, using good judgment in working with the people concerned to discern relevant and powerful things for them to imitate, and being aware of what therefore constitutes negative modelling for that person or group, including, hardest of all perhaps, one's own capacity for this, the strategy does not preclude teachers, or trainers, from using their skills in the traditional way. What is important is to remember the power of imitation in one's own life and bring the knowledge of this power to bear to address devaluation. To do this, as we have said, requires the presence of people to act as models, in the physical settings where the relevant behaviour normally takes place. This leads us on to the penultimate theme of social integration and valued social participation.

9

The ten themes of SRV:
Personal social integration and valued social
participation; The conservatism corollary

Introduction to the theme of personal social integration and valued social participation

As in the USA and most industrialised countries, the English experience of the wounds of distantiation, via segregation and congregation, of various groups of people, the elderly, people with mental health problems and people with learning disabilities, had resulted, by the time normalization appeared on the scene in the fifties and sixties, in a powerfully established service model of the institution (Wolfensberger 1969). In the English experience these were the descendants of the workhouse and the asylum, often actually using the same buildings, but bolstered in the period between the wars, at least as far as learning disability was concerned, by the mass building of 'colonies' to cater for the greater numbers institutionalised as a result of eugenic ideas embodied in the Mental Deficiency Act, 1913 and its successor policies (Race 1995). By the time normalization was being seriously discussed, at least in academic circles, in the late sixties and early seventies institutions for people with learning disabilities were almost all controlled by the National Health Service, largely in the same buildings as the pre-war colonies, now called hospitals. As we discussed in chapter 1, the impact of normalization, then and later, was largely confined to services for people with learning disabilities, although there was a more general anti-institution movement in other areas, especially in the mental health field, was also voiced (Jones 1971)

  The importance of this historical reminder to our exposition of the ten themes of SRV is that the strength of the anti-institution movement, and contribution of normalization to it, was then seen by many to have resulted in 'success' in what came to be called 'community care' and the closure of many long-stay hospitals (Hatton & Emerson 1996). The fact of those hospital closures, and the many reactions to those changes in the learning disability world (Cox & Pearson 1995) produced a very firm, but rather one dimensional, association between 'normalisation' (what was being taught through PASS and PASSING workshops and their spin-off events) and 'ordinary housing' i.e. the residential model offered by the service system as an alternative to segregated institutions. That lack of depth of understanding of the breadth of normalization, and even more so of SRV as it developed, led to a further simplification in some people's minds; namely that 'normalisation' equalled 'integration'. This is scarcely surprising, given that the theme of social integration had been consistently argued in most versions of normalization, especially Wolfensberger's (1972). It also was prominent among the 'seven themes' of normalization, as taught in varying ways in England in the eighties (Race 1987). When this teaching is combined with the obvious changes to the service system and the physical changes of buildings and their locations resulting from community care policies then the assumption that 'normalisation', 'ordinary housing' and 'integration' were all the same thing was understandable. It had its dangers, however, and the two most relevant to our attempt to describe SRV theory are that, firstly, such beliefs oversimplify and reduce to mere physical presence the import both of this theme, and of SRV as a whole. It has always been taught, even as part of the seven themes of normalization, and in the O'Briens' *Framework for Accomplishment* (1989), that what was often shortened to the one word 'integration' was not just about people being physically present in society, but being fully participating social members as well. Several studies have, however, shown that some services, while located in 'ordinary housing' went very little further than mere presence in communities, with social participation at a minimum (Hatton & Emerson 1996). Reasons for this include an acknowledgement of the much more difficult task of achieving social as well as physical integration. Some of these studies (e.g. Sinson 1993.) go on to blame 'normalisation' for this state of affairs, thus reinforcing the inadequate analysis described above. Few, if any, acknowledge the development of SRV, and its emphasis on social participation via valued social roles, and so no serious discussion has taken place in the English academic literature about this theme, beyond the 'collectivity of oppression' argument described earlier (Szivos 1992). Where reference is made to 'normalisation' it tends to be a reference to the O'Brien 'Accomplishments' and that tool of implementation has certainly been applied in far more services, though sometimes in the 'name' of SRV or 'normalisation'. This leads us to the second danger that a narrow understanding of 'normalisation' as 'integration' and a narrow understanding of 'integration' as 'ordinary housing' has brought to the English experience. It is an argument that runs as follows. 'Normalisation', which has merely been 're-named' as SRV, was about getting people with learning disabilities out of hospitals and into ordinary houses. That has now been achieved, so SRV is now redundant. The argument, though rarely expressed so bluntly, is also expressed in naive interpretations of the term 'inclusion'. Just as 'integration' is naively assumed to have been achieved by physical presence, so 'inclusion' is assumed to follow from action to ensure 'rights of access' for certain groups to facilities available to the rest of society. In fact 'inclusion' is often assumed to be an 'evolution' from 'integration' as it also is interpreted as participation in society by different groups who may still retain a distinct 'identity', even the identity which caused their 'exclusion' in the first place (Borland and Ramcharan 1997).

These are dangers that spring from naive and one-dimensional interpretations, both of SRV and 'inclusion,' but to read the current literature it is not just the service world that is making these interpretations, but academics as well. Readers who have got this far will, it is hoped, be clear that there is much more to SRV than just 'integration', and what follows is an attempt to show that there is much more to this theme than the simple promotion of ordinary housing for people with learning disabilities. Put at its simplest it is about the participation of all individuals and groups at risk of devaluation in as wide a range of valued activities, relationships and roles as possible. For that to happen those activities, roles and relationships need to be predominantly with ordinary, valued people in ordinary, valued settings. Those seeking to use SRV theory to address devaluation need, therefore, to attend not only to the physical presence of vulnerable people with others in their society, though that is a prerequisite, but to the nature and quantity of interactions, and the settings in which they take place. The links with the themes of mindsets and expectancies and interpersonal identification should be clear, as should the benefits to people's competency, especially via imitation and role expectancy, and their image, through all the various media that we discussed under that theme. Because of the key part that this theme, and misunderstanding of it, has played in the English experience, however, we need to examine these links and benefits in more depth.

Benefits Of Personal Social Integration And Valued Social Participation

Those engaged in analysing change processes (e.g. Handy 1984) point to a seemingly inherent capacity in individuals, and more especially in organisations, to initially resist change. Part of this is expressed by the tendency of those to whom a change is proposed only to accept the change if they perceive it to be considerably better, not just better in some aspects. Hence when studies such as Hatton and Emerson (1996) show that some people who were moved out of hospital had few or no friends in community settings, this is seized on as 'proof', not that the change did people good in other areas, but that they are 'worse off' than they were before. The same applies to the benefits of personal social integration and valued social participation. Since, like SRV theory, they rely on probabilistic outcomes rather than deterministic ones, it will always be possible to point to individual examples where the empirical data does not 'fit' the argument. Readers are, therefore, urged to consider the balance of probabilities, rather than specific examples when evaluating the benefits outlined below.

Benefits to individuals and groups at risk of devaluation

A common, if sad, feature of English human services in recent decades has been the regularity of abuse, both physical and sexual, of people in residential care (e.g. Gilleard 1994). Ironically, this clearly illustrates the risks of social segregation, regardless of the location in which that segregation takes place, in that the abuse has occurred in a range of physical settings, from large remote institutions to ordinary houses in communities. Obviously if a harmful regime takes hold in a larger and more remote institution, then the damage will be more widespread than in a smaller establishment. The physical presence of smaller settings in communities has not, however, prevented similar severity of abuse. Real social integration offers the benefit of preventing or reducing the likelihood of abuse in that it presupposes the presence of non-service people in the lives of users of the service and a wide range of interactions taking place in common facilities used by the ordinary community. There would therefore be many more people in a position to notice signs of abuse, and many more whose capacity to act was unaffected by obligations to the service system (Bayley 1997).

Second, there are a number of benefits of social integration to individuals and groups in terms of the development of their competencies, the importance of which was discussed in detail in chapter 8. These benefits stem, first, from an increased likelihood that services open to the general public are likely to be of a higher quality than those for devalued groups. As our age becomes increasingly consumer led, the financial and social power of valued groups is pushing a response from such common services as leisure centres, pubs and restaurants. This is also generally true of transportation and tourism services. With all these services, it is true, financial considerations have often prevented devalued people from participation and the effect of the wound of involuntary poverty also needs to be taken into account (Russell 1995; Lister 1990). However, the money spent on providing segregated, 'specialist' equivalents of community facilities, or even specialist facilities that have no community equivalents, such as 'snoezelens' (Whittaker 1992) could go a considerable way towards enabling more vulnerable people to take advantage of the improvements of the various facilities open to the public at large.

As well, of course, as the quality of publicly available services they offer far more chances than segregated settings for observation and imitation of appropriate behaviour which in turn can assist in peoples' competency enhancement.Besides the possibility of imitation, ordinary settings, as we have seen earlier, can be very effective in eliciting positive expectancies of those who use them, not just from the physical environment, but from those other conveyors of role expectancies, namely: the people present in the settings; the behaviour expected, if not demanded; and the language used to and about people in those settings. All of these argue strongly for the use of facilities available to the general public, at times that the public use them, and in activities that valued people carry out there, as powerful reinforcement of the sort of competency development that is part of SRV's strategy to address the devaluation of vulnerable people. This competency development can then lead to an even wider range of role models and activities than that which encouraged the initial contact with any particular community based service.

A corollary of this range of experiences in a range of valued settings is a higher probability that vulnerable people can exercise, and be seen to exercise, increasing autonomy and choice in their activities, and exercise increasing freedom and independence in doing so (Bayley 1997). As an address of the wound that talks of the loss of such autonomy and freedom this is an important benefit, but it needs to happen as a corollary of all the opportunities being offered and supported by those who wish to address devaluation. As we have seen, simply 'abandoning to choice' has been one of the service responses to 'normalisation,' without regard to the development of access to the range of activities that will enable people to make real choices, about which they have some information and personal experience (Peters 1996). This again means that a true interpretation of this theme would not simply 'put' people in normative settings and expect social integration to occur, but must work hard at preparation, support and reinforcement of all the opportunities presented, including account being taken of the experience of vulnerable people in initiating or taking the lead in social contact. In particular, the opportunity to meet as wide a range of people as possible, with attention being paid to enhancing interpersonal identification, is not going to just happen by people being physically present in an integrated setting. It is not going to happen at all in a segregated setting, of course, but the importance of providing the opportunity for mutual relationships to develop is such that detailed attention to all aspects of the encounter is vital.

As well as benefits to vulnerable peoples' competency, social integration and valued social participation also have benefits in terms of their image. It should be clear by now that the proximity of valued people to vulnerable ones, especially if it is in a valued setting, is likely to transfer various aspects of the image of those valued people to the vulnerable. In many integrative settings, many valued roles, with associated valued images, are present. Membership of a sports club, for example, is one such role, but it then offers further roles such as secretary, committee member or even chairperson. So the likelihood of the individual being seen as being part of a set of services available by right to people as members of a community, rather than as some sort of charity, is increased. This in turn is likely to have an effect on the wound of low self esteem, in that seeing themselves in a number of valued settings, with valued people, and in valued roles has a powerful impact on the image that people hold of themselves (Twine 1994). A review of the theme of imagery should demonstrate, once again, that it is the combined effect of the setting, the activities, the expectations and the people with whom one is grouped that affects perceptions of others, which can then emerge as valuing or devaluing. So attention and effort is again required in looking at all aspects of the various opportunities in integrative settings, without assuming that such settings automatically convey positive images. This will be covered in more detail as part of the last theme, the conservatism corollary to SRV.

Benefits to families, and those in close personal relationships with vulnerable people

As the themes of SRV theory overlap and interact, so too do the benefits of social integration, in that many expressions of such integration and valued social participation can have benefits to different people. For families, and those in close personal relationships with vulnerable people, the involvement of one's relation in ordinary, valued activities in ordinary, valued settings can, first of all, be a strong reinforcement of the relationship, and act powerfully against the social pressure, recounted in family studies (e.g. Ayer and Aleszewski 1984; Barnes 1997) to deny or even reject the vulnerable member. The pressure also to keep away from public events, or to be moved, by anger at public reaction, to confrontational tactics, which ultimately reinforce the devaluation of both one's relation and oneself, is much reduced when the vulnerable person, by virtue of increased competencies and expectations such as we have just discussed, does not 'stand out' in the same way. Of course, as we have repeated often, we may wish that this should not be necessary, and in the benefits to society described below it could well be that a greater tolerance of difference emerges. As things stand now in terms of devaluation, families are faced with such pressures almost daily that any reduction in that pressure is welcome. So too, is the feeling that they are not alone, as family members, in trying to help the vulnerable person to be part of their community. In ordinary, valued settings and activities the opportunities for family members of other, less vulnerable, people, similar in age and with possibly similar interests to those of the vulnerable person, to meet and make contact is that much greater, to the extent that families become more identified as themselves, and less as a function of the vulnerable person, something again that family studies have shown is an important issue (Barnes 1997).

Benefits to society, or at least the wider community

As we mentioned above, the increasing presence of vulnerable people in ordinary, valued settings participating in ordinary, valued activities has benefits to the wider community, perhaps even to society as a whole. The vulnerable person or group is, first of all, provided with a much greater opportunity to contribute to their community and society, possibly only in small ways, but possibly, too, in ways in which their particular talents and gifts can be used, something that segregation tends to deny to society, Wolfensberger (1988). As before these talents and gifts are unlikely just to emerge by mere presence, though they cannot emerge at all by segregation, but need support, reinforcement, and a positive interpretation of people to have their fullest effect.

This also goes for the effect of social integration on society in terms of moving it, or at least significant sections of it, to become more tolerant of differences. At an individual level the presence of a vulnerable person in, say, a mainstream school, can have a dramatic effect on particular teachers, breaking down stereotypes and replacing negative expectations with positive ones (Hegarty 1993), but it also introduces, young children naturally to the idea of toleration and valuing of difference, and the many more things that their fellow pupil has in common with them, as opposed to highlighting their differences negatively. Evidence from societies where such integration is more widespread than England, suggests that such results are possible (Inclusion International 1995). In England, as chapter 1 hinted, a period dominated by individualism has had its effects on the school system as elsewhere, and league tables and a national curriculum predicated on certain levels of academic ability have been powerful counter forces to social integration and valued participation in the school system (Fulcher 1989). Nevertheless, where it has occurred, the probability of an effect on society exists.

Where it has occurred, too, there have been some instances where not only the service of education, but other integrated services have been provided to vulnerable people at a lower cost than segregated ones, and this is a third possible benefit to society of social integration. Unfortunately, the 'cost' argument has also been used, in the English experience, both to justify inadequately staffed community based services and, paradoxically, as part of the case of those who would continue segregation. The latter, of course, use costs from the most expensive of community services (Cox and

Pearson 1995), and have been answered by more independently produced figures (Cronshaw 1996), but it is important to bear in mind that cost savings are probably the least of the arguments in favour of social integration. Much more important are the benefits outlined above, most of which have good evidence to support them. It remains to be seen whether a new government, whose commitment, at least in their rhetoric (Blair 1998) to a values position which endorses social integration will find that evidence enables them to put their espoused values into action. More globally, it will be interesting to see if, as part of the so-called 'Third Way' there is a reversion to at least some aspects of the Western Judeo-Christian ideals of mutual assistance, self-sacrifice and responsibility for others, which tie in, at the level of values, with the importance of personal social integration and valued social participation.

Strategies for assisting vulnerable people in achieving social integration

Whatever the global developments, it still seems very likely that devaluation, and vulnerability to it on the part of certain individuals and groups, will continue to be present in our society. So whatever one's individual stance in relation to the historical values of Western society, there is still a reaction at the level of values to devaluation, as we have discussed. Assuming that this reaction, perhaps informed by SRV theory, is to seek to address devaluation, then the theme of social integration offers one of the key strategies suggested by SRV for doing so. Again, these are not the only strategies, and one's values will ultimately determine which of the various courses one adopts. This is especially important in this theme, since details of the strategy have caused some of the key reactions to 'normalisation'. In particular the idea that, as well as looking at the physical location of people, one should also address their personal impression, and as well as ensuring their presence in integrated community facilities one should support and model appropriate behaviour in those settings, has raised accusations of prescriptiveness (Dalley 1992). We have, of course been here before in this book, and it is hoped that the arguments used in a number of chapters, especially those covering the themes of imagery, mindsets and expectancies, role expectancy and interpersonal identification will have convinced the reader that a) SRV is a multilayered understanding of devaluation and its address, which b) reflects observations and evidence from the real world, not the world as one might like it to be and c) leaves those who study it free to decide, on the basis of values, what action to take, if they take any at all, to counter devaluation. What then follows as suggestions for a strategy to assist vulnerable people achieve social integration should not be taken in isolation from the rest of SRV, and should be considered in the light of the readers experience of the real world and their own values.

In fact the strategy will come as no surprise to those who have read thus far. As with other strategies it is based, first of all, on a discerning and detailed examination, with the vulnerable person or group concerned, of their physical and social environment, and the possibilities for social integration and valued social participation that it offers. This includes, of course, a detailed examination, with the person or group themselves, of their own characteristics, wishes, competencies, images and image risks in relation to that physical and social environment.

Issues to consider in the physical environment

Such an analysis can, of course, take place at the planning level for a whole service to a particular group of people, and then be more and more detailed and individualised as the analysis gets closer to the person. At the broad level, it can be subdivided into the headings we have used before, particularly the location, size and features of the physical environment. Even if they knew very little about the individual or group concerned, service planners could pay attention to these issues. They are, of course, some of those contained in the PASSING instrument, and readers who wish to go into the level of detail that is beyond our scope here should refer to that instrument. We will merely point to the effect that the physical environment has on possibilities for integration. It's size will affect both the image of people using it, and therefore the mindsets of those in the locality. Size also affects the potential for individualised activities, which have their effect on the competency of those using the service, and also their potential to get out and use community facilities. Of course, the potential of siting some services actually in community facilities, or indeed of merely integrating the individuals or groups in existing community facilities is also an important consideration for planners, and one which is particularly likely to be a possibility in day services for various groups. Then the location of the physical setting can be examined for its integrative potential. The resources of that location can be such that ease of access is assured, and a range of opportunities opened up.

At the level of an individual service, assuming that it is beyond the planning stage and actually exists, then again there are some issues on the physical environment that relate to integration. The size of the building may be a matter for the planners, but its image, both inside and outside, can be such as to invite people in or put people off. A welcoming environment is far more likely to evince interaction with the community, even in the reserved neighbourhoods of middle England, and within a setting there are many things that can be done to facilitate individual interactions. As we have noted above, however, physical presence, even a welcoming one and one set in a community with many resources, is only the prerequisite to social integration, not a guarantee of it. Increasing the probability of such integration requires the next group of issues, namely actions within the social environment.

Issues to consider in the social environment

More detail can be found in the PASSING instrument, but again there are issues that can be taken up at all levels of a service organisation. Planners, in considering the size and location of the physical environment, also need to consider the social effects of those decisions. The size, number, and make up of groupings and sub-groupings within a service can have a crucial impact on the nature and frequency of social interactions. Large groups of vulnerable people do not, on the whole, produce a positive response from the outside community, so the planner seeking to facilitate integration needs to think small. Even those services who use or are part of community facilities need to be planned on the basis of a close examination of the integrative potential of the ratio of the numbers of vulnerable people and the numbers of the rest of the community using the facility.

At the service unit level, again assuming the overall group size is set, action on sub-group size and individualised activities can have a major effect on the social environment. Support for individuals and groups to take advantages of the facilities in most communities in sufficiently small numbers as to maximise their chances of positive interactions is very important. Unfortunately, many services in the English experience have taken this issue as a reason for not doing anything with people. Because of low staff levels, it has not been possible to use community resources except in groups, so managers have cited 'normalisation' as a reason for keeping people within the physical confines of the service, especially in residential services. So we need to be clear here what SRV is suggesting. Paying attention to grouping issues is important in predicting the likely effect of activities in communal settings, but the detailed analysis, described above, of the physical and social environment of vulnerable people may be such that the weight given to the grouping issue is outweighed by the prospect of people having no possibility of interaction because they are not allowed to go out in a group. Basically, a degree of subtlety and common sense is called for in deciding on a course of action, plus, of course, action much earlier by planners in determining the overall size of the groups concerned, so that front line staff are faced with less 'no-win' situations.

Issues to consider in specific integrative contacts and activities

Assuming that the detailed and discerning analysis of the social and physical environment of individuals and groups has taken place, certain things will have been revealed to work on, in terms of an individual's image and competency, which are more likely to facilitate positive social integration. As we have discussed on the issue of imagery, and in the initial analysis of devaluation, characteristics which elicit negative valuation, reinforce stereotypes and confirm mindsets are very powerful, though it could be wished that the situation was otherwise. In helping people to participate in a valued way, therefore, strategies suggested by SRV include paying attention to personal characteristics, such as grooming, dress, bodily hygiene and social habits. It is ironic that such suggestions have produced howls of outrage from those claiming to represent the interests of vulnerable people, when politicians and others anxious to create a good image spend thousands of pounds on 'image consultants' to pay attention to those very same personal characteristics. Of course, as we have noted already, this is more easily done when vulnerable people are dispersed in communities, rather than being congregated in groups, but even groups of people can be helped in terms of their personal impression and behaviour. Other negative images associated with people which exist in the physical and social environment can also be addressed, including how staff of the service deal with and present the individuals concerned to the community at large. Similarly, developing integrative contacts is much easier if people already have one or more valued roles in a given community, so the potential for confirming or creating these should also be part of the analysis.

Work can also be done, however, on the community outside the service, despite the simplistic account of 'normalisation' that only the vulnerable person is the object of change. One starting point is to look for individuals or groups who share the interests and activities of the vulnerable individuals or groups as revealed by the analysis. In an integrated environment, another is to use the possibilities of 'pairing up' for particular tasks, particularly those where success is reasonably likely and not too taxing. More specifically, eliciting direct long or short term commitments by valued individuals to vulnerable people has been shown, at least through studies of citizen advocacy (Butler et. al. 1988; Simons 1995) to have important spin-offs for integration, as the person making such commitments is usually part of many other community groups, some of which offer potential for the vulnerable person. All of these strategies help in interpersonal identification and, as we state under that theme, need support and reinforcement, in terms of their chances of success.

The whole exercise of social integration is certainly a massive task, and as we noted at the beginning, some services have not attempted it at all, some have given up once the physical presence has been achieved, and some, perhaps many, have struggled with the task and achieved varying levels of success. Yet since, by its very essence, devaluation is about people in a society rejecting other people in that society, an address of devaluation has to try and address that rejection. Those who seek to do that by laws and procedures may well help the process, not least in requiring the presence of devalued people in settings from which they have been excluded, but unless one addresses the minds of those doing the rejecting, the devaluation will still occur, in fact it may build up to resentment of those very laws that force the presence of vulnerable people. That this has happened, to varying degrees, in schools that have had inclusive policies forced upon them, or in societies where policies to close hospitals have resulted in people being 'dumped' on them, is indicative of the power of devaluation. That will not be solved by repealing those laws, nor by returning to the institutions. Instead, SRV would suggest that for social integration and valued societal participation to become a reality, at least for some groups, attention should be paid to all those things which affect devaluation; the physical environment, the social environment and, yes, people's personal presentation and behaviour. The final theme discusses the importance of this attention being paid with great sensitivity.

Introduction to the theme of positive compensation for disadvantage, or the conservatism corollary of SRV

In chapter 3 we noted that, while most people have some experience of some of the wounds of devaluation, usually only occasionally or for a short period of time, the true effect of those wounds on people we have called devalued comes because of the frequency, severity and relentlessness of their application. Devaluation is therefore experienced by such people in so as to become, in some cases, life-defining. Even those without quite this degree of devaluation will have their lives dramatically affected by it. A group, such as people with learning disabilities, that have been or still are systematically and collectively devalued, may have members who only experience a mild degree of personal devaluation. Nearly all the group, however, are likely to have experienced extra 'costs', both financial and psychological, as a result of devaluation, with the same often applying to family and other close relations. Some, especially where the devaluation has been long term, are likely to have developed responses to it that become deeply embedded, and yet which themselves cause further devaluation when they are perceived by the rest of society (see Wolfensberger [1998a] for a more detailed account of individual responses to devaluation.)

When this is combined with the probability that with one set of wounds comes a greater chance of others, against which devalued people have lesser defences, then the need for sensitivity as to the risks of any action referred to in previous themes becomes that much greater. This does not just apply to strategies for social integration, but all the strategies suggested by SRV to address devaluation. Thus many actions that may be ordinary, or even valuing, to most people might only serve to heighten the devaluation of those described above.

This then, is the root of the final theme, and is summed up in a number of phrases from history. *Afflicto afflictio non est addenda* is a Latin tag from early Christianity, that translates as 'one must not further afflict the already afflicted.' 'Don't add insult to injury' is a phrase in more common usage, and the section of the Hippocratic oath, 'at least do no harm', mentioned in chapter 3, is another way of expressing the view, held at least as an ideal in Western societies, that to those already suffering, great care needs to be taken not to make matters worse. This theme takes such ideas further with the notion of positive compensation, whereby devalued people require more than the average or routine option when it comes to enhancing their image and competency, but the best, most valued option to counterbalance as much as possible the negative effect of their wounding experiences.

In the English experience of 'normalisation', extended by assumption to SRV, it is ironic that this theme, which is in effect no more than a rider to bear in mind, when applying the strategies of SRV, should have generated some of the most trenchant criticism. It is possible that, as I suggested in an earlier publication (Race 1987) that the very use of the word conservatism, or conservative, collided with the mindsets of many academics and others suffering the effects of the mid eighties and a Thatcher government in full service cutting flow, but it also seems to be an underlying theme of many critics that such a title reveals the underlying paternalism and maintenance of the status quo of 'normalisation' (Dalley 1992).

As we noted in chapter 1, it also says something about how 'normalisation' was taught and implemented, in certain parts of the country, that action at the level of, usually hypothetical, individuals could be used to challenge a whole theory, as if finding a case that didn't fit disproved the whole edifice. Some of this has been covered in earlier chapters, specifically the notion that SRV is 'imposing' actions on people or that it is not challenging the status quo, and much of it is answered more succinctly in Wolfensberger's 1995 article, 'Is SRV too conservative? No it is too radical' so we will not reiterate those arguments here. What it is important to state however, is the continuing appeal to values in judging actions, and to empiricism when judging theory. The reader should by now be in a position to do the latter, at least as far as SRV is concerned, and is again urged not to be put off by hypothetical 'case-studies'. This last theme should, in fact, be read with the full understanding of the tensions between different actions that may result from the various themes, and taken as an attempt to bring to the discerning analysis of an individual or group's wounds and identities a sensitivity based on the historical maxims cited above.

Implications of the conservatism corollary

Put at its simplest, the conservatism corollary asks that, for each action being considered to address devaluation, the analysis of the individual or group's identities and wounds be used to add what could be called a 'sensitivity test' of the actions. This test then acts as an extra way of judging different actions in terms of their likely effects on devaluation. The test then goes as follows. The more devalued is an individual or group, and the longer they have been so devalued, then the more sensitive should be the judgement of actions in terms of a) preventing further devaluation, b) reducing the devaluation, and vulnerability to it, that already exists, and c) compensating for existing devaluation by choosing the most highly valued option, in terms of image and competency, that is available. Of course this fits entirely with the overall strategy of SRV of enhancing image and competency, to enable more valued roles to be held by people, and thus increase their chances of the 'good things in life' that was discussed in chapter 5, but adds a fine tuning, or extra sensitivity, the more devalued people are.

This means that some conditions or activities that are ordinary, or normative, may, under this extra analysis be not sufficient to address the particular wounds of a devalued person or group. For example, certain normative forms of dress, such as trainers, which are worn by many adults, may reinforce the particular stereotype of an older person or a person with learning disabilities who have been cast into the child role. Or a normative activity, such as a 'quiz night' at a pub, may focus attention on the negatively valued low intellectual ability of a person with learning disabilities. Some normative and even helpful conditions can, in fact, add to the experience of people's wounds by accidentally accentuating a key wound in their life. So when someone who needs help with personal care needs to use public toilets then, even if there is some privacy in an adapted cubicle, the public image of the impairment and their 'dependency' is emphasised. Some normative conditions that impose competency demands on most people can, in addition, actually impair an already diminished competency in devalued people, such as steep steps for someone who has difficulty with heights acting as a pressure to be, or feel, incapable of attempting any stairs.

All of these are exceptional situations, and all may have other benefits that outweigh the costs to the devalued person. What the conservatism corollary asks is that sensitivity and consciousness be applied in weighing up the likely effects. So, if one is following the strategy of addressing a person's personal impression, the conservatism corollary would ask for extra care as to the potential image risks to an already devalued person. When there is a choice of options, the conservatism corollary would suggest the most valued or least risky, in terms of devaluation potential in relation to the particular group or culture into which one is aiming the social integration. This would then influence action even if some other benefits might be greater. Where decisions are being made about grouping of people, the conservatism corollary would suggest extra attention be paid to the make up of the group, in terms of the images that might transfer to devalued people, and that might transfer from valued people.

So all the conservatism corollary is saying, in effect, is be even more aware of devaluation issues when dealing with more devalued people. Such is the complexity of devaluation of course that there will inevitably be occasions where a 'least worst' option results from this analysis, and these contradictions should not be used to prevent good things happening in people's lives. As we have emphasised throughout, SRV has experience of good things as its major goal. What the conservatism corollary provides is a final fine tuning of the detailed analysis of the likely effects of actions on the valuation and devaluation of vulnerable people. Ultimately, those who act on it, as those who act on all SRV strategies, are coming up against the most powerful forces in the opposite direction, namely the forces of societal devaluation. As we have seen, these are largely unconscious, seemingly built into human nature, and act more powerfully on groups than individuals. It therefore requires action at all levels of society to address such forces. Whether the English experience of SRV will encourage people to take such action, and whether such action will be to apply SRV strategies, or something else, remains to be seen. Those who decide not to do so may like to reflect on the high probability that they will fall into at least one of the categories of people vulnerable to devaluation, that is elderly people, and consider the following quotation from Pastor Niemoller, written when devaluation was taking one of its grossest forms.

'First they came for the Jews
And I did not speak out -
Because I was not a Jew

Then they came for the communists
And I did not speak out -
Because I was not a communist.

Then they came for the trade unionists
And I did not speak out -
Because I was not a trade unionist.

Then they came for me -
And there was no one left
To speak out for me.

(Pastor Niemoller 1938, cited in Rosen and Widgery 1991)

11

Conclusion and epilogue

Introduction

Apart from the theoretical and not so theoretical critiques of the English experience of SRV that this book has attempted to address, there is a final, dismissive cry to the effect that there is little evidence that SRV makes a difference in real people's lives. 'It's all just a theory' is the refrain. It would, of course be surprising if SRV alone, like any other set of ideas operating in isolation, could be clearly and solely responsible for developments in people's lives, because ideas (and theories) do not work like that. In the whole range of examples that could be given of some effect of SRV there would, inevitably be other influences at work. This should not, however, be taken to imply that SRV is an impractical theory, with no applicability in the real world unless bolstered by other unrelated actions. Equally, though the account of the 'wounds' given in chapters 3 and 4 gives an understanding of devaluation that is crucial to an appreciation of SRV, that account has been equally crucial, in my view, in leading to other actions to address devaluation. Taking up those other options does not imply a rejection of SRV, nor does success with other options invalidate SRV. Still further, the ten themes outlined above help, as we have said, to deepen our understanding of devaluation and the strategies offered by SRV to address it, but action taken as a result is not dependent upon those ten themes. If it is action following the applications of SRV, towards providing and safeguarding valued roles for people so that they are more likely to have access to the 'good things of life' and if this is done through attention being paid to issues of imagery and competency, then that action is more likely to be informed by the ten themes than other influences, but ultimately people will measure the utility of SRV by the difference those actions make to people's lives, not how rigorously they stuck to one or any of the themes.

SRV, like normalization, has always been intended to be an applied theory, as the account of its primary and secondary goals make clear, but one of the difficulties in writing a book of this kind that attempts to explain

SRV theory is that however clear or otherwise one's explanations are, and however much, as one goes through the theory, one includes examples of aspects of its application or effect in the real world, there is still clamour for definitive examples of the whole theory 'in practice.' This last chapter will largely resist those clamours, for the reasons given above, i.e. that very few actions in the real world of services are solely attributable to one single idea or theory and that acceptance of SRV as a valid theory should not be based solely on examples from real life, with its inherent flaws of understanding and application. What we will do, however, as a prelude to a few concluding remarks on this book and the possibilities of SRV having a place in influencing conditions for devalued people, is to give a couple of examples, one about an individual and one about a service organisation, which resulted, over a significant period of time, in major changes in the lives of vulnerable people. As I write this, the advance programme for the second international conference on SRV, to be held in Boston in June 1999 and entitled 'The Difference SRV Makes' contains the promise of many more real life examples from the range of countries in which SRV has been taught, as well as an examination of the theoretical issues. Readers who wish to look for something beyond the examples from the English experience that I have been able to give in the course of this book may therefore like to look for any published proceedings .

SRV in practice - two stories

The two stories which follow also reiterate the points made in chapter 2 on the relentlessness and universality of devaluation. For though both reveal positive changes in the lives of vulnerable people as a result of SRV, these outcomes have not got rid of devaluation, either in the lives of the individuals concerned or in the wider society. What has happened, though, has made a difference that is unlikely to have occurred without the influence of SRV.

The first story concerns a young man, now in his late teens, who by the help of another individual for most of his school life and in the early part of his time at a Further Education College, was able to be part of his community, despite some impairments that might in other circumstances have resulted in his being completely segregated. In particular, both at home and in school, he would regularly, and without warning, vomit. This was so frequent that over time much physical damage has been done to the young man, and he has been in hospital many times and received all sorts of diagnoses for his condition. As well as the vomiting, mental impairments affected the young man's ability, when younger, to develop either basic academic skills or social skills. His behaviour would cause other children to either be afraid or hostile. When the woman who was to help him came into contact with the family, he was still of primary school age, and was attending a segregated special school, with frequent time out due to sickness. All the devaluing roles were a possibility, and most a reality, for the young man. The sick role, the menace role, the subhuman role, the eternal child role, even at some points the holy innocent role were all cast on him. What happened over the next ten to fifteen years did not, as we noted above, stop all of those role perceptions being held by some people, but did, for some of the time, and for significant periods in his life, give him access to some of the 'good things of life. The woman who helped the young man effectively followed the steps outlined by SRV theory, though of course she would not have articulated it in that way. What she actually did was to spend time with the young boy, first in terms of simply being a friend of the family, then being his classroom assistant for some of the time he spent at the special school. She then strongly advocated for, and obtained, time for him first at the mainstream primary school, and later at a mainstream secondary school. This was never completely full-time , and there were many battles and setbacks over the years. The young man did, however, get to the point where his vomiting was drastically reduced, where some of the rudiments of academic skills were attained, and where the expectations of social behaviour of a mainstream school pupil were sufficient to develop in him a range of social skills. When I met him, in his early teens, the impression that presented itself to me was of a maturing young man, well behaved and interesting to talk to, with a number of attributes that I could compare positively with my own teenage sons.

The second story concerns an organisation, originally set up in the early seventies by parents of children with learning disabilities to provide what was called 'respite care.' The organisation, as so many services were, was based around a building, a large Victorian house in the suburbs of a major city. The service housed up to thirteen people at any one time, mostly children. By the time the organisation was set up as a limited company in 1990, following the broader developments in services described in chapter 1, many of the original children had grown to be adults, and new young children had come on to the books. This presented, in SRV terms, all the devaluing possibilities of a segregated setting, with a grouping of young children, teenagers and even older people under one roof and in numbers which meant that most of the activities that took place were within the house. Increasingly, parents of younger children saw dangers in the often bored and restless activities of the older people, and therefore stopped using the service. The service system increasingly saw the house as a resource to ease some of their own pressures as more adults came out of hospital. So the manager undertook a major review of what was going on, again with strong influence from SRV, though other guides to action were also examined and utilised. Part of this review involved detailed discussions with a wide range of people, including the people with learning disabilities who used the service. The result has been a major change in all the aspects of the service that convey role messages about those who use it. Changes took place in the setting, in that the large house gradually ceased being used for respite care and eventually became offices, with the residential part of the service being replacing by smaller satellite houses. There were also changes in the groupings of the service, in that much more attention was paid to normative age groupings for certain parts, and individualised attention in others. Activities, too, changed considerably, in that the visits to the service were much more focused on individualised activities in integrated settings. One young man, for example, was helped to join the local air cadets, trained for a number of the aircraft recognition and other technical exams and was fully involved with the other cadets of his own age. Another teenager, who had come to the service with a great deal of hostility and anger, refusing to go out of the big house, was gradually introduced to being with other teenagers in ordinary settings, which initially involved two support workers being with her, to the extent that she was later able to go away from her town for a weekend holiday. The service began to develop networks of exchanges with other such services, enabling people to visit parts of the country that they had never seen and to which they would rarely have been able to afford to go. The service expanded, attracted back the parents of young children, and is recognised at least locally as providing positive options for people with learning disabilities.

These two examples at least show the chance of success in addressing devaluation by applying SRV measures. The scale of the two is different but both started by a very clear examination, including the vulnerable people involved, of the 'risk' factors for those people, of their current roles, and current social standing. For the young man at the start of this chapter these were largely negative, as we explained. For those attending the respite service before its review, roles and social standing were equally negative, especially with regard to the 'child role' and the 'menace role' By focusing on what they were able to address, and not trying to change the world, the woman who helped the young man and the manager of the residential service were able to achieve a great deal. For the young man, moving him, at least for part of the time, to the valued role of mainstream pupil with all the attendant expectations and opportunities to imitate appropriate social behaviour had a major impact. Changing the perception of those using the residential service from being 'respite residents' to 'guests' or 'visitors' again resulted in changed expectations and activities that related more to the sort of things one would do with visitors than 'service users'. Trying to address the young man's vomiting by clear expectation and modeling was some defense against his falling further into the sick role, and by separating this role to those occasions when real medical intervention was needed, even the playing of this role became a less devaluing aspect of his life. By focusing on changing from the large building to the smaller ones and looking at spending time in integrated settings, the former respite service prevented, to some extent, those using the service from falling into further devalued roles, particularly a deepening of the 'eternal child' role or becoming seen as an 'object of charity'. The young man was enabled to enter some positively valued new roles, such as college student, member of a teenage group, as were many of the users of the service, such as the person mentioned above. The service also, by varying the options available to people and involving them in the changes, was able to reduce some of the negativity inherent in the role of 'service user' Exchanging the role of visitor with some aspects of the role of host, as occurred in the network that the service began to set up, was another SRV strategy that was demonstrated in practice. Overall, therefore, although not specifically expressed in this way by the people concerned, both the story of the young man and of the former respite service illustrate the potential for increased access to some of the good things of life that a strategy of creating, enhancing and defending valued social roles for people can bring. So the reader is asked to bear this in mind, though as noted above not to focus totally on these examples, when considering their response to the theory that this book has tried to explain. We end with some thoughts on the possibilities for its future, both as an academic theory and as something that can affect people's lives.

Epilogue : 'From normalisation to where?' - How about SRV?

This book set out with the two objectives of providing a detailed, though not definitive, account of SRV theory and a response to what has almost become the 'accepted wisdom' in academic circles in England, that 'normalisation,' which encompasses SRV in the thinking of those circles, is either finished, outdated, or only applies to services for people with learning disabilities. Two recently published textbooks illustrate the tendency, in the current English experience, to accept second or third hand sources and opinions on 'normalisation.' In one, Clarke and Clarke dismiss SRV without citing any supporting sources, as a 'moralistic stance with an allegedly scientific basis' (Clarke & Clarke 1998, p20). In another Barnes and Oliver (1998, p52), the critics of 'normalisation' are cited as authorities on the work of the 'Canadian theorist' [sic] Wolfensberger, and all the familiar criticisms that we have covered in this book are produced, with the whole of 'normalisation's' contribution being dismissed in two pages. Ironically, there is acknowledgment, by reference to Wolfensberger's other work, that he, like them, believes that forces beyond the individual may be at work in devaluation, though even here what is cited as 'later work' is something that Wolfensberger has been discussing and publishing about for many years (see, for example, Wolfensberger 1983b).

These are only the latest examples of the reaction from various quarters to 'normalisation' and the reality of the power, both perceived and real, that it had over services in the English experience.

Chappell's 1997 paper, whose title forms the first part of the heading of this epilogue, continues this accepted wisdom, and then goes on to criticise what she takes as the accepted successor, the so-called social theory of disability, for not 'including' people with learning disabilities.

It is hoped that those critics, as well as getting Wolfensberger's nationality right, will at least consider the notion that there is a distinction between normalization and SRV, and that this book will help them to do that, but that it will also help them to consider whether their criticisms of 'normalisation' still apply in the case of SRV theory. For many, the lack of a 'stance' from SRV on the relative power position of those receiving services and those delivering them will still lead to rejection, even if they acknowledge the reality of devaluation and wounding. To those all one can say is that moral outrage is fine for generating action, but can also be very debilitating if that action is confined to refusal to engage with the 'wicked world', because that world is where vulnerable people are. SRV theory is offered as an analysis of that real world, with some strategies to address the devaluation that it contains, especially but far from exclusively within the service system. Let it be said for the last time in this book, however, that SRV does not dictate the final actions of individuals and groups to address devaluation, they are determined by reference to values.

There will be others reading this book, however, to whom its first objective is much more important. They will be those who have either not heard of SRV, or have only come across it as enshrined in mission statements or job descriptions, sometimes with a very tenuous connection to the theory outlined in the previous ten chapters. To those, the account of the theory is offered as something to reflect on and explore, alongside other theories such as the social theory of disability, and see how it accords with their everyday reality. In particular, those from other service fields than learning disability can come to this reflection without the baggage that the English experience of 'normalisation' has cast around the neck of that particular area of human services. As this is written, there are signs of a small, but growing interest in the theory from people involved in the mental health field, and also those involved with elderly people, and it may be through that channel that an alternative academic reaction, as well as an effect on individuals and services, can come. It is hoped that those who look for more opportunities for reading will follow the advice in the prologue, and complement this book with study of Wolfensberger's 1998 monograph, and those who want a more interactive analysis will seek out SRV, PASS and PASSING workshops, which still take place at various locations in the UK, to compare their understanding of the theory with others, and to see the possibilities of SRV in practice.

For both groups, the book is offered as a contribution, not an answer, to efforts to engage with the reality of devaluation and the effects it has on the lives of many people. If it recruits one more person to those efforts, then regardless of its academic acceptability the effort will have been worthwhile.

References

Acts of Parliament
Mental Deficiency Act (1913), London, HMSO.
Education (Handicapped Children) Act (1971), London, HMSO
National Health Service and Community Care Act (1990), London, HMSO
Mental Health Act (1959), London, HMSO

Abberley, P. (1987) The concept of oppression and the development of a social theory of disability, *Disability, Handicap and Society*, 2 (1), 5-22.

Abrahams, R., Metiuk, O., and Race, D.G. (1996) Threats to the lives of devalued and vulnerable people: the potential victim's viewpoint, in: Adams, R. (ed.) *Crisis in Human Services: National and International Issues* - selected papers from a conference held at the University of Cambridge, September 1996, Lincoln, The University of Lincolnshire and Humberside.

Abrams, D. and Hogg, M. (eds.) (1990) *Social Identity Theory*. Hemel Hempstead, HarvesterWheatsheaf.

Airedale NHS Trust v Bland (1993) (The Tony Bland Case) 2 WLR, 316

Aleszewski, A & Ong, B.N. (1990) *Normalisation in Practice: Residential care for children with profound mental handicap*, London, Routledge

Alvarado, M. and Thompson, J. (eds.) (1990) *The Media Reader*, London, British Film Institute.

Angers, M. (1992) 'Created' Communities and 'Natural' Community. Special Issue: The Clubhouse Model, *Psychosocial Rehabilitation Journal*, 16(2) 117-123.

Atkinson, D. and Williams, F. (eds) (1990) *Know me as I am - an anthology of prose, poetry and painting by people with learning difficulties*, London, Hodder and Stoughton.

Ayer, S. and Aleszewski, A. (1984) *Community Care and the Mentally Handicapped:*

Baldwin, S. (1985) Sheep in wolf's clothing: Impact of normalisation teaching on human service providers, *Int. J. Rehab. Research*, 8(2) 131-142.

Baldwin, S. (1989) Applied Behaviour Analysis and Normalization: New Carts for Old Horses, *Behavioural Psychotherapy*, 17, 305-308.

Baldwin, S. & Hattersley, J. (1991) *Mental Handicap: Social science perspectives*, London, Tavistock/Routledge

Baldwin, S. and Stowers, C. (1987) Normalisation and Elderly Persons: In Whose Best Interests? *American Archives of Rehabilitation Therapy*, Spring, 34-42.

Bano, A., Crosskill, D., Patel, R., Rashman, L. and Shah, R. (1993) Dark Shadows on a White Wall: A Black Perspective on Wolfensberger's Theory of Normalisation, in: Bano, A., Crosskill, D., Patel, R., Rashman, L. and Shah, R., *Improving Practice for People with Learning Disabilities*, London, Central Council for Education and Training in Social Work.

Barnes, C. (1990) *Cabbage Syndrome: The Social Construction of Dependency*, London, Falmer Press.

Barnes, C. and Oliver, M. (1998) *Disabled people and Social Policy: From Exclusion to*

*Inclusion,*Longman Social Policy in Britain Series, Harlow, Addison Wesley Longman.

Barnes, M (1997) Families and Empowerment, in:Ramcharan, P., Roberts, G., Grant, G. and Borland, J (eds.) (1997) *Empowerment in Everyday Life: Learning Disability,* London, Jessica Kingsley.

Barton, L. (ed.) (1996) *Disability and Society: Emerging Issues and Insights,* London, Longman.

Bayley, J. (1998) *A Memoir of Iris Murdoch,* London, Duckworth.

Bayley, M. (1973) *Mental Handicap and Community Care: a study of mentally handicapped people in Sheffield,* London, Routledge & Kegan Paul.

Bayley, M. (1991) Normalisation or 'Social Role Valorisation': an adequate philosophy?, in Baldwin, S. & Hattersley, J. (1991) *Mental handicap: Social science perspectives,* London, Tavistock/Routledge.

Bayley, M. (1997) Empowering and Relationships, in: Ramcharan, P., Roberts, G., Grant, G. and Borland, J (eds.) (1997) *Empowerment in Everyday Life: Learning Disability,* London, Jessica Kingsley

Bechtel, W. (1990) Connectionism and the Philosophy of Mind: An Overview, in: Lycan, W.G. (ed.) *Mind and Cognition - A Reader,* Oxford, Blackwell.

Bignell, J. (1997) *Media Semiotics - an introduction,* Manchester, Manchester University Press.

Blair, A. (1998) Speech to Labour Party Conference, Blackpool, September 1998.

Blonsky, M.(ed.) (1985) *On Signs: A Semiotics Reader,* Oxford, Blackwell.

Blunden, R. & Smith,H. (1988) Leaving long-stay hospitals; caring in patches, *Community Care Supplement,* 27 Oct, i-ii

Booth, A. (1988) Challenging Conceptions of Integration, in Barton, L.(ed) *The Politics of Special Educational Needs.* Lewes, Falmer Press

Booth, T., Simons, K., and Booth, W. (1990) *Outward Bound: Relocation and community care for people with learning difficulties,* Milton Keynes, Open University Press.

Borland, J. and Ramcharan, P. (1997) Empowerment in informal settings: the themes, in: Ramcharan, P., Roberts, G., Grant, G. and Borland, J (eds.) (1997) *Empowerment in Everyday Life: Learning Disability,* London, Jessica Kingsley

Brandon, D. (1991) *Innovation Without Change: Consumer power in psychiatric services,* London, Macmillan.

Brechin, A. & Walmsley, J.(eds)(1989) *Making connections; reflecting on the lives and experience of people with learning disabilities,* London, Routledge

Brown, H. (1994) 'An Ordinary Sexual Life': a review of the normalisation principle as it applies to the sexual options of people with learning disabilities, *Disability, Handicap and Society,* 4(2), 123-44.

Brown, H. and Smith, H. (1989) Whose Ordinary Life is it anyway? - a feminist critique of the normalisation principle, *Disability, Handicap and Society,* 4(2), 105-19.

Brown, H. and Smith, H. (1992a) Postscript, in: Brown, H. and Smith, H. (eds.) *Normalisation, A Reader For The Nineties,* London, Routledge.

Brown, H. and Smith, H. (1992b) Assertion, not assimilation. in: Brown, H. and Smith, H. (eds.) *Normalisation, a Reader for the Nineties,* London, Routledge.

Brown, R. (1996) Intergroup Relations, in: Hewstone, M., Stroebe, W. and Stephenson, G.M. (eds.) *Introduction to Social Psychology,* 2nd Edition, Oxford, Blackwell.

Burda, M. and Wyplosz, C. (1997) *Macroeconomics: A European Text,* 2nd Edition, Oxford, Oxford University Press.

Burton, M. (1994) Towards an alternative basis for policy and practice in community care. *Care in Place ,* 1(2)

Butcher, T. (1995) *Delivering welfare; the governance of the Social Services in the 1990's.* Buckingham, Open University Press

Butler, K., Carr, S., and Sullivan, F. (1988) *Citizen Advocacy: A Powerful Partnership,* London, National Citizen Advocacy.

Campaign for the Mentally Handicapped (1973) *Listen: a weekend conference held at the Greenwood Centre.* London, CMH Publications.

Capie A.C.M., Taylor P.D. & Perkins E.A. (1980) *Teaching Basic Behavioural Principles,* Kidderminster, B.I.M.H.

Carling, A. (1991) *Social Division,* London, Verso.

Cattermole, M., Jahoda, A., and Markova, I. (1988) Leaving Home: the experience of people with a mental handicap, *Journal of Mental Deficiency Research,* 32, 46-57.

Chappell, A.L. (1992) Towards a Sociological Critique of the Normalisation Principle, *Disability, Handicap and Society,* 7(1), 25-51.

Chappell, A.L. (1997) From Normalisation to Where? in Barton, L. & Oliver, M. (eds) *Disability Studies: Past, Present and Future,* Leeds, The Disability Press.

Clarke A.D. B. (1966) *Recent Advances in the Study of Subnormality,* National Association for Mental Health

Clarke A.M. & Clarke A.D.B. (1958) *Mental Deficiency: The changing outlook* (1st ed.) London, Methuen.

Clarke A.M. & Clarke A.D.B. (1974) *Mental Deficiency: The changing outlook* (3rd ed.) London, Methuen

Clarke, A.M. and Clarke, A.D.B. (1996) The Historical Context. in: Stratford, B. and Gunn, P.(eds.) *New Approaches to Down Syndrome,* London, Cassell.

Comley J. (ed.) (1975) *Behaviour Modification with the Retarded Child,* London, Heinemann Medical

Condor, S. (1990) Social Stereotypes and Social Identity, in: Abrams, D. and Hogg, M. (eds) *Social Identity Theory: Constructive and critical advances,* Hemel Hempstead, Harvester Wheatsheaf.

Cooper, R (1990) Organization/disorganization, in: Hassard, J. and Pym, D. (eds.) *The theory and philosophy of organizations: Critical issues and new perspectives,* London, Routledge.

Cox, C. and Pearson, M. (1995) *Made to Care,* London, The Rannoch Trust.

Cronshaw, P. (1996) *Residential Provision for People with Learning Disabilities: Report of a research study into the cost of village communities,* Economics and Operational Research Division at the Department of Health with the Personal Social Services Research Unit, University of Kent, London, Department of Health.

Crossman, R. (1977) *The Diaries of a Cabinet Minister,* Vol 3, London Hamish Hamilton.

Cuff, E.C., Sharrock, W.W., and Francis, D.W. (1992) *Perspectives in Sociology,* 3rd Edition, London, Routledge.

Dalley, G. (1992) Social Welfare Ideologies and Normalisation, in: Brown, H. and Smith, H. (eds.) *Normalisation, A Reader For The Nineties,* London, Routledge.

Dawson, A.D. (1996) *The Two Faces of Economics,* London, Longman.

Decalmer, P. and Glendinning F (1997) *The Mistreatment of Elderly People,* London, Sage.

Denham, M.J. (ed.) (1997) *Continuing Care for Older People,* Cheltenham, Stanley Thomas.

Department of Health and Social Security (1971) *Better Services for the Mentally Handicapped,* London, HMSO

Department of Health and Social Security (1973) *Local Authority Building Note No. 2,*

London, HMSO

Eayrs, C. and Ellis, N. (1990) Charity Advertising - for or against people with mental handicap, *Brit.J.Social Psychology*, 29(4) 349-66.

Eco, U. (1977) *A Theory of Semiotics*, London, Macmillan.

Elks, M.A. (1994) Valuing the Person or Valuing the Role? Critique of Social Role Valorization Theory, *Mental Retardation*, 32(4) 265-71.

Emerson, E. (1992) What is Normalisation, in Brown, H. & Smith, H. (eds) *Normalisation: A reader for the nineties*. London, Routledge.

Emerson, E. and McGill, P. (1989a) Normalization and Applied Behaviour Analysis: Values and Technology in Services for People with Learning Difficulties, *Behavioural Psychotherapy*, 17, 107-17.

Emerson, E. and McGill, P. (1989b) Normalization and Applied Behaviour Analysis: Rapprochment or Intellectual Imperialism? *Behavioural Psychotherapy*, 17(4) 309-13.

Evans, K. (1985) *The Development and Structure of the English School System*, London, Hodder and Stoughton.

Fiedler, K. (1996) Processing Social Information, in: Hewstone, M., Stroebe, W. and Stephenson, G.M. (eds.) *Introduction to Social Psychology*, 2nd Edition, Oxford, Blackwell.

Fiske, S.T. and Taylor, S.E. (1991) *Social Cognition* (2nd Edn.), London, Mcgraw Hill.

Firth, H. and Rapley, J. (1990) *From Acquaintance to Friendship: Issues for People with Learning Disabilities*, Kidderminster, BIMH Publications.

Flaker, V. (1994) On the Values of Normalization, *Care in Place*, Vol. 1, Number 3.

Fleming, I. and Kroese, B.S. (1993) *People with Learning Disability and Severe Challenging Behaviour: New developments in services and therapy*, Manchester, Manchester University Press.

Foss, N.J. and Knudsen, C. (1996) *Towards a Competence Theory of the Firm*, London, Routledge.

Friere, P. (1972) *Cultural Action For Freedom*, Harmondsworth, Penguin

Fulcher, G. (1989) Integrate and Mainstream? Comparative issues in the politics of these policies, in: Barton, L. (ed.) *Integration: Myth or reality?*, Lewes, The Falmer Press.

Gabriel, Y and Lang, T. (1995) *The Unmanageable Consumer: Contemporary consumption and its fragmentations*, London, Sage Publications.

Garling, T. and Evans, G. (1991) *Environment, Cognition and Action: An Integrated Approach*, Oxford, Oxford University Press.

Gibson, E.J. (1991) *An Odyssey in Learning and Perception, A Bradford Book*, Cambridge MA, The MIT Press.

Gilbert, T. (1993) Learning Disability Nursing: from normalisation to materialism - towards a new paradigm, *Journal of Advanced Nursing*, 18, 1604-9.

Gilleard, C. (1994) Physical abuse in homes and hospitals, in: Eastman, M. (ed) *Old Age Abuse: A new perspective*, London, Age Concern England/ Chapman and Hall.

Gilroy, P. (1997) Diaspora and the Detours of Identity, in: Woodward, K. (ed.) *Identity and Difference*, London, Sage Publications

Goffman, E. (1961) *Asylums*, New York, Anchor.

Goffman, E. (1963) *Stigma: Notes on the management of spoiled identity*, New York, Prentice-Hall.

Goffman, E. (1974) *Frame Analysis: An essay on the organization of experience*, New York, Harper and Row.

Gunzburg, H.C. (1968) *Social Competence and Mental Handicap*, London, Balliere, Tindall and Cassell.

Gunzburg, H. C. (1970a) Editorial, *British Journal of Mental Subnormality*, Dec 1970

Gunzburg, H.C. (1970b) The Hospital as a Normalising Training Environment. *British Journal of Mental Subnormality*. Dec 1970

Gunzburg H.C. (ed.) (1973) *Advances in the Care of the Mentally Handicapped*, London, Bailliere Tindall

Gunzburg, H.C. (1978) Editorial, *British Journal of Mental Subnormality*, Vol 24 Pt 1

Gunzburg H.C. & Gunzburg A.L. (1973) *Mental Handicap and Physical Environment: the application of an operational philosophy to planning*, London, Bailliere Tindall

Hadley, R. and Clough, R. (1996) *Care in Chaos: frustration and challenge in community care*, London, Cassell.

Hall, S. (ed.) (1997) *Representation: cultural representations and signifying practices*, London, Sage/ The Open University.

Handy, C. (1984) *Taken for Granted; Understanding Schools as Organisations*, York, Longman.

Hansard (1998) *The Welfare of former British Child Migrants*, Select Committee on Health Third Report, London, HMSO

Harris, J. (1985) *The Value of Life*, London,Routledge.

Hastie, R. (1980) Memory for information that confirms or contradicts a general impression, in: Hastie, R., Ostrom, T.M., Ebbeson, E.B., Wyer, R.S, Hamilton, D.L.and Carlston, D.E. (eds) *Person Memory: The cognitive basis of social perception*, Hillsdale NJ, Erlbaum.

Hattersley, J. (1991) The future of normalisation, in: Baldwin, S. and Hattersley, J. (eds.) *Mental Handicap: Social science perspectives*, London, Tavistock/Routledge.

Hatton, C. & Emerson, E. (1996) *Residential Provision for people with learning disabilities: A review of research*. Manchester, Hester Adrian Research Centre.

Hegarty, S. (1993) *Meeting Special Needs in Ordinary Schools*, 2nd Edition, London, Cassell.

Heller, H.W., Spooner, F., Enright, B.E., Haney, K. and Schilit, J. (1991) Classic Articles: A Reflection into the field of Mental Retardation, *Education and Training in Mental Retardation*, 26(2), 202-6.

Heron, A. & Myers, M. (1983) *Intellectual impairment: The battle against handicap*. NY/ London, Academic Press

Hilliard L.T. & Kirman B.H. (1965) *Mental Deficiency* (2nd. ed) , London, Churchill

Hirschi, T. and Gottfriedson, M. (1994) *The Generality of Deviance*, New Brunswick, Transaction Publishers.

Hobson, R.P. (1993) *Autism and the Development of Mind*, Hove, Lawrence Erlbaum Associates.

Hogg, J. (1995) Assessment methods and professional directions, in: Malin, N. (ed.) *Services for people with learning disabilities*, London, Routledge.

Hogg, M. and Vaughan, G.A. (1995) *Social Psychology: An Introduction*, London, Prentice Hall/Harvester Wheatsheaf.

Home Office, Department of Education and Science, Ministry of Housing and Local Government, Ministry of Health (1968) *Report of the Committee on Local Authority and Allied Personal Social Services* (The Seebohm Report), Command 3703, London HMSO

Howe Report (1969) *Report of the Committee of Inquiry into Allegations of Ill-treatment of Patients and other Irregularities at the Ely Hospital*, Cardiff (chairman: Geoffrey

Howe), London, HMSO

Inclusion International (1995) *Inclusion (ILSMH News)*, May, No 17.

Jackson, R. (1994) The Normalisation Principle: Back to Basics?, *British Journal of Developmental Disabilities*, 40(2), 175-9

Jay Committee (1979) *Report of the Committee of Enquiry into Mental Handicap Nursing and Care*, Command 7468-I, London, HMSO

Jay, P with Tizard, J (1996) EXODUS: Bringing children out of hospital. in: Mittler, P. with Sinason V. (eds) *Changing Policy and Practice for People with Learning Disabilities*, London, Cassell

Jenkins, P. (1998) *An Introduction to Social Role Valorisation - A Package of Information to Promote Education in Social Role Valorisation*, prepared for the course on SRV, Plymouth, March 1998, (unpublished)

Johansen, L.N. (1986) Welfare State Regression in Scandinavia? The Development of the Scandinavian Welfare States from 1970 to 1980, in: Oyen, E. (ed.) *Comparing Welfare States and their futures*, Aldershot, Gower.

Jones, K. (1971) *A History of the Mental Health Services*, London, Routledge and Kegan Paul.

Jones, R. and Withers, J. (1991) Normalisation and Clinical Psychology: From Infatuation to Scepticism, *Clinical Psychology Forum*, 35(9), 18-20

Kiernan C. & Woodford F.P. (1974) *Behaviour Modification with the Severely Retarded:* Study Group 8 of the Institute for Research into Mental and Multiple Handicap, Oxford, North-Holland Publishing Co.

King R.D., Raynes N.V. & Tizard J. (1971) *Patterns of Residential Care: Sociological studies in institutions for handicapped children*, London, Routledge, Kegan Paul

King's Fund Centre (1980) *An Ordinary Life; Comprehensive Locally-based Residential Services for Mentally Handicapped people*. London, King's Fund Centre

Klein R.D. (1973) *Behaviour Modification in Educational Settings*, Manchester University Library.

Korman, N. and Glennerster, H. (1990) *Hospital Closure: A political and economic study*, Milton Keynes, Open University Press.

Kovel, J. (1988) *White Racism: A psychohistory*, London, Free Association Books.

Kuhn, T.S. (1970) *The Structure of Scientific Revolution* - 2nd Edition (enlarged), Chicago;London, University of Chicago Press.

Kushlick A., Felce D., Palmer J. & Smith J. (1976) *Evidence to the Committee of Inquiry into Mental Handicap Nursing and Care from the Health Care Evaluation Research Team*, Winchester, HCERT

Kushnick, L. (1998) *Race, Class and Struggle: Essays on Racism and Inequality in Britain, the US and Western Europe*, London, Rivers Oram Press.

Laclau, E. (1990) *New Reflections on the Revolution of our Time*, London, Verso.

Lemay, R.A. (1995) Normalization and Social Role Valorization, in: Dell Orto, A.E., and Marinelli, R.P. (eds), *Encyclopedia of Disability and Rehabilitation*, pp 515-521. New York: Simon and Schuster.

Lemay, R.A. (1996) *Social Role Valorization and the principle of normalization: Guidelines for the implementation of social contexts and human services for people at risk of social devaluation*. SRV/VRS Vol 2.2..

Lemay, R.A. (in press) Roles, identities and expectancies: Contributions of role theory to Social Role Valorization Theory, in: Flynn, R.J. and Lemay, R.A. (eds), *Twenty-five years of normalization and Social Role Valorization: Past accomplishments and future prospects*, Ottawa, Canada, University of Ottawa Press.

Levy, A. and Kahan, B. (1991) *The Pindown Experience and the Protection of Children: The report of the Staffordshire Child Care Inquiry*, 1990, Stafford, Staffordshire County Council.

Lewis, J. & Glennerster, H. (1996) *Implementing the New Community Care*, Buckingham, Open University Press

Lewis, D. (1990) What Experience Teaches, in: Lycan, W.G. (ed.) *Mind and Cognition - A Reader*, Oxford, Blackwell.

Lifton, R.J. (1987) *The Nazi Doctors: Medical killing and the psychology of genocide*, London, Papermac.

Lindley, P. & Wainwright, A. (1992) Normalisation training: conversion or commitment? in Brown, H. & Smith, H. (eds) *Normalisation: A reader for the nineties*, London, Routledge

Lister, R. (1990) *The Exclusive Society: Citizenship and the Poor*, London, Child Poverty Action Group.

Llewelyn-Davies, Weeks Forester-Walker & Bor (Company) (1971) *Building for Mentally Handicapped People*, Report for DHSS, London HMSO

Loizos , P. (1996) How Ernest Gellner got mugged on the streets of London, or: civil society, the media and the quality of life, in: Hann, C. and Dunn, E. (eds.) *Civil Society: Challenging Western models*, London, Routledge.

Lycan, W.G. (1990) *Mind and Cognition: A Reader*, Oxford, Basil Blackwell.

Lynch, B. and Perry, P. (1992) *Experiences of Community Care: Case Studies of UK Practice*, London, Longman.

Maclean, M. and Groves, D. (eds.) (1991) *Women's Issues in Social Policy*, London, Routledge.

Macmillan, M. (1992) The Sources of Freud's methods for gathering and evaluating clinical data, in: Gelfand, T and Kerr, J. (eds.) *Freud and the History of Psychoanalysis*, Hillsdale NJ, The Analytic Press.

Marques, J.M. (1990) The black-sheep effect: out-group homogeneity in social comparison settings. in: Abrams, D. and Hogg, M.A.(eds.) *Social Identity Theory*, Hemel Hempstead, Harvester Wheatsheaf.

Martin, J. (1984) *Hospitals in Trouble*, London, Blackwell.

Martin, J. (1990) Breaking up the mono-method monopolies in organizational analysis, in: Hassard, J. and Pym, D. (eds.) *The Theory and Philosophy of Organizations: Critical issues and new perspectives*, London, Routledge.

McCourt Perring, C. (1993) *The Experience of Psychiatric Hospital Closure: An anthropological study*, Aldershot, Avebury.

McGill, P. and Cummings, R. (1990) An analysis of the representation of people with mental handicaps in a British newspaper, *Mental Handicap Research*, 3(1) 60-69.

McGill, P. and Emerson, E. (1992) Normalisation and applied behaviour analysis: Values and technology in human services, in: Brown, H. and Smith, H. (eds.) *Normalisation, A Reader for the nineties*, London, Routledge.

McKnight, J (1995) *The Careless Society: Community and its counterfeits*, New York, Basic Books.

Mickelson, R.A. (1992) Why does Jane read and write so well? The anomoly of women's achievement, in: Wrigley, J.(ed.) *Education and Gender Equality*, London, The Falmer Press.

Miller, A. (1982) *In the Eye of the Beholder: Contemporary issues in stereotyping*, New York, Praeger.

Moore, M., Beazley, S. and Maelzer, J. (1998) *Researching Disability Issues*, Buckingham,

Open University Press.

Morris, J. (1991) *Pride Against Prejudice: Transforming attitudes to disability*, London, The Women's Press.

Morris, P. (1969) *Put Away: A sociological study of institutions for the mentally retarded*, London, Routledge & Kegan Paul.

Nirje, B. (1970) The Normalisation Principle - Implications and comments, *British Journal of Mental Subnormality*, Dec 1970

Noakes, J. (eds.) *Challenging Behaviour in Schools: Teacher support, practical techniques and policy development*, London, Routledge.

North Western Regional Health Authority (1983) *Services for People with Mental Handicap: A model district service*, Manchester, NWRHA

Norwich, B. (1990) *Special Needs in Ordinary Schools: Reappraising Special Needs Education*, Special Needs in Ordinary Schools Series, London, Cassell Educational.

O'Brien, J. (in press) Education in applying the Principle of Normalization as a factor in the practical arts of improving services for socially devalued people, in: Flynn, R.J. and Lemay, R.A. (eds), *Twenty-five years of Normalization and Social Role Valorization: Past accomplishments and future prospects*, Ottawa, Canada, University of Ottawa Press.

O'Brien, J. and Lovett, H. (1993) *Finding a way towards everyday lives: The contribution of person-centred planning*, Harrisburg PA, Department of Public Welfare.

O'Brien, J. & O'Brien, C.L. (1989) *Framework for Accomplishment*. Version 1, Responsive Systems Associates. Georgia

O'Connor, N & Tizard J (1956) *The Social Problem of Mental Deficiency*, London, Pergamon Press.

Oliver, M. (1990) *The Politics of Disablement*, London, Macmillan.

Oliver, M. (1996) *Understanding Disability: From theory to practice*, London, Macmillan.

Oswin, M. (1971) *The Empty Hours*, London, Allen Lane

Oswin, M. (1984) *They Keep Going Away*, London, King Edward's Hospital Fund.

Palmer, J. (1994) *Taking Humour Seriously*, London, Routledge.

Perrin, B. and Nirje, B. (1985) Setting the Record Straight: a critique of frequent misconceptions of the normalization principle, *Australia and New Zealand Journal of Developmental Disabilities*, 11(2), 69-74.

Peters, S. (1996) The politics of disability identity, in: Barton, L. (ed.) *Disability and Society: Emerging issues and insights*, Harlow, Addison Wesley Longman.

Pilling, D. (1995) Do PASS and PASSING pass? in: Pilling, D. and Watson, G. (eds) *Evaluating Quality in Services for Disabled and Older People*, London, Jessica Kingsley

Pilling, D., and Watson, G. (eds) (1995) *Evaluating Quality in Services for Disabled and Older People*. London, Jessica Kingsley.

Pinker, R. (1971) *Social Theory and Social Justice*, London, Heinemann.

Pinker, S. (1994) *The Language Instinct: The new science of language and mind*, London, Allen Lane/ The Penguin Press.

Pizzat F.J. (1974) *Behaviour Modification in Residential Treatment for Children*. Manchester University Library.

Race, D.G. (1977) *Investigation into the effects of different caring environments on the social competence of mentally handicapped adults*, Unpublished PhD Thesis, University of Reading.

Race, D.G. (1987) Normalisation - Theory and Practice, in: Malin, N. (ed.) *Reassessing Community Care*, London, Croom Helm.

Race, D.G. (1995) Historical development of service provision, in Malin N (ed) *Services for People with Learning Disabilities,* London, Routledge.

Race, D.G. (1999) Values and services: in Malin, N. Manthorpe, J., Race, D.G. and Wilmot, S., *Community Care for Nurses and the Caring Professions,* Buckingham, Open University Press.

Race, D.G. and Race, D.M. (1979), *The Cherries Group Home: A Beginning,* London, H.M.S.O.

Ramcharan, P., Roberts, G., Grant, G. and Borland, J (eds.) (1997) *Empowerment in Everyday Life: Learning disability,* London, Jessica Kingsley.

Ramon, S. (1988) Skills for Normalisation Work, *Practice,* 2(2).

Rapley, M. and Baldwin, S. (1995) Normalisation - Metatheory or Metaphysics: a conceptual critique, *Australia and New Zealand Journal of Developmental Disabilities,* 20(2) 141-57.

Reddy, V. (1991) Playing with other's expectations: Teasing and mucking about in the first year, in: White, A. (ed.) *Natural Theories of Mind,* Oxford, Blackwell.

Richardson, A. and Ritchie, J. (1989a) *Letting Go: Dilemnas for parents whose son or daughter has a mental handicap,* Milton Keynes, Open University Press.

Richardson, A. and Ritchie, J, (1989b) *Developing Friendships: Enabling People with Learning Difficulties to Make and Maintain Friendships,* London, Policy Studies Institute.

Riddell, S.I. (1992) *Gender and the Politics of the Curriculum,* London, Routledge.

Robinson, T. (1989) Normalisation: The Whole Answer? in: Brechin, A. and Walmsley, J. (eds.) *Making Connections: Reflecting on the lives and experience of people with learning disabilities,* London, Routledge.

Rosen, M. and Widgery, D. (1991) *The Chatto Book of Dissent,* London, Chatto and Windus.

Royal College of Psychiatrists (1976) Royal College of Psychiatrists' Memorandum to the Jay Committee, *British Journal of Psychiatry.* October 1976

Russell, J. (1995) Leisure and Recreation Services, in: Malin, N. (ed) *Services for People with Learning Disabilities,* London, Routledge.

Russell, J. (1996) *Agency: Its role in mental development,* Hove, Erlbaum (UK).

Ryan, J. & Thomas, F (1987) *The Politics of Mental Handicap* - revised edition, London, Free Association Books.

Salaman, G. (1995) *Managing,* Buckingham, Open University Press.

Schwartz, D. (1992) *Crossing the River: Creating a conceptual revolution in community and disability,* Cambridge MA, Brookline Books.

Schwartz, D.B. (1997) *Who Cares? - Rediscovering Community,* Oxford MA, Westview Press.

Shapiro A. (1974) Fact and Fiction in the Care of the Mentally Handicapped, *British Journal of Psychiatry,* 125, 286-92

Shearer A. (1972) *Normalisation?* - a paper given at the 5th International Congress on Mental Retardation of the International League of Societies for the Mentally Handicapped, CMH Discussion Paper Number 3, London, CMH Publications.

Sidell, M. (1995) *Health in Old Age: Myth , mystery and management,* Rethinking Aging Series, Buckingham, Open University Press.

Simons, K. (1995) Empowerment and Advocacy, in: Malin, N. (ed) *Services for people with Learning Disabilities,* London, Routledge.

Sinclair, I. (ed.) (1987) *The Research Reviewed - Literature surveys commissioned by the Independant Review of Residential Care* (Chair, G.Wagner), London, N.I.S.W./ H.M.S.O.

Sinson, J. (1990) Micro-institutionalisation? Environmental and managerial influences in ten living units for people with mental handicap, *British Journal of Mental Subnormality*, 36, 71-86.

Sinson, J. (1993) *Group Homes and Community Integration of Developmentally Disabled People: Micro institutionalisation?*, London, Jessica Kingsley.

Sloper, P. and Turner, S. (1993) Determinants of parental satisfaction with disclosure of disability, *Developmental Medicine and Child Neurology*, 35, 816-25.

Smith, H. and Brown, H. (1992) Defending Community Care: can normalisation do the job? *British Journal of Social Work*, 22(6), 685-93.

Smith, J., Glossop, G., Hall, J. and Kushlick, A. (1977) *A Report on the First Six Months of a Home Teaching Service for Pre-school Handicapped Children*, (The Wessex Portage Project), Winchester, Health Care Evaluation Research Team.

South Western Regional Health Authority (1986) *Achieving high quality community based services for people with learning disabilities* in the South West., Bristol, SWRHA

Stroebe, W. and Jones, K. (1996) Attitude Formation and Strategies of Change, in: Hewstone, M., Stroebe, W. and Stephenson, G.M. (eds.) *Introduction to Social Psychology*, 2nd Edition, Oxford, Blackwell.

Swain, J., Finkelstein, V., French, S. and Oliver, M. (1993) *Disabling Barriers - Enabling Environments*, London, Sage/ Open University.

Szivos, S.E. (1992) The limits to integration? in: Brown, H. and Smith, H. (eds.) *Normalisation, A Reader For the Nineties*, London, Routledge.

Szivos, S.E. and Travers, E. (1988) Consciousness raising among mentally handicapped people: A critique of the implications of normalisation, *Human Relations*, 41 (9) 641-53.

Tawney, R. (1938) *Religion and the Rise of Capitalism: A historical study; with a prefatory note by Charles Gore*, Harmondsworth, Penguin.

Taylor-Gooby, P. and Lawson, R. (eds.) (1993) *Markets and Managers: New issues in the delivery of welfare*, Buckingham, Open University Press.

Thomas, D., Firth, H. & Kendall, A. (1978) *ENCOR - A Way Ahead*, London, CMH Publications

Thomas, S. and Wolfensberger, W. (in press) An overview of Social Role Valorization (SRV), in: Flynn, R.J. and Lemay, R.A. (eds), *Twenty-five years of normalization and Social Role Valorization: Past accomplishments and future prospects*, Ottawa, Canada, University of Ottawa Press

Tizard J. (1967) *Survey and Experiment in Special Education: An inaugural lecture delivered at the University of London Institute of Education 5th December 1996.* Published for VLIE by Harrap 1967

Tizard, J. (1972) Research into Services for the Mentally Handicapped: Science and policy issues, *British Journal of Mental Subnormality*, October

Traxson, D. (1994) Helping children to become more self-directing in their behaviour, in: Gray, P., Miller, A. and Noakes, J. (eds.) *Challenging Behaviour in Schools: Teacher support, practical techniques and policy development*, London, Routledge.

Tredgold A.F. (1956) *A Textbook of Mental Deficiency*, London, Balliere Tindall & Cox

Turner, B. (1990) The rise of organizational symbolism, in: Hassard, J. and Pym, D. (eds.) *The Theory and Philosophy of Organizations: Critical issues and new perspectives*, London, Routledge.

Twine, F. (1994) *Citizenship and Social Rights: The Interdependence of self and society*, London, Sage.

Tye, M. (1993) Blindsight, the Absent Qualia Hypothesis, and the Mystery of

Consciousness, in: Hookway, C. and Peterson, D. (eds.) *Philosophy and Cognitive Science: Royal Institute of Philosophy Supplement;* 34, Cambridge, Cambridge University Press.

Tyne, A (1978) *Looking at Life in a Hospital Hostel, Home or Unit,* London, CMH Publications.

Tyne, A. (1987) Shaping community services: The impact of an idea: in Malin N (ed) *Reassessing Community Care,* London, Croom Helm

Tyne, A. (1992) Normalisation: from theory to practice: in Brown, H. & Smith, H. (eds) *Normalisation: A reader for the nineties,* London. Routledge.

Vanier, J. (1971) *Eruption to Hope,* Toronto, Griffin House.

Wagner, G.(1988) *A Positive Choice - Report of the Independant Review of Residential Care,* (Chair, G.Wagner), London, N.I.S.W./H.M.S.O.

Walker, C. (1993) *Managing Poverty: The limits of social assistance,* London, Routledge.

Ward, L. (1987) *Getting Better all the Time? Issues and strategies for ensuring quality in community services for people with mental handicap.* London, King's Fund Centre

Watts,P. and Olsen, P. (1994) Moving from consumer survey to service evaluation, in: Gray, P., Miller, A. and Noakes, J. (eds.) *Challenging Behaviour in Schools: Teacher support, practical techniques and policy development,* London, Routledge.

Weeks, J. (1994) *The Lesser and the Greater Good: The theory and politics of social diversity,* London, Rivers Oram Press.

Weinert, F.E. and Scheider, W. (1995) *Memory Performance and Competencies: issues in growth and development,* Mahwah NJ, Erlbaum.

Wertheimer, A. (1981) *Living for the Present: Older parents with a mentally handicapped person living at home,* London, CMH Publications.

Whittaker, J (1992) Can anyone help me to understand the logic of Snoezelen?, *Community Living,* 6(2), 15.

Williams, P. (1993) *Speak Out, Issue 17,* August, Trowbridge, CHMERA.

Williams, P. (1995a) *The History of SRV in Britain - Part 3,* CMHERA Newsletter, Issue 15, Jan

Williams, P. (1995b) The results of PASS and PASSING evaluations, in Pilling, D. and Watson, G. (eds) *Evaluating Quality in Services for Disabled and Older People,* London, Jessica Kingsley

Williams, P & Race, D.G. (1988) *Normalisation & the Children's Society,* London, CMHERA

Wistow, G., Knapp, M., Hardy, B., Forder, J., Kendall, J. and Manning, R. (1996) *Social Care Markets: Progress and prospects,* Buckingham, Open University Press.

Wolfensberger, W. (1969) The origin and nature of our institutional models, in Kugel R B and Wolfenberger W. (eds) *Changing Patterns in Residential Services for the Mentally Retarded,* Washington DC: President's Committee on Mental Retardation.

Wolfensberger, W. (1972) *The Principle of Normalisation in Human Services,* Toronto, NIMR

Wolfensberger, W. (1983a) *Guidelines for Evaluations during a PASS, PASSING or Similar Assessment of Human Service Quality.* Toronto, NIMR

Wolfensberger, W. (1983b) *Voluntary Associations on behalf of Societally Devalued and/ or Handicapped Persons,* Toronto, NIMR

Wolfensberger, W. (1983c) Social Role Valorization: A proposed new term for the Principle of Normalization, *Mental Retardation,* 21, 234-9.

Wolfensberger, W. (1984) A reconceptualization of normalisation as Social Role Valorization, *Mental Retardation* (Canadian), 34, 22-5.

Wolfensberger, W. (1985) Social Role Valorisation, a new insight and a new term for normalisation, *Australian Association for the Mentally Retarded Journal* 9 (1) 4-11

Wolfensberger, W (1988) Common assets of mentally retarded people that are commonly not acknowledged, *Mental Retardation*, 26 (2), 63-70.

Wolfensberger, W. (1990) A Most Critical Issue: Life or death, *Changes, An International Journal of Psychology and Psychotherapy*, 8(1), 63-73.

Wolfensberger, W. (1991) Reflections on a lifetime in human services and mental retardation, *Mental Retardation* 29(i)

Wolfensberger, W. (1992a) *A Brief Introduction to Social Role Valorization as a High-Order Concept for Structuring Human Services*, 2nd (revised) edition, Syracuse, NY, Training Institute for Human Service Planning, Leadership and Change Agentry, Syracuse University.

Wolfensberger, W. (1992b) *The New Genocide of Handicapped and Afflicted People*, 2nd (revised) edition, Syracuse, NY, Training Institute for Human Service Planning, Leadership and Change Agentry, Syracuse University.

Wolfensberger, W. (1995a) An 'If this, then that' formulation of decisions related to Social Role Valorization as a better way of interpreting it to people, *Mental Retardation*, 33(3), 163-9.

Wolfensberger, W. (1995b) Social Role Valorization is too conservative. No, it is too radical, *Disability and Society*, 10 (3), 365-68.

Wolfensberger, W. (1996a) major obstacles to rationality and quality in human services in contemporary society, Keynote Address, in: Adams, R. (ed.) *Crisis in the Human Services: National and International Issues - selected papers from a conference held at the University of Cambridge, September 1996*, Lincoln, The University of Lincolnshire and Humberside.

Wolfensberger, W. (1996b) *A History of Human Services*, presentation given at the University of Cambridge, September 1996 (unpublished)

Wolfensberger,W, (1998) *A Brief Introduction to Social Role Valorization as a High-Order Concept for Addressing the Plight of Societally Devalued People and for Structuring Human Services*, 3rd (revised) edition, Syracuse, NY, Training Institute for Human Service Planning, Leadership and Change Agentry, Syracuse University.

Wolfensberger, W. and Glenn, L. (1975) *Programme Analysis of Service Systems: Handbook and Field Manual*. 3rd edition. Toronto NIMR.

Wolfensberger, W. and Thomas, S. (1983) *Program Analysis of Service Systems, Implementation of Normalisation Goals*, Toronto, NIMR.

Wolfensberger, W, Thomas, S. and Caruso, G. (1996) Some of the universal 'good things of life' which the implementation of social role valorization can be expected to make more accessible to devalued people, *SRV/VRS*, 2(2), 12-14

Wolfensberger, W. and Tullman, S. (1982) A brief outline of the principle of normalization, *Rehabilitation Psychology*, 27, 131-145.

Woodward, K. (ed.) (1997) *Identity and Difference*, London, Sage Publications.